FUNDAMENTAL PRINCIPLES OF LAW

KV-034-640

The Law of Tort

AUSTRALIA AND NEW ZEALAND
The Law Book Company Ltd.
Sydney : Melbourne : Perth

CANADA AND U.S.A.
The Carswell Company Ltd.
Agincourt, Ontario

INDIA
N.M. Tripathi Private Ltd.
Bombay
and
Eastern Law House Private Ltd.
Calcutta and Delhi
M.P.P. House
Bangalore

ISRAEL
Steimatzky's Agency Ltd.
Jerusalem : Tel Aviv : Haifa

FUNDAMENTAL PRINCIPLES OF LAW

The Law of Tort

by

W. V. H. Rogers, M.A.
of Gray's Inn, Barrister
Professor of Law in the University of Leeds

LONDON
SWEET & MAXWELL
1989

Published in 1989 by
Sweet & Maxwell Limited now of
South Quay Plaza, 183 Marsh Wall, London.
Laserset by P.B. Computer Typesetting, N. Yorks.
Printed by BPCC Hazell Books
Aylesbury, Bucks, England
Member of BPCC Ltd.

Reprinted 1990

British Library Cataloguing in Publication Data

Rogers, W. V. H.
Tort
1. England. Tort. Law
I. Title
344.2063

ISBN 0–421–36480–7
ISBN 0–421–36490–4

PREFACE

The aim of this book is to provide, in a reasonably small compass, an introductory account of all the aspects of tort law which a student is likely to encounter in a degree course. I hope that it strikes a suitable balance between stating enough "rules" for the structure of the law to be understood before study in greater depth is undertaken, while at the same time putting the law in its context. It is based on English law, but the proportion of authorities cited from other common law jurisdictions is high, for I respectfully endorse the spirit of the remarks made by Sir Anthony Mason upon his swearing-in as Chief Justice of Australia (February 6, 1987):

> "In stating the law for Australia, we now pay closer attention to the common law as reflected in the judicial decisions and academic writings of other countries. Despite differences in principle and technique, courts in countries following the common law tradition inherited from England have achieved a remarkable degree of uniformity in evolving principled answers to common problems."

Two tort decisions of the House of Lords handed down on the same day (*Fitzgerald* v. *Lane* [1988] 3 W.L.R. 356 and *D. & F. Estates* v. *Church Commissioners* [1988] 3 W.L.R. 368) were decisively influenced by cases from Australia and the U.S.A. respectively.

Since this book is about fundamentals there would be no point in fixing a precise date at which it states the law, as is the custom in larger texts. Suffice it to say that I hope it gives a fair view of English law in the summer of 1988. The *Vesta* case (p. 76) and the question of the effect of the Unfair Contract Terms Act on disclaimers (p. 88) are likely to reach the House of Lords before

v

publication. Mr. Browne's Protection of Privacy Bill is perhaps unlikely to reach the statute book but one never knows.

It is a pleasure to record my sincere thanks, as on other occasions, to Mrs. Christine Taylor, whose excellence and indispensability increases year by year, and to the publishers for their patience and help.

Finally, a mention should go to Mr. M. Boya of Benin, for providing what is surely the ultimate proof that fantastic chains of events occur in the real world as well as in the fevered imagination of law teachers. According to *The Times* of December 17, 1988, a mis-placed golf drive by Mr. Boya, who was practising near an airstrip, resulted in the destruction of an entire flight of five jet fighters valued at £44 million. The government decided not to pursue its civil claim.

W.V.H.R.

LEEDS
December, 1988

CONTENTS

TABLE OF CASES

TABLE OF STATUTES

CHAPTER ONE

Introduction

The law of torts is concerned with the redress of wrongs or
injuries (other than breaches of contract) by means of a civil
action brought by the victim. This redress most commonly
takes the form of damages, that is to say, monetary compensation. This definition has no pretensions to being complete
or watertight and a definition which was would be extremely
cumbersome and so full of qualifications that it would be
incomprehensible to all except those who already knew
enough to recognize the province of torts without difficulty. It
is more helpful to the beginner to provide some illustrations which will indicate the types of case in which tort law
operates. The law of torts would be the basis of a claim for
compensation for injuries suffered in a road accident or as a
result of a medical error in the course of an operation (in both
cases the tort of negligence); for loss caused by being tricked
into buying worthless shares (fraud or deceit); for injury to
reputation caused by a false accusation of misconduct or
incompetence (defamation); for deprivation of liberty following an unjustified arrest (false imprisonment); for interference
with the enjoyment of one's garden caused by persistent
smoke or noise (nuisance); for loss caused by a strike outside
the protection of trade union legislation (inducing breach of
contract); or for leading the public to believe that your goods
are manufactured by a competitor who is the leader in the
field (passing off). This random list hints at two important
characteristics of "tort" in the common law systems—it is
extraordinarily diverse and it cuts across other practical, historical and theoretical systems of legal classification.

1

This diversity contrasts with the more unified concept of contract, the common law's other great source of "obligation." It is true that a system which applies the same general theory of contract to the charter of a tanker and the purchase of fish and chips sometimes shows signs of strain; it is also true that the detailed rules developed behind the general law for particular types of contract are indispensable for the solution of most practical problems. Nevertheless, it is possible to expound the law of contract with a beginning, a middle and an end. But where are we to find the connexion between defamation and highway accidents or between inducing breach of contract and assault? Not only are the social problems dealt with by the law utterly different, so also are the rules developed in response to them: as the next Chapter shows, there is a wide variety of levels of legal duty and of specialized defences in tort. It is widely believed that tort law has been in a crisis for a number of years as its doctrines have come into contact with other, competing principles and institutions but the nature of the crisis changes as we pass from one tort to another. There is a serious issue whether the high degree of protection (in particular the high level of damages) afforded by the common law to personal reputation is compatible with a free press; it is an even more serious, but nevertheless completely different issue whether negligence is an apt mechanism for allocating compensation for personal injuries by accident in societies with comparatively highly developed systems of private and social insurance. The diversity within the English system (from which this book takes its stance) is now being matched by a growing diversity within particular areas of liability as other common law systems have come to maturity and developed their own responses. The greatest divergences have occurred in the United States and in some areas the law is now virtually unrecognizable against the original model, two striking examples being the rigorous controls imposed on the law of defamation since 1964 by the application of the constitutional guarantee of freedom of speech and the rapid development of strict liability for dangerously defective manufactured goods.[1] Within the Commonwealth, New Zealand has produced the most dramatic reform of torts by casting it out altogether in personal injury cases and replacing it with social insurance and there are more modest versions of the same idea for motor accidents in parts of Australia and Canada. As a

---

[1] England has now enacted legislation on similar lines as a result of an E.E.C. Directive: see Chap. 6.

matter of doctrine, there is almost as much tort law in New Zealand as in England (because the same principles continue to apply to non-personal injury cases) but its importance as a social institution has been much diminished.

If we turn to classification, a continental lawyer trained in a more systematic tradition would be surprised at tort's "table of contents." If he had been reared on the French Civil Code he would recognize a good deal of our law of negligence, our law about defective buildings, dangerous things and fierce animals as part of his law of obligations known as *la responsabilité délictuelle*. If he went further into a typical textbook, however, he might be surprised to find a goodly proportion of the law governing the acquisition of property (trespass and "ejectment," conversion) and its use (nuisance), elements of the law of trade competition (passing off) and of the law guaranteeing civil liberties (assault and false imprisonment). The common law in its historical origins was a remedial or "actions-based" system which looked at the law in terms of the remedies to be granted in various types of commonly recurring situations rather than in terms of general rights to which remedies were merely ancillary. The specialized remedies (the "forms of action") were abolished in the middle of the last century and there has unquestionably been a shift towards thinking in terms of rights and duties rather than remedies, but the shape of the law is still governed by its history—there has been no systematic codification such as that to which other European systems have been subjected since 1800. As a result, and always subject to statute, a tort is a wrong which in former times would have been remediable by one of the actions of "trespass" (for direct wrongs) or "trespass upon the case" (for indirect wrongs). From the point of view of exposition this is not a happy state of affairs!

The question of what to include in an introductory book and how to organise it must, however, be faced. One approach is to concentrate heavily upon "accident law," which is dominated by the comparatively modern tort of negligence. This has a good deal of coherence and is the most important tort in practice—indeed, it shows recurrent signs of ambitions to swallow the rest of tort and a slice of contract at the same time. However, one should not necessarily structure one's study of the law along the lines of the scores in the Judicial Statistics: murder is a statistically insignificant offence alongside driving with an excess of blood alcohol but it would be an unusual criminal law course in which a good deal more attention was not paid to the former than to the latter. (There are those who would reverse this situation, but this is not the place to pursue that point). The lawyer who knows all about employer's liability for industrial accidents and nothing about interference with trade by unlawful means has little understanding of the *structure* of English law even though the information he does have is likely to be called on a good deal more frequently in practice than that which he lacks. It is perfectly true that the restrictions adopted by English law on the recovery of purely financial loss present the plaintiff who claims in respect of a loss of trade with a difficult task and successful suits will be rare but this does not render the area in any way an improper subject of study: it has been fairly said that it is as much the concern of tort to say when the defendant is *not* liable as it is to impose liability. A respectable case can be made that the correct approach is to study segments of the law of torts when dealing with those areas which provide their raw material. On this basis, interference with trade would belong in labour law because in England (though not elsewhere, particularly the United States) industrial strife has been the basis of most of the case law; similarly, assault and false imprisonment might be examined in the context of civil liberties. This may well be the best way of going about things at an advanced level, but it is unlikely that the student will have the opportunity to make a detailed study of all the specialised areas of law which it would be necessary to cover on this approach. For the foreseeable future the view is likely to prevail that a fairly broadly based study of torts is a necessary part of a legal education, ramshackle and random as the structure of the subject may be, and this book attempts to give an outline of all those topics likely to be encountered in an undergraduate torts course. There is a good deal of "accident law" in the Chapter on negligence and elsewhere and another Chapter looks at the long-running debate on alternatives to tort law but an attempt has been made to give proportionate space to other areas of tort law—which, incidentally, are often very difficult.

If we now return to our very broad definition, the student will soon find that he is less concerned with what tort is in the abstract than with distinguishing it from other sources of legal obligation or liability. Not only can we not understand the function of tort without an idea of where it stands in relation to the territory of, say, contract, but the enquiry may sometimes have a distinctly practical purpose. For example, legislation governing time limits within which claims must be brought ("limitation of actions," see Chap. 14) is likely to have separate provisions for tort and contract so we have to decide into which category our claim falls.

There is usually little difficulty in distinguishing tort from crime but every teacher of the subject will be familiar with the desire of first year students to inject criminal law into their answers so it would be wise to start with a word or two on that. Criminal proceedings are brought by the State (or by some person authorised to act on behalf of the State) and have as their object "punishment" (though that word must be used in a very broad sense so as to include objects like reform of offenders and deterrence of others) of an "offence." The offence may, of course, have involved the infliction of some harm upon an individual victim and may also be—indeed is very likely to be—a tort against him, but the main object of the criminal proceedings is not the compensation of the victim and his part in the proceedings is as a witness, not that of a person in control, and able to withdraw or settle the case.[2] The rules of procedure will be distinctively different from those applicable in courts settling civil disputes and the rules of evidence are likely to be a good deal more restrictive. Furthermore, the whole terminology is different: we speak of "guilty" and "innocent" rather than "liable" and "not liable," "prosecute" rather than "sue." No lawyer now or for a good many years past would have much difficulty distinguishing civil and criminal proceedings but the line has not always been so clear. In the Middle Ages trespass, which to us is exclusively a tort (whether it be to land, goods or the person), had a strong criminal flavour in the sense that proceedings might end in (i) the award of damages to the victim *and* (ii) the imposition of a fine payable to the Crown *and* (iii) the imprisonment of the offender. European legal systems generally have a less sharp procedural distinction between the civil and criminal elements of a case (see, for example, how the victim may claim compensation in French criminal proceedings as *partie civile*) and even the common law may be moving back towards blurring the distinction. In England, for example, there has been, since 1973, legislation whereby a criminal court may order the defendant to pay compensation (currently up to £2,000) for "any personal injury, loss or damage" resulting from an offence. Losses arising from most road accidents are excluded and the criminal courts should not utilise the power where there are complex issues of law, but in the generality of small cases of assault, theft or fraud the victim is much more likely to make informal representations for compensation to the criminal court (which will cost him nothing, or next to nothing) than to mount separate civil proceedings. About 120,000 such orders are made in England each year and the relative importance of this method of compensation is likely to increase rather

---

[2] The right to bring a private prosecution to some extent contradicts this, but they are comparatively rare.

than diminish. Indeed, the criminal court must now explain a decision *not* to award compensation.

The criminal process impinges on tort litigation in a less obvious but this time supportive rather than competitive way in the context of evidence. Many tort cases arise from road accidents and a serious case is likely to be not less than a couple of years in coming to trial. If there has been negligence (and there can be no civil claim unless there has been) it is quite likely that there will have been a criminal prosecution for breach of the road traffic legislation. Originally, the common law so strictly separated the civil and criminal processes that the defendant's conviction in the criminal case could not even be given in evidence in the civil proceedings. However, this rule has been abrogated by statute in some jurisdictions (in England the Civil Evidence Act 1968) so that the conviction is now prima facie evidence in the civil action. Thus if, for example, the defendant has already been convicted by the magistrates of the offence of careless driving he is unlikely to be able to defend himself against an allegation of negligence when sued for damages. This does not remove all the plaintiff's difficulties of proof, for the civil suit may involve issues of causation or amount of damages or of contributory fault on the plaintiff's part which were not relevant in the earlier proceedings, but the legal machinery of the state designed primarily for the enforcement of general standards via the criminal law will have gone some way towards assisting the victim with his claim for compensation.

The relationship between tort and contract is likely to cause the law student and the practising lawyer a good deal more conceptual difficulty. Putting aside the special category of "contracts" under seal, a contract is an agreement which the law will enforce by an action for damages (though other remedies may be available in some cases). It must be supported by "consideration," that is to say, by something which the law regards as having value, for a gratuitous promise is not generally enforceable. In principle, the requirement of consideration applies as much to the modification of an existing agreement (say, an agreement to increase the price for building work or to allow a debtor more time to pay) as to its initial creation, but the courts have developed a doctrine whereby a promise to modify an existing legal obligation, if relied upon by the other party, may be binding in the sense that there is a defence against a claim to enforce the promise in its original terms. In the United States the courts have gone further and allowed the recipient of the modifying promise actually to sue upon it.

Traditionally, it has been said that the distinction between contract and tort is that liability in tort arises from a duty imposed on persons generally by the law, whereas contractual duties arise from the agreement between the parties, are defined by the agreement and bind only the parties. Now there are clearly situations which are the exclusive province of one or the other head of liability. Suppose A agrees on Monday to sell electric pumps to B and then immediately reneges on his promise. There is a breach of contract which allows B to sue A for the difference between the contract price and the higher price he has to pay to find a substitute consignment, but A has committed no tort against B—there is no general duty to deliver pumps, only duties arising from particular contractual promises to do so. Equally, if A on leaving B's premises ran down a pedestrian, X, that is a tort but not a breach of a contract, for X has no contract with A. Unfortunately, this explanation of the distinction can only be maintained with the aid of a certain amount of fiction. Many contractual duties arise only nominally from agreement because they are based on terms "implied" into the contract even though the parties have given no thought to the matter. Indeed, these implied terms may, by statute, be unexcludable so that even an express agreement to depart from them will be ineffective. In such cases the duties only arise from the agreement of the parties in the sense that they have manifested an intention to enter into an agreement of a particular type, the legal content of which is supplied "off the shelf" by the law. On the other side, a duty in tort may arise when a person is asked for information or advice in circumstances in which it is reasonable for the inquirer to place reliance on the response. At least where there is no legal obligation to respond, the tort duty may be said to arise from the agreement by the respondent, inferred from the unqualified nature of his response, to undertake the duty to take care.

Contract and tort may "overlap" in the sense that the same set of facts may give rise to legal obligations under both heads and, generally speaking, the plaintiff may sue for either or both, though he cannot of course recover damages twice over. In our example of the electric pumps, if the pumps were negligently manufactured and caught fire, destroying B's factory, B would have an action in tort for negligence as well as his action in contract under the Sale of Goods Act on the ground that the pumps were unfit for their purpose. Since the contract duty would not require proof of negligence the tort would add nothing of substance; in other cases (for example, that of a fare-paying passenger injured by the careless driving of a bus) the duties may be the same under each head. In some cases the law of contract might provide an unfavourable answer for the plaintiff but the application of tort doctrine might point the other way. The courts are often reluctant to allow tort to "trump" contract in this way.

In *Tai Hing Cotton Mill* v. *Liu Chong Hing Bank*[3] a company's accounts clerk forged the managing director's signature on 300 cheques totalling HK $5.5 million. When this was discovered the company claimed that the bank was not entitled to debit these forgeries against the company's account—as it clearly was not, unless the bank could establish some breach of duty by the company. It was well established that the contractual duty of a customer to his bank for this purpose required the customer to exercise due care in drawing cheques so as not to facilitate fraud by alteration and to notify the bank of any forgeries of which he was *aware*. But neither of these duties had been broken. The tort of negligence, however, had developed to the stage whereby it might very broadly be said that one must take reasonable care not to cause damage to persons likely to be affected by one's conduct. Could it not therefore be said that the slackness of the company's financial control in allowing the forgeries to go undetected for so long constituted negligence? The Privy Council replied in the negative, saying that while it might be possible to analyse the rights and duties of the parties "as a matter of legal semantics" in terms of tort as well as contract, their mutual obligations in tort could not be greater than those found expressly or by necessary implication in their contract. The idea seems to be that contract, as the creation of the parties, is the "superior" legal institution and is not to be contradicted or subverted by tort. The courts have traditionally shown themselves particularly reluctant to impose liability in tort where the defendant has *failed* to act to benefit the plaintiff or where the plaintiff's loss is purely economic (as it was in the *Tai Hing* case) involving no injury to person or property. Both areas are regarded as peculiarly the province of contract and we shall have to return to look in more detail at the relationship of tort to them.

Where it is not the substance of the defendant's obligation which is in issue but ancillary matters such as the rules which govern the extent of liability or the time limits within which claims must be brought the current tendency seems to favour the plaintiff. In *Midland Bank Trust Co.* v. *Hett, Stubbs & Kemp*[4] there was an allegation of negligence against a solicitor in failing to register a transaction concerning land. Since the statutory time limit of six years ran against a contract claim from the time when the contractual duty was broken but ran against a tort claim only from the time when the plaintiff suffered damage, it was possible for the contract claim to be time-barred before the tort claim, for the damaging effects of the breach might lie dormant until some

---

[3] [1986] A.C. 80.
[4] [1978] Ch. 384.

further transaction with the land was attempted. Although on the facts the contract claim was held not to be time barred, Oliver J. was prepared, if it had been necessary, to give judgment for the plaintiff in tort, the content of the solicitor's duty (to exercise proper professional care), being the same under both heads.[5]

At one time the law was that if A owed a contractual duty to B this precluded any concurrent tort duty by A to a third party, C. Thus if A manufactured a defective product which he sold to B and this was transferred to C, whom it injured, A would not be liable in tort to C. This "privity of contract fallacy" has long since been exploded.

The other sources of obligation known to the courts under the English system are statute, restitution and trusts. Where a statute expressly imposes an obligation to pay damages for breach of a duty to the plaintiff it is largely a matter of chance or tradition whether we classify it, for the purposes of exposition, as part of the law of torts. The Occupiers' Liability Act 1957 and the Torts (Interference with Goods) Act 1977 would be found in any reasonably comprehensive book dealing with the subject. It is possible (the point is not clear) that statutory breach of copyright is a tort but the subject is highly specialised and contains so much that is not directly concerned with *liability* that it is treated as a subject in its own right.[6] A rather different question is whether a statute imposing a duty *impliedly* gives rise to a civil action for damages. Though this might just as well be regarded as part of the law of statutory interpretation it is customarily considered in an account of the law of torts.[7]

It is difficult to convey briefly the idea of the law of restitution, but its central theme is the prevention of "unjust enrichment." It covers matters such as the recovery of a price paid in advance under a contract which has not been performed or the recovery of money paid by mistake. It is formally distinguishable from tort in that the sums recoverable are not "damages" and are generally measured by the defendant's unjustified gain rather than by the plaintiff's loss, but the law of restitution has some impact upon tort because in certain cases (principally those involving

---

[5] Some subsequent cases suggest that even in tort time might begin to run before the damage in such a situation is manifest, but the law has anyway been affected by the Latent Damage Act 1986 (see Chap. 14).

[6] There are some topics governed by judge made law the proper classification of which is subject to some doubt: it is not clear for example, how far the law of confidence and the law of bailment are within the law of torts. From a practical point of view the point is most likely to arise in the context of time-bars on claims.

[7] See Chap. 5.

misappropriation of property) the plaintiff may sue in restitution as an alternative to tort. This is now of limited practical importance and falls outside the scope of an introductory book. Finally, there is the law of trusts. This is commonly regarded as falling within the law of property but it does impose liabilities which have some passing similarity with those of the law of torts: a trustee may have a duty to take care in connection with the management and investment of the trust fund and will have a duty to pay compensation for loss caused by breach of that duty. Again, however, what is payable is not technically damages. But more significant than this formal distinction is the fact that the law of trusts has developed from the jurisdiction of the courts of equity, a source wholly different from that of tort, which was the child of the common law courts. Even today, although law and equity are formally "fused" and the High Court considers both, actions for breach of trust are heard in a separate division of the Court. The remedy of injunction is historically based in equity: otherwise, the equitable "input" into torts has been minimal.

Even the simplest practical legal problems cut across these classifications. A lawyer can practise in "personal injuries" or "commercial law" or "Chancery" but he cannot practise in "Tort" or "Contract" or "Trusts" even though each of the three might spend most of his time considering those topics respectively.[8] For the purposes of learning and exposition the classifications are necessary but it is to be hoped that the student will make as much effort to look at situations "in the round" as is consistent with (a) his progress through the curriculum and (b) what, in a particular instance, he is asked to do.

The reader may have noticed that the singular "tort" and the plural "torts" have been used throughout this Chapter with little apparent regard to anything except grammatical sense and euphony. This is because it does not really matter very much which we say. A century and a half ago the law was undoubtedly one of torts in the plural because different wrongs were remediable by resort to different writs, so that if the plaintiff was complaining of his neighbour's intruding tree roots and brought an action for trespass he lost because he had made the wrong choice of action even though he might have an unquestionable basis on which to bring an action on the case for nuisance. Modern procedure is much less strict and one does not have to identify one's claim by name in the formal steps which bring the action to court (though it would be usual to do so). Nevertheless, the rules of liability do differ from one situation to another and for

---

[8] An extreme example of conceptually diverse litigation is the "Ocean Island" case ([1977] Ch. 106), which traverses half of English private law.

this reason it remains necessary to use labels such as trespass and nuisance to identify the rules upon which the plaintiff bases his claim. In this sense, therefore, it is still a law of torts and is most unlikely ever to be anything else. Even the most avid proponent of the theory of separate torts could not, however, deny that this branch of the law is capable of expansion or modification by decisions of the courts and that for this purpose they may be influenced by broad themes or principles of liability. The most easily recognisable in this generation has been the tendency to intrude negligence both into the rules of older torts and into new fields of conduct. Some have attempted to find a broad principle whereby all infliction of harm is tortious unless there is some justification for it. If "justification" simply means all those situations in which one is *not* at present liable in tort such a principle tells us nothing. If, on the other hand, it means that in a case not already covered by one of the "named" torts the defendant who has caused loss to another is liable unless he satisfies the court that his action was justified that would be incompatible with the present law, particularly that governing interference with contractual and business relations.[9] One might say that there was less of a "general part" to tort law than to say, contract or crime, but it would be wrong to think that one can never speak of a "tort rule" of more or less general application despite the diversity of individual torts. For example, the court's power to apportion responsibility among co-defendants[10] is applicable to all torts, as is the concept of vicarious liability,[11] and damages in tort cases have the common theme that they are designed to put the plaintiff in the position he would have been in if the tort had not been committed.[12] Certain defences, such as consent/assumption of risk and default of the plaintiff also appear across the whole range of torts, though their detailed application may differ.

---

[9] See Chap. 13.
[10] See p. 25, *post.*
[11] See p. 29, *post.*
[12] See Chap. 14.

CHAPTER TWO

Fundamentals of Liability

A. STANDARDS OF CONDUCT

It is often said that the law of torts rests upon "fault." This is broadly true in the sense that there are comparatively few situations in which liability is incurred by a defendant who can be said to be truly blameless, but it is misleading in that it suggests a unified law with a single standard of fault—again perhaps the influence of the pervasive law of negligence. In fact, the law of torts is a series of points along a scale of conduct with liability only for intentionally caused harm at one end and for purely accidental and even unforeseeable harm at the other. The tort of malicious prosecution is an example of liability at the top, or, from the plaintiff's point of view, demanding, end of this scale. It is committed where the defendant initiates an unfounded criminal prosecution against the plaintiff, but the plaintiff can succeed only if he can show that the defendant (a) on the facts as he, however erroneously, believed them to be did not have grounds for thinking that the plaintiff was probably guilty of the crime charged *and* (b) he was actuated by malice rather than a desire to vindicate the law. Lack of reasonable cause for the belief may be evidence from which the court may infer that the defendant was malicious but if it concludes that he was actuated by stupidity rather than malice he escapes liability. This onerous burden on the plaintiff is designed to protect accusers (who perform a useful social function in putting the law in motion) from the risk that they may incur liability in a case of genuine error or that they may be harassed over a perfectly wellfounded charge. The policy favours law enforcement over individual

12

rights and certainly seems to be effective, judging from the dearth of successful claims even in the days before the practice of awarding costs to successful defendants in criminal cases removed much of the incentive to sue. Close to the other end of the scale (rather to the surprise of many law students) is the tort of conversion: if I deal with your goods without your authority I may incur liability to you for their value even if I acted in all innocence and even if the reason they came into my hands was that you were careless enough to let someone steal them.

To complicate the matter further, we cannot even really speak of *a* tort standing at a particular point on this scale because different aspects of a tort may lie at different points along it. For example, since the decision in *Letang* v. *Cooper*[1] it is fairly clear in England that the variety of trespass known as battery is an intentional tort requiring something in the nature of a blow—a careless, accidental contact will not do. However, in many cases the victim of battery is not likely to sue unless he has suffered some harm which justifies the risk and expense of litigation. Must the defendant have intended this harm as well as the blow which led to it? The answer is no, so that rough and bullying horseplay to which the plaintiff is known to object may lead to liability for consequences more serious than the defendant intended. The tort is one requiring intention as to one of its aspects but not as to another. Again, battery or its close relation, false imprisonment, may be committed by a person seeking to exercise a power of lawful arrest which justifies what would otherwise be a tort. The powers of a police officer are a good deal more extensive than those of a private citizen, but the fundamental principle is that an arrest is lawful where the "offender" has committed a serious offence *or* where the arrester reasonably believes that he has done so, *the burden of proving justification being upon the arrester.* Accordingly, far from the plaintiff having to show that the defendant intended to act unlawfully he need only show that the interference with his liberty was intentional and the arrester must then show that there were grounds which justified his action.

Defamation provides an even richer source of complexity. One cannot even say, for example, that it is necessary that the defendant intends his defamatory words to refer to the plaintiff, for if the words fall outside the protection of the Defamation Act 1952 he acts at his peril, even if he thought he was writing about a fictional character. For the cases within the Act, however, a negligence standard is imposed. Is it necessary that the defendant should know that what he says is untrue (truth being a complete defence) or be negligent as to its untruth? Generally no,

---

[1] [1965] 1 Q.B. 232. See further p. 133 *post.*

again he acts at his peril; but when the occasion on which he spoke gives rise to a "privilege," his honest belief in the truth of his words protects him, even if it is the product of gross prejudice.

Bearing this further complexity in mind we can nevertheless group torts into three broad categories by reference to their central features—those requiring intention, those requiring negligence and those which may be committed without either intention or negligence.

Torts Requiring Intention

The principal members[2] of this group are (a) the torts having their origin in the old writ of trespass and which protect personal liberty and security (assault, battery, false imprisonment) (b) fraud and injurious falsehood (c) a group of torts which protect against interference with contractual relations and trade.

As to the trespass torts there has been remarkably little judicial discussion of the meaning of intention. In this respect tort stands in sharp contrast to the criminal law, where intention is the subject of constant and rather bewildering refinement and redefinition by the courts. The paucity of civil cases on the point is probably to be explained by two factors. First, it is only comparatively recently that the requirement of intention has been clearly established: in earlier times less attention was paid to the mental element than to the requirement that the injury be "direct." Furthermore, the establishment of the significance of intent came at a time when trial by jury in civil actions had all but disappeared, removing the opportunity for appellate challenge to a decision for inadequate or improper explanation of technical terms to the jury.[3] Secondly, the absence of any tangible harm to the victim is likely to substantially reduce the chance of his bringing a civil action for trespass; but if there is some harm it will hardly matter whether the defendant acted intentionally because even if he did not there may be liability for negligence. Suppose that D, as a stupid practical joke, fires an air rifle into a crowd of people and the pellet hits P in the eye, blinding him. It is unlikely that D *desires* to hit anyone. He probably realises in a vague way that he may do so but he thinks that the chance of serious injury is small. Now some might classify his state of mind as intentional with regard to injury or (which comes to much the same thing)

---

[2] Another, malicious prosecution, has been mentioned above.
[3] But in the criminal law there is now a tendency towards saying that intention is something which does not normally *need* explanation: see *R. v. Moloney* [1985] A.C. 905.

equate him for the purposes of the law with someone who acts intentionally. In the law of torts, however, since D would be liable for negligence if he carelessly *but wholly inadvertently* discharged the gun into the crowd he must be liable here. As we have seen, the plaintiff is not, under modern conditions, obliged to choose a form of procedure unique to the liability on which he relies and provided his statement of claim is adequately drafted (containing, preferably, alternative allegations of trespass and negligence) then the court, if satisfied that D was at least negligent, need not really consider whether his conduct was intentional. Some courts in the United States have been forced into more precise attempts at definition by the existence of different time limits for bringing actions for trespass and negligence. The English legislation is not a model of clarity on this point, but the courts have interpreted it in such a way that the period is the same for both torts. However, there are other issues on which the courts might not be able to avoid the question of whether the conduct was intentional, for example the application of the law of contributory negligence and the award of aggravated or exemplary damages. Until the matter is settled by authority it seems reasonable to surmise that intention in these torts covers the situation where the defendant desires to produce the results forbidden by law *and* that where he foresees that it may happen and presses on regardless—what is sometimes called recklessness (though that word has fallen into such confusion in the criminal law that it is perhaps best avoided).

For fraud the law is clearer. The tort is based on the making of a false statement upon which the recipient relies and it is clear that the defendant must know the statement is untrue or be aware that it may be untrue. That the mental element was defined with such precision was no doubt due to the fact that until 1963 English law did not recognise liability for negligence in this area.[4]

The narrowest form of intention is to be found in the third group. It is the tort of conspiracy if A and B combine together and act to cause injury to P. However, it is not enough that A and B are aware even that the inevitable consequences of their actions will be to harm P, it must be their *purpose* to bring this about and if their purpose is wholly or mainly to advance their own interests by promoting their trade at the expense of the plaintiff's they are not liable in this tort. In other words, liability is confined to disinterested malice and successful claims are rare. Where, however, the defendant interferes with some existing contractual right of the plaintiff (for example by persuading the plaintiff's supplier not to fulfil a binding order), that is the different tort of

---

[4] See *Hedley Byrne* v. *Heller* [1964] A.C. 465.

interference with contract and it is enough that the defendant knows that his conduct will have this effect.[5]

Negligence

Negligence is a tort in its own right, in practical terms the most important tort in the system, but it is also a description of a type of conduct ("state of mind" is hardly apt since it is normally marked by the absence of advertence) which is an element of the tort of negligence and which is a foundation of legal responsibility in other torts and in branches of the law other than torts: a negligence standard plays a major role in the law of contract, in crime and in the law of trusts. Indeed, it seems to be almost the modern lawyer's instinctive reaction to use the question "was he negligent" as the determinant of a wide range of issues. In this respect the law finds itself at odds with some current social and economic thinking, which favours efficiency of transfer of resources and broad distribution of losses at the expense of traditional notions of justice based upon fault. A negligence based system will have the consequences that those accident victims who are unable to show that their injuries are attributable to the fault of the defendant will go uncompensated and in any case considerable expense may be involved in the investigation of facts necessary to establish fault. A legal system can in practice go a good way to avoid these results by setting high standards of care and manipulating the burden of proof. However, critics may respond that what one ends up with is a "false" system, the practical operation of which has cut loose from its theoretical basis and which will still involve an irreducible minimum of uncompensated victims and wasted expenditure.

We shall have to return to the relative merits of negligence when compared with other compensation systems.[6] For the moment, the cornerstone of the legal concept of negligence is that it sets an objective standard. The defendant must comply with the standard which the *law* sets for the conduct of activity—it is not enough that he has done his best, if that best falls below the objective standard. This standard is sometimes described as that of the reasonable man, no doubt because in the formative years of the law of negligence it was set, within broad limits of judicial control, by juries. The instruction that they should determine whether the defendant had acted with the care to be expected of a reasonable man was hardly a formula which they could apply scientifically or mechanically and was in fact an implied invitation

[5] See Chap. 13.
[6] See Chap. 15.

to apply their own standards of prudence. Bearing in mind that a nineteenth century jury was likely to be drawn from the more "substantial" elements of society it is perhaps not surprising that the formula should have survived the transition to a system in which, in England, trial is always by judge alone.

Because the concept of negligence is founded upon what the courts perceive to be fundamental community feelings of fairness and justice there are instances where this pure objective standard has been departed from. For example, when it was held that a landowner was obliged to take steps to remove a danger arising naturally on his land even though there had been no act on his part bringing the danger about, the Privy Council adopted an intermediate standard requiring the defendant to do what was reasonable in the light of *his* physical abilities and financial resources—no doubt because some allowance was thought necessary for the fact that the duty had been forced upon the defendant.[7] The situation of a landowner faced by trespassers endangered by a hazard on his land evoked a similar response from the House of Lords in *B.R.B.* v. *Herrington*.[8] It must, however, be remembered that being "fair" to the defendant in this way increases the chance that the harm to the plaintiff will go uncompensated and this sometimes leads to a court's rejecting any modification of the objective standard even when logic appears to point strongly the other way. In *Nettleship* v. *Weston*[9] the plaintiff, a non-professional driving instructor, recovered damages against his pupil on the basis that the pupil—*ex hypothesi* an experienced driver—had failed to drive with the skill of an experienced driver! The reason, quite baldly stated by Lord Denning M.R., was that the existence of compulsory liability insurance for car drivers assured the plaintiff of compensation at no direct cost to the defendant.

Where the defendant's conduct is at issue, instances of departure from the objective standard are comparatively few. However, the plaintiff's conduct may also be in issue because failure by the plaintiff to take care for his own safety (contributory negligence) may reduce or even extinguish his damages. Here the almost universal practice is to modify the objective standard fairly readily, at least to the extent of basing it on the capacity of the group to which the plaintiff belongs, so that, for example, a child will probably be judged by the standard of the "reasonable child" of his age. Some courts have gone so far as to ask whether the plaintiff acted reasonably according to *his* capacity if that is

---

[7] *Goldman* v. *Hargrave* [1967] 1 A.C. 645.
[8] [1972] A.C. 877. See now the Occupiers' Liability Act 1984.
[9] [1971] 2 Q.B. 691.

lower than that of his group (see, for example, the Canadian case of *Finbow* v. *Domino*[10] concerning a child of eight with a mental age of three-and-a-half). Originally the more generous view taken towards the plaintiff's conduct may have been a reaction against the common law rule that *any* contributory negligence amounted to a complete defence but that rule has all but disappeared and the courts' attitude is now perhaps to be explained by the relatively greater impact upon plaintiffs of findings of contributory negligence than of findings of liability upon defendants, who will usually be insured.

Strict Liability

As we have seen, there may be elements of "strict" liability in many torts, but some do not require fault even as to their core elements. Even an honest and reasonable mistake as to ownership may not provide a defence to wrongful interference with another's goods. In the area of accidents the best known example is the so-called rule in *Rylands* v. *Fletcher*[11] whereby a person who collects dangerous things may be liable without proof of fault for damage done by their escape. However, the judicial trend in England and the Commonwealth has been to water down this rule by restricting the range of activities to which it applies and introducing defences which in effect allow the defendant to escape liability by showing positively that he was not at fault. What might have been a means of imposing liability upon defendants for the creation of unusual risks is well on the way to being not much more than a sub-heading of negligence, albeit one requiring a high degree of care. Strict liability now more often arises from statute and examples will be found in section 14 of the Factories Act 1961, in the Merchant Shipping (Oil Pollution) Act 1971 and in the Nuclear Installations Act 1965. However, the coverage appears random and arbitrary. For example, a public water undertaking incurs strict liability for damage caused by a burst main (see the Water Act 1981), presumably on the basis of one or both of two ideas: that it is best able to insure against the risk and that the cost, including damage, of water supply is best spread among the community by the higher charges which the water undertaker will be able to exact. Now much the same is true of a company manufacturing dangerous chemicals or explosives, but in England a "Bhopal" or a "Flixborough" would be left to the common law rule with all its qualifications and uncertainties. The sole modern instance of a

[10] (1957) 11 D.L.R. (2d) 493.
[11] See p. 112, *post*.

significant *judicial* creation of strict liability has been the American development of product liability. England has now followed the same lines, but by statute.[12]

B. CAUSATION

Most torts require that the plaintiff should have suffered damage and it is for this damage that the law gives compensation.[13] It is therefore a fundamental requirement that the damage should have been caused by the defendant's tortious act or omission. Otherwise, the damage is a mere coincidence for which the defendant bears no responsibility. This link of cause and effect runs right through the law (for example, a plaintiff can only recover more than nominal damages for breach of contract if the breach caused his loss) but for some reason it is crime and tort that have spawned the overwhelming mass of authorities and in tort nearly all the cases are about negligence or the closely related tort of breach of statutory duty. The problems are in fact greater in tort than in crime because in the latter there may be a conviction for an attempt to commit the crime even if the causal connection is not established, but there is no law of attempted tort.

In the majority of cases the causative link is so obvious that it is assumed instinctively rather than arrived at by a process of logical thought (it has been said that causative concepts are "latent in ordinary thought and speech"[14]) and even where the courts have expressly adverted to the question there has been little attempt to put forward scientific or philosophical formulae of general application. However, some principle there must be and that which has been most commonly adopted if not acknowledged is that sometimes known as the "equivalence" theory, the condition *sine qua non*, or, in more homely language, the "but for" test. According to this the defendant's wrong is a cause of the damage if the damage would not have occurred if his wrongful act or omission had not taken place. One states the facts of the case, removes the element of the defendant's conduct which is wrongful and asks, "What would have happened if the defendant had conformed his conduct to the law?" Thus suppose the stopping distance (including "thinking distance") of a well

---

[12] See Chap. 6.

[13] The principal exceptions (or "torts actionable *per se*") are the varieties of trespass (Chap. 8) and libel. To some extent the exceptions are more apparent than real: if someone has been wrongfully arrested or his reputation has been grossly traduced he may not be able to point to a loss directly measurable in money but the man in the street would probably say he had been "harmed."

[14] *Haber* v. *Walker* [1963] V.R. 339.

maintained bus travelling at 50 m.p.h. to be 100 metres and that of one travelling at 80 m.p.h. to be 200 metres. When the bus is 25 metres from a junction, travelling at 80 (the speed limit being 50) a motor cyclist emerges from the side road without priority, is struck by the bus and killed. Now exceeding the speed limit by 30 m.p.h. near a junction is pretty powerful evidence of negligence, but the negligence is not a cause of the death because even if the bus had been doing 50 it could not have stopped in time. Had the bus been 150 metres away when the motor cyclist emerged, then, since there would have been no accident at 50 m.p.h. the speeding *is* a cause of death. It is important to note that we are only asking whether the speeding was *a* cause, not *the* cause of death. The motor cyclist's own negligence was also undoubtedly a cause and perhaps it even amounts in law to the sole effective cause, but that is a further stage of the process of allocating responsibility and one which we cannot even reach until we have established that the defendant's act was a contributory factor in the purely "factual" or "scientific" sense.

The principal difficulty with the "but for" test is that it may lead to results which defy commonsense when applied to cases of multiple causation. If D1 and D2 simultaneously shoot P through the heart no legal system can deny that both caused his death but our test would lead to the exclusion of both as causes of death because the act of each would, alone, have been sufficient to cause death. There are numerous contexts in which the law recognises that there may be concurrent sufficient operative causes. The point is implicit in the cases on misrepresentation. If the plaintiff seeks to recover damages for a fraudulent or negligent misrepresentation he must show that he suffered loss by relying on the misrepresentation. However, it is clear that the misrepresentation does not have to be the sole or even the dominant factor leading to his decision. As long as it was regarded by him as a substantial factor, albeit together with others, that is enough. *Baker* v. *Willoughby*[15] points the same way where the factors involved in causation are separated in time. P was injured by D in a road accident and suffered a permanently stiff leg. Before his action came to trial he was shot in that leg during a robbery at his place of work and the leg was amputated. The House of Lords held that D's liability for the loss of capability and enjoyment involved in having a stiff leg continued in the period after the amputation: the robber had removed his leg but he had not removed his loss, he had made it worse. Before the amputation he was X per cent. disabled as a result of what D had done; afterwards, he was 2X per cent. disabled as a result of what

---

[15] [1970] A.C. 467.

D and the robber had done. However, in *Jobling* v. *Associated Dairies*[16] the House of Lords came to the opposite conclusion where the subsequent cause was non-tortious—an illness unconnected with the disabling injury which would anyway have caused as great a degree of disablement as the injury. When the illness struck, the tort ceased to be a cause of the plaintiff's loss. The reasoning is compelling. If a court is asked to assess damages for future loss likely to be suffered by the plaintiff as a result of a tort it makes a discount for the "vicissitudes of life"—damaging contingencies like premature death or disabling illness which might in any event have cut the plaintiff off in his prime at a later time than the tortfeasor has in fact done.[17] Accordingly, it is impossible to ignore such an event when it is not a contingency but has actually occurred before trial. The status of *Baker* v. *Willoughby* is unclear. Possibly it still stands as authority for a different rule for successive sufficient tortious injuries. It could be argued that the prospect of a second tortious injury was so much more unlikely than illness or pure accident that it would not form part of the contingencies taken into account in assessing future damages in a normal case and therefore it should not be regarded as extinguishing the effect of the first tort in this situation, but this is not very convincing. If there is a different rule for multiple tortious injuries it is much more likely to rest upon policy. The second tortfeasor (*i.e.* the robber) in *Baker* v. *Willoughby* would (probably) be liable only for the already reduced "value" of the plaintiff's stiff leg so that if the first tortfeasor's liability were terminated at the time of the shooting there would be a gap in compensation even though the totality of the plaintiff's loss is undoubtedly attributable to the combined effect of the acts of the two tortfeasors. It is wrong that the plaintiff should suffer in this way as against two undoubted wrongdoers. In other words, reasons of fairness and policy are allowed to modify apparently more "scientific" rules of factual causation.[18]

A further problem is that our approach to causation involves a hypothetical enquiry ("but for this what *would* have happened?") to which the answer must to some extent be speculative. It has usually been said that the plaintiff must prove on a balance of probabilities that he would not have suffered the harm if the defendant had fulfilled his duty. In *McWilliams* v. *Arrol*[19] the

---

[16] [1982] A.C. 794.
[17] See p. 211, *post*.
[18] The robber in *Baker* v. *Willoughby* was not sued, though he was undoubtedly a tortfeasor. It is not known if P made a claim on the Criminal Injuries Compensation Board (p. 143 *post*) but his compensation from that source would have been assessed in much the same way as damages in an action against the robber.
[19] [1962] 1 W.L.R. 295.

defendants were under a statutory duty to provide safety belts for their steel erectors. They withdrew them and a few days later the deceased fell to his death, an event which the defendants admitted would not have occurred if he had been wearing a belt. For various reasons steel erectors very rarely wore belts when provided and though the enquiry was not as to what the deceased did but what he would have done in circumstances which never arose, the evidence led to a "natural, and indeed almost inevitable," inference that he would not have worn a belt on that day even if one had been available. Hence there was no proof of a causal connection between breach of duty and death. The opposite decision might, of course, have had the effect of encouraging employers to ensure that safety devices were actually used, but such a result would be better brought about by imposing a direct statutory duty to this effect. In any case, the defendants had committed a criminal offence by failing to *provide* belts and lack of a causal connection with the death would not be a defence to this charge even though the death might have been what prompted the prosecution.

The court in *McWilliams* v. *Arrol* could feel fairly confident in its answer to the hypothetical question but other situations give rise to formidable difficulties. Consider the causation of disease. Cigarette smoking causes lung cancer but many people who do not smoke contract cancer (and not merely from other people's smoke). An accurate medical diagnosis may simply be that a particular individual may well have contracted cancer as a result of smoking because it is known that there is a higher incidence of cancer among smokers. Long term radiation injury presents an acute example of this problem for the risk to health of ionising radiations is expressed in terms of percentage increases, often very small, of cancers already found in the community. A scientist asked to say whether a particular cancer had been "caused" in the lawyer's sense by radiation might answer that the question was impossible. In such a situation the law faces a choice between turning away virtually all cases or attributing a causal connection in an individual case on some basis other than a finding that the defendant's act is more likely than not to have produced the result. A liberal approach was taken in *McGhee* v. *N.C.B.*[20] The plaintiff contracted dermatitis after the defendants, in breach of duty, had failed to provide washing facilities to remove dust to which he had been exposed in doing his work. The medical evidence was that it was not possible to say that the plaintiff would not have suffered dermatitis had the facilities been provided but their absence "materially increased" the risk

[20] [1973] 1 W.L.R. 1.

of contracting the disease. The House of Lords held that this entitled the plaintiff to succeed. It was quickly perceived that this decision had implications for medical negligence cases and for the growing number of claims alleging side effects from drugs and vaccinations and an attempt was made to develop it into a principle of compensation for "loss of a chance."

In *Hotson* v. *East Berks Health Authority*[21] the plaintiff was injured in a fall but the hospital to which he was taken failed properly to examine him. He then developed a serious hip condition leading to permanent deformity. Had the hip injury been discovered on full examination the trial judge concluded that there was a 25 per cent. chance that immediate treatment would have prevented the deformity. He therefore, following *McGhee's* case, awarded the plaintiff 25 per cent. of his loss,[22] in which decision he was upheld by the Court of Appeal. However, the House of Lords reversed this decision on the ground that it was inconsistent with the general proposition that the plaintiff must prove his case on a balance of probabilities.

The consequence of the case seems to be that if the plaintiff fails to show on a balance of probabilities that he would have recovered he receives nothing but if he shows that it is more likely than not that he would have recovered he receives 100 per cent. of his loss, notwithstanding that recovery may be only very slightly more likely than non-recovery. Certain contract cases which have given damages for loss of a chance are perhaps to be explained on the basis that the plaintiffs *had* suffered a loss as a result of the breach and the court was concerned to quantify that loss.[23] *Hotson* was unsatisfactory in that it barely mentioned *McGhee's* case. However, the House of Lords in *Wilsher* v. *Essex Area Health Authority*[23a] has now said that *McGhee's* case lays down no new rule and does not challenge the basic proposition that the burden of proof of causation lies upon the plaintiff. Rather, it was a case in which the court, applying "a robust and pragmatic approach to the undisputed primary facts of the case," concluded that it was a legitimate inference of fact that the defendants' negligence had materially contributed to the plaintiff's injury.

There is no doubt that in medical negligence cases the courts must rely largely on statistical evidence but a plaintiff cannot found a case on mathematical probability alone. Suppose the

---

[21] [1987] 3 W.L.R. 232.

[22] There was no such discount in *McGhee's* case because it was not possible to quantify the risk in this way.

[23] For example, *Chaplin* v. *Hicks* [1911] 2 K.B. 786 (wrongful exclusion from beauty contest). Possibly the tort case of *Davies* v. *Taylor* [1974] A.C. 207 rests on the same basis.

[23a] [1988] 2 W.L.R. 557.

plaintiff is hit at night by an unknown vehicle. It is certain that there were only four vehicles in the vicinity, three of which belonged to and were driven by the servants of D (who would be liable for their driving) and one of which was driven by X. That evidence would no more justify a finding that one of D's vehicles had hit the plaintiff than would the knowledge that most men do not die of cancer justify a conclusion that a particular man had not. In a famous criminal case an American court overturned a verdict which was largely based upon evidence that the chance of anyone else possessing the identifying characteristics of the defendants was only one in twelve million. Even assuming that this assessment was accurate (which it almost certainly was not) that still meant there was one other "identical" couple in the Greater Los Angeles area and the court remarked that "urging that the [defendants] be convicted on the basis of evidence which logically establishes no more than this seems as indefensible as arguing for the conviction of X on the ground that a witness saw either X or X's twin brother commit the crime."[24]

Multiple Defendants

P, a pedestrian, is knocked down by the careless driving of D1 and left lying in the gutter. He is stunned, his expensive suit is ruined, but he has suffered no significant injury. A few moments later, along comes D2, driving too fast, and runs over the legs of the prostrate P, breaking them. D1 is certainly liable for the suit. D2 is equally certainly liable for the broken legs—and for nothing else, for that is all he has caused.[25] But it is possible, depending on the circumstances, that D1 is also liable for the broken legs. His driving was certainly a causal contribution (without it P would not have been lying there to have his legs broken by D2). It is true, as we shall see in the next Chapter, that the law limits the extent of D1's liability by requiring that the further damage must not be too "remote" but the second accident here is probably sufficiently immediate and foreseeable to satisfy that requirement. If so, both D1 and D2 have contributed to the same damage (the broken legs) and are "jointly and severally" liable for it. In other words, each is in principle liable to pay the whole sum of damages flowing from the broken legs even if the court concludes that the act of one is more causally important than that of the other. It is wrong to look

---

[24] *People* v. *Collins* 438 P. 2d 33 (Cal. 1968). A tort case rejecting a claim based on mathematical probability is *Smith* v. *Rapid Transit Inc.* 58 N.E. 2d 754 (Mass. 1945).

[25] Had D1 caused significant personal injury the question might be more difficult because it might not be possible to apportion P's loss of earnings to the acts of D1 and D2.

for the "main" cause and attach responsibility solely to that. The plaintiff can sue either or both of them and enforce his judgment against each for all or part of his loss as he chooses, though he cannot of course collect more than he has lost. Since multiple cause losses are common (consider a motorway "pile-up"; a situation where a manufacturer puts out a dangerous product and a distributor omits a pre-delivery inspection; or the appearance in a newspaper of a libellous letter which has found its way there as a result of the acts of writer, proprietor, editor, printer and so on) this principle of joint and several liability is of great importance. If the plaintiff chooses to collect his judgment from one defendant the developed common law systems (contrary to the original rule) allow that defendant to recover a proportionate contribution from other defendants liable (see the Civil Liability (Contribution) Act 1978) and there is usually a procedural mechanism whereby if only one defendant is sued he can bring in the others to have the question of contribution settled without separate proceedings. But this is not the direct concern of the plaintiff, who has a separate right of recovery in full against each. This is crucial where some tortfeasors are insolvent and unable to meet their share of liability, for the effect of the rule is to throw upon the solvent defendant the burden of the insolvency of his fellows. In the United States, where damages awards are high and where liability insurance is often held up to only fairly modest limits this has become a serious problem for public entities such as highway authorities, who may find that on the basis of a very small share in the responsibility for a road accident they carry the lion's share of a multi-million dollar award. This has led some states to abolish or drastically modify the joint and several liability rule so that each defendant is liable to the plaintiff only for his proportionate share of the loss. So far, however, the joint and several rule remains the law in Britain and the Commonwealth.

The principal difficulty in applying the joint and several rule is to know when the defendants have caused the same damage, for it is only to that that it applies. In many cases the exercise will be performed in a fairly broad way because that is the only practical approach: if the plaintiff suffers multiple injuries in a car crash involving vehicles driven by three defendants it is unlikely that it will be feasible to say that such and such an injury was attributable to one defendant and such and such to another. Diseases and degenerative conditions, however, once again raise greater problems. Suppose P has worked for a number of years in the employ of D1, D2 and D3, all of whom have contravened legislation designed to minimise noise in the workplace. Hearing impairment through exposure to excessive noise is a gradual process and may take some time before it manifests itself in disability. Suppose at the end of his employment with D3 P has become partially deaf, a condition which is valued in damages at £X. Assuming the periods of employment and the level of damaging noise to be about equal,[26] is each defendant jointly and severally liable for £X or only for his "proportion," say £1/3X? It will be appreciated that this is the very sort of situation where the choice may be crucial because the earlier employers may have gone out of business, not to mention the difficulties which may arise over the statutory time limits for bringing claims. The predominant view is that there is no joint and several liability, for to impose it would be to ignore the fact that D2 and D3 took over a plaintiff whose hearing was already impaired by the acts of their predecessor (even though that impairment might not yet have manifested itself in disability) just as in *Baker* v. *Willoughby* the robber would have been liable for the amputation of a damaged leg, not a sound leg. The result reflects that in cases where the defendant's act has caused the plaintiff's death but the plaintiff was already susceptible to premature death, whether from natural causes or some earlier injury. The defendant is liable for that death but in valuing the lost life for the purposes of damages the court takes into account the pre-existing weakness, because it might have been triggered by some other factor, and makes a deduction accordingly. Nevertheless, in neither case is it entirely obvious why the result should be different from that of the case where the plaintiff is the victim of concurrent tortious acts, for there no account is taken of the fact that either would have been sufficient.

In one area of concurrent cause some American jurisdictions have cut loose altogether from traditional notions of cause and effect and abandoned any attempt to trace a factual link between what the defendant did and what the plaintiff suffered. This started in a modest way in a shooting party case where one of two negligent defendants had shot the plaintiff but it could not be determined which one: the court held that each was obliged to show that his shot had not caused the injury and if neither could do so both were liable.[27] This seed developed into a startling growth in *Sindell* v. *Abbot Laboratories*.[28] The Supreme Court of

---

[26] In real life, of course, the relationship of noise, age, hearing impairment and disability is very much more complex and uncertain. See *Thompson* v. *Smiths Shiprepairers* [1984] Q.B. 405, which concerned the slightly different situation of a continuous employment with one employer during only part of which was there a practical possibility of taking effective steps against noise.

[27] *Summers* v. *Tice* 199 P. 2d 1 (Cal. 1948). This might represent the law in England, as it does in Canada: *Cook* v. *Lewis* [1952] 1 D.L.R. 1.

[28] 607 P. 2d 294 (Cal. 1980). At least 1,000 actions were filed in this litigation, some of them "class" actions on behalf of numerous plaintiffs.

California had to deal with a claim arising out of the prescription of the drug D.E.S. to the plaintiff's mother twenty years before, which the plaintiff alleged had caused her (the plaintiff) to develop cancer. The passage of time, combined with the fact that the drug had been prescribed generically made it impossible for the plaintiff to identify which of about 200 manufacturers was responsible for the batch in question. Abandoning the stance in previous cases that the burden of proof might be reversed in the plaintiff's favour if all possible defendants were sued, the court laid down that the plaintiff could proceed against companies having a "substantial share" of the D.E.S. market and recover against each in proportion to its share of the market unless the particular defendant could prove that it had not manufactured the consignment in question. The decision is controversial. It is certainly not the law in England and it has been widely rejected in the United States, being described by one court as "repugnant to the most basic tenets of tort law." On the other hand, it must be pointed out that although in an individual case one manufacturer would be held responsible for the products of another, yet over the market as a whole the liability of each would be approximately equivalent to the damage it caused.[29] This is an extreme form of loss spreading and what the court virtually does is to create a form of loss insurance financed by a levy on the industry. There can be little doubt that if this is the goal desired it would be better achieved by a direct legislative scheme of compensation, but *Sindell* is nevertheless a remarkable example of the adaptation of tort to deal with a type of litigation which traditional principles are incapable of handling.

C. WHO CAN SUE OR BE SUED?

There is little to say on the first question. Any legal person, natural (a human being) or artificial (such as a company or the Crown) may be the victim of a tort and sue for it, though in the nature of things some torts could not be committed against some legal persons (for example, assault against a company or a local authority).[30] It has been held in several jurisdictions that a person may sue for bodily harm suffered by him before he was born, but while the English courts would almost certainly have come to the same conclusion the matter is now governed by statute, the Congenital Disabilities (Civil Liability) Act 1976.

---

[29] For this reason the market share approach should not be applicable where the product was not inherently unsafe but the defect related to the manufacture of a particular batch.

[30] But a company or local authority may sue for defamation.

As to the second question, the most important instance of a privileged position is that of the Crown. In England until the Crown Proceedings Act 1947 there was no Crown liability for tort though in practice the relevant government department usually satisfied a judgment against an individual Crown servant, who generally enjoyed no immunity. The 1947 Act went far towards equating the Crown with other legal persons and further legislation in 1987 repealed the controversial section 10 of the 1947 Act, which had restricted the Crown's liability to members of the armed forces. Crown immunity was exported to the former colonies but there too it has been abrogated in varying degrees.[31] The former immunity of the Crown no doubt had some connection with the fact that it was the Crown's courts which were dispensing justice and perhaps for this reason the doctrine was not extended in England (though it was in the United States) to local government bodies. However, it should be noted that all organs of government, central and local, possess a large element of discretion in relation to many of their functions and this may make their conduct difficult or impossible to challenge via the law of torts.[32]

The Crown is not liable for judicial acts and the judge himself enjoys a personal immunity for things done in the exercise of his office. This is partly based on the need to preserve judicial independence without fear of vexatious claims but there is a further, and perhaps more compelling, reason in the need to protect the integrity of judicial decisions and to prevent the use of tort actions against judges as a "back door" route of appeal. For these reasons a similar immunity attaches to other participants in the judicial process, counsel conducting a case, witnesses (even perjured witnesses) and jurors.

As to children, the law of torts, unlike contract or crime, has no particular age of responsibility. One can predict with some confidence that no court would impose liability for fraud or defamation on a five-year-old, though to say that this is because of a lack of capacity to form the intent required is perhaps to ignore the rather simple mental elements of these torts. As for negligence, the predominant view is that some allowance must be made for the child's age, notwithstanding that the general standard is the objective one of the reasonable man. It should not be too readily assumed that a child's liability for negligence is theoretical and unenforceable in practice: parents are not

---

[31] The American legislation, the Federal Tort Claims Act, restricts those features of American procedure which are widely thought to be responsible for large awards—trial by jury and contingency fees.

[32] See p. 90, *post*.

responsible for their children's torts (as opposed to their personal negligence for failing to supervise their children) but it is quite common for the child himself to be covered by an extension of the common form household policy provision which gives cover against liability other than for motoring and work-related accidents. Mental disorder is not a defence as such in tort: an insane person is liable for an intentional tort if he can form the requisite intent and he gets no special treatment from the law of negligence.

Far more important than any of the above is the doctrine of vicarious liability which is the cornerstone of the utility in practice of many of the principles of tort and which the student would do well to grasp at the outset. Where a tort is committed by a person in the course of his employment then his employer is also liable for it. The employer may absorb the cost of legal liability into his prices either directly by carrying the liability himself (as the Crown and public corporations do) or by purchasing liability insurance. The individual employee would not have the resources to follow the first course and in many situations would not have the access to the specialised insurance market to take the second. Even if he did, the level of risk in a hazardous enterprise would put cover beyond his means. Nor would it make much sense for an employer of one hundred tanker drivers earning £10,000 a year to increase the wages of each by £5,000 so that each could effect his own insurance. The "channelling" of responsibility to one defendant and his ability to spread its cost are powerful arguments in favour of vicarious liability. Furthermore, since the employer has ultimate control of the organisation of work in his enterprise he is in the best position to correct dangerous practices and maximise safety, and the imposition of liability upon him should encourage this. This, of course, assumes that tort liability even when filtered into the form of increased insurance premiums has a deterrent effect, a somewhat controversial question in itself. All this is not to say that the judges consciously developed vicarious liability with ideas of loss distribution and safety promotion in mind: it is much more likely to have arisen from a rather vague feeling that an employer should have to pay for the harm generated by his enterprise, the popular instinctive reaction that "they" should pay. But whatever its origins, vicarious liability, in conjunction with liability insurance, is what keeps tort afloat. Without it, the system would either atrophy in some areas or become intolerable.

The central feature of vicarious liability in its developed form is that it is strict and requires no fault on the part of the employer. It is truly vicarious, that is to say, the employer stands "in place of" the actual wrongdoer. The employer may have taken all possible care in the selection, training and supervision of his workers and the accident may have occurred as a result of a momentary lapse of attention away from the employer's premises, but liability is still imposed. It may be, of course, that there has been some deficiency in the organisation or supervision of the work. If so, there is added a further basis for liability, which is personal rather than vicarious—the employer is at fault in creating a situation in which it was foreseeable that others might act without due care and cause an accident. This theoretically simple distinction is blurred by the fact that the majority of modern employers are corporations, which can only act via human agents. Suppose the A Co. employs a safety inspector, B, who fails to carry out his duties efficiently so that he fails to observe and check the slapdash methods being used by an employee, C, in operating his machine. These lead to injury to P. A Co. is liable to P because it is vicariously liable for C's negligence. The claim could also be framed as invoking vicarious liability for the negligence of *B* at one step removed and this would be perfectly acceptable in theory. In practice, however, the alternative claim might be framed as an allegation of a direct failure by A Co. to ensure a safe system of work at its factory. At one time the distinction between the employer's personal duty and his truly vicarious liability was of vital importance because of the doctrine of "common employment," restricting the scope of vicarious liability where one employee injured another. The abolition of common employment certainly reduced the importance of the personal duty but it is still of importance where the employer has entrusted a task to someone outside his company, for whom he is not vicariously liable. The idea has also surfaced in medical negligence cases, where it has been suggested that a hospital authority may be under a duty, independent of vicarious liability, to take care to ensure that its treatment units are properly staffed and equipped.[33]

Though vicarious liability does not require any fault on the part of the employer it only comes into play if the employee has himself committed a tort[34] and that will normally require fault on *his* part. In effect the doctrine is ancillary to a fault-based system and in an effort to ensure a financially responsible defendant

---

[33] See *Wilsher* v. *Essex Area Health Authority* [1987] Q.B. 730. The House of Lords ordered a new trial in this case on the causation issue: see p. 23, *ante*.

[34] A handful of cases adopt the "master's tort theory" whereby the employer commits a tort through the act of his employee. But even on this theory there must be an act by the employee which would normally amount to a tort. The point has only been of importance where there has been some procedural bar to suing the employee.

shifts the fault-based liability of the employee to the faultless employer. When we say "shifts" that is theoretically untrue, for the actual wrongdoer remains personally liable (on a joint and several basis) for his wrong and, since the tort will almost inevitably be a breach of his contract of employment, he is liable to indemnify his employer should the latter be sued to judgment. It is, however, unlikely that the plaintiff will press his rights against the employee to a conclusion where the employer is solvent (a point reflected in the fact that the employer's liability insurance will rarely cover the employee's personal liability) and the practicalities of industrial relations render the employer's right of indemnity nowadays more theoretical than real.[35] The real sanction is dismissal.

The law must seek some criterion for identifying the relationships which entail vicarious liability; it must then determine which acts within that relationship will bring the doctrine into play. As is implicit in the terminology adopted above, the central relationship attracting vicarious liability is that of employer and employee or "master and servant" in the traditional language of the common law; the relationship arising from a contract of service, as opposed to the legally distinct category of a contract for services. There is a huge amount of case law on this question, though most of it in modern times has arisen not in the context of vicarious liability but in other areas of the law (for example, social security taxation and employment security) where the legislation makes the existence of a contract of service the determinant of rights and duties. It seems, however, to be assumed that the expression has the same meaning wherever it occurs. Sometimes the distinction between the two types of contract can be very fine. My chauffeur is employed under a contract of service even though I may only use him once a week; but the local haulage firm is operating under a contract for services even though it carries all my factory production and has very little other business. The classical approach to the task of identifying a contract of service was to ask whether the person doing the work was under the control of the employer as to how the work was to be done. Such a test would tend to confine vicarious liability to situations where the work was of a simple, routine nature but modern expectations of effective compensation for injury have caused the net to be cast a good deal more

---

[35] For the indemnity see *Lister* v. *Romford Ice etc. Co.* [1957] A.C. 555. An employer's liability insurer who has satisfied a judgment against the employer would be subrogated to (*i.e.* could take over and enforce) the employer's right of action, but in England no attempt would be made to do so unless there was wilful wrongdoing. In parts of Australia the employer's right of indemnity has been abrogated by statute.

widely so that, for example, a hospital authority is now vicariously liable for the negligence of its full-time medical staff even though the hospital managers have no medical skill. Sometimes this extension has been achieved by attenuating the control test so as to require control only of the organization of the work but not detailed supervision.[36] Other cases have thrown over the control test in favour of asking whether the wrongdoer was an integral part of the defendant's business. Perhaps the dominant approach now is to pay some regard to the control test but to look in addition at other factors to see if they are consistent with the existence of a contract of service—method of payment, risk of loss, provision of materials and so on. The issue is so heavily dependent upon the facts of the particular case that the response is inevitably impressionistic. One judge has said that a contract of service is something easier to recognize than to define and perhaps we cannot do better at the end of the day than pose the question, albeit circular, "is the person doing the work acting as an employee or as a person in business on his own account?"

If one concludes that the wrongdoer is employed under a contract of service there may be a further problem if, on the occasion in question, his services have been "lent out," for the issue may then arise of whether he is in the service of his general or temporary employer. The law is that he remains in the service of the general employer for vicarious liability purposes unless the temporary employer has the power to direct not simply what shall be done but how it shall be done, and this is a context in which the control test has not been watered down. Where the worker is a skilled man in charge of the general employer's machinery this burden is exceedingly difficult to satisfy and even where the work is unskilled it has been said that the general employer's task is a "formidable" one if he is to shift responsibility. It is, however, very common for the two employers to make specific contractual provision for the consequences of negligence. Except in so far as it provides evidence that the temporary employer had control this contract has no effect upon the position of the injured plaintiff, though if it provides for indemnification of the general by the temporary employer it will, of course, determine where ultimate financial responsibility lies.

If the relationship is not a contract of service it is customary to call it that of employer and "independent contractor" and the general rule is that there is no vicarious liability in this situation. Provided the employer has taken reasonable care in selecting the

---

[36] But even on this basis a building contractor or sub-contractor is not employed under a contract of service.

contractor, and thereby fulfilled his own duty, then the contractor alone is liable. What amounts to reasonable care in selection varies according to the nature of the work. You do not have to ask for testimonials when hiring a taxi or sending your car to be serviced for in effect you are entitled to assume competence from a person in the trade unless you have actual and compelling notice to the contrary. On the other hand, the developer of a major building complex would be expected to make extensive enquiries, though he would certainly do so anyway for the protection of his own interests. The reason for the general absence of *vicarious* liability is probably that as a class independent contractors are far more likely to be claimworthy than are employees, so there is less need for the ''back up'' of vicarious liability. Indeed to impose vicarious liability would often be startlingly inconvenient and inefficient—imagine all the old ladies, non-car owners, who would need to buy insurance cover against the day they picked an inattentive taxi driver. Yet it must be admitted that insolvent and uninsured contractors do exist and that their financial irresponsibility may be the reason they can drum up business with attractive prices. Logically, there would be nothing to prevent an enquiry into the contractor's financial responsibility being built into the requirement of reasonable care in selection, as some American courts have held. Again, such a duty to enquire would for practical purposes be non-existent in the day-to-day dealings of private individuals and in a major contract the matter is likely to be taken care of by express requirements as to insurance. The sort of case which under the present law gives rise to difficulty is that where a major concern uses a small firm for minor tasks like window cleaning or roof repairs. There might be something to be said for a general rule that a person who employs a contractor in the course of a business should be vicariously liable for his torts, but aside from difficulties of definition this might require both employer and contractor to insure and hence be inefficient.[37]

Notwithstanding the general rule, there are situations in which the employer is responsible for the contractor's negligence although no fault can *in fact* be attributed to him. Strictly speaking these do not involve true vicarious liability[38] for the predominant view is that the employer's liability arises from a personal, ''non-delegable'' duty which he discharges through the contractor, so that if the contractor is negligent the duty is automatically

---

[37] Contrast the situation under a contract of service, where, the employer's right of indemnity being a dead letter, liability will stop with the employer.
[38] But plenty of judicial statements can be found referring to it as a vicarious liability.

broken—not a duty to take care but a duty that care be taken, something quite distinct from the employer's duty in selection. The distinction between this and vicarious liability has little practical consequence and we probably speak in terms of a non-delegable duty because it makes it easier to justify a situation in which liability is the exception rather than the rule. It would, however, be difficult to draw up a definitive list of non-delegable duties[39] and harder still to find a convincing rationale for their imposition in some cases but not in others. Perhaps the most practically important is the duty of an employer to take care for the safety of persons employed by him under a contract of service—if he entrusts the performance of this to someone outside his organisation he is responsible for that person's negligence. In imposing this non-delegable duty the courts have been influenced by the fact that if the law were otherwise the employee might be adversely affected by the technicalities of corporate organisation. For example in *McDermid* v. *Nash Dredging and Reclamation Co.*[40] the plaintiff was injured by the negligence of the master of a tug owned by S Co. Technically, the plaintiff was employed by N Co., a wholly owned subsidiary of S Co., the function of which was to employ English crew to serve on S Co.'s vessels. Had the accident taken place on the following shift the master would have been an Englishman, C, who was employed by N Co. It is hardly surprising that the House of Lords held N Co. were liable to the plaintiff because they had delegated their duty to S Co.'s servant. In certain areas the imposition of a non-delegable duty may owe something to the existence of an undertaking, contractual or near-contractual, by the defendant. This would explain cases where bailees have been held liable for sub-bailees and possibly also the view that a hospital might be liable for doctors (not directly engaged by the patient) who are not on the full-time staff. Of course, if there is a contract it may impose upon the defendant a duty not merely that care be taken but to secure a particular result, in which event one need not worry about whose act or fault actually caused the loss: the duty of a seller is to deliver the contract goods, not to guarantee due care by his suppliers.

A related and extremely obscure area concerns the liability of a principal for the torts of his agent. Agency is primarily a contractual concept concerned with the power of the agent to

---

[39] Further, there might be variations from one common law jurisdiction to another. For example, certainly in the U.S.A. and probably in England such a duty arises if the work is "extra-hazardous" but the existence of this category has been doubted in Australia.

[40] [1987] 3 W.L.R. 212.

create and modify relationships between his principal and third parties. Since torts involving misrepresentation (*e.g.* fraud) are commonly committed in a contractual context it is not surprising that they should involve the principal in vicarious liability for his agent even though the latter is not employed under a contract of service. Beyond this, however, despite many unguarded dicta, it is unlikely that there is any general liability of principals for torts of non-servant agents, though there may be further isolated instances. One is the rule that the owner of a motor vehicle is liable for the driving of the vehicle by a person acting as his agent. Mere permission to drive is not enough to bring this into play, the driver must be performing some task (though not necessarily a commercial one) on behalf of the owner; for example in one of the earlier cases the driver was taking a friend's car to Monte Carlo for him preparatory to starting a touring holiday there. Though this doctrine is found in most common law jurisdictions its scope and significance varies according to local arrangements for satisfaction of judgments against uninsured drivers,[41] for this is the area par excellence where the law hardly conceals its purpose of a search for a claimworthy defendant. In the United States, where such machinery tends not to exist, many courts apply a "family car" doctrine, making the owner liable for the negligence of any member of his household; some states have simply legislated to make the owner vicariously liable for any person driving with his permission. Here, the decision in *Morgans* v. *Launchbury*[42] smothered any development along these lines by requiring a genuine agency.

If the relationship between the parties is such as to give rise to vicarious liability there must obviously be some connection between the relationship and the tort. There is no reason why a haulage company should be liable for the careless driving of one of its drivers while on holiday: the risk is in no way created by the employer's enterprise and in any case it would be difficult for it to insure against it. In the case of persons employed under a contract of service the required link is expressed by asking whether the act was done "in the course of employment." This does not limit the employer's liability to acts which the employee is fully entitled to do (for that would stultify the doctrine of vicarious liability altogether—who is entitled to be negligent?) but extends to cases where the conduct of the employee can be described as an improper mode of doing what he was employed to do. Hence smoking by a petrol tanker driver during delivery is

---

[41] In England, the Motor Insurers' Bureau Agreement. The owner is personally liable for breach of statutory duty in allowing an uninsured person to drive.
[42] [1973] A.C. 127.

within the scope of employment even though it is negligence so crass as to justify instant dismissal[43]; but a blow given by him in an altercation with the garage owner on his late arrival would not be. The non-liability in the latter case is not simply because the tort is intentional but because the employment is merely the background against which it is committed. If, however, the same blow had been struck in a mistaken or excessive attempt to protect the employer's property against theft, then liability might be imposed. Similarly, if a car is entrusted to the safe-keeping of a garage, the garage would be responsible if the night watchman took it on a joyride, since the security of the vehicle has been put in his hands and making off with it is just a highly improper way of performing the task. If, however, the vehicle had been taken by someone in the accounts department the employer would not be liable even though the employment certainly facilitated the wrong. It will be appreciated that this approach may lead to a person being both within and without his employment at the same time. If the night watchman on his joyride not only damages the car but injures a pedestrian at the same time the garage would not be liable for this: the night watchman is not employed to drive, although the act of driving may be an improper way of doing what he was employed to do for the purposes of the car owner's claim.

Course of employment is a question of law, but so much turns on the facts that the court's conclusion may be hard to predict. One may, however, recognise two general approaches to the question. Some cases define what the employee was employed to do in very broad terms, which makes it easy to describe very serious acts of misconduct or disobedience as improper modes of doing an authorised act; others take a narrower view and treat the employee's instructions as defining what he is authorised to do. Though outright conflict is avoided by saying that every case turns on its own facts the student will soon come to recognise the two approaches. For example, it is often said that instructions which limit the manner, time or place of his work will not limit the scope of the employment. Thus in *Bugge* v. *Brown*[44] an Australian "rouseabout" was held within the course of his employment when, although instructed to go to a house at K to cook his meal he did so instead at a hut at F. On the other hand, there has been a tendency to refuse to impose vicarious liability where a driver entrusted with his employer's vehicle has caused a road accident while making a substantial deviation from his authorised route for private purposes. It may seem obvious that in such a case the

---

[43] *Century Insurance Co.* v. *Northern Ireland Road Transport Board* [1942] A.C. 509.
[44] (1919) 26 C.L.R. 110.

driver is no longer on his employer's business because he is employed to drive from A to B and not from A to C. But why should it not be said that the core of his employment is to have charge of the vehicle so that he is still engaged in that while deviating? One might equally well say that an employee entrusted with goods for safe keeping was not employed to steal them, but as we have seen such an act *does* involve the employer in liability. Of course, the line would have to be drawn somewhere—for example the employer should not be liable for an accident caused by his driver after he has decamped with the vehicle intending never to return.

If the employee acts with the purpose of promoting the employer's business that will certainly be a factor pointing towards the employer's liability. For example, numerous cases have held that a driver is outside the course of his employment in picking up unauthorised passengers (in other words the prohibition on the giving of lifts is regarded as limiting the scope of the employment) but in *Rose* v. *Plenty*[45] liability was imposed where a milk float driver, in breach of orders, carried a child on the float to help him with deliveries. An intention to promote the employer's business is, however, neither sufficient nor necessary for the imposition of liability. In the well-known case of *Poland* v. *John Parr & Sons*[46] a blow to a boy whom a carter mistakenly thought to be pilfering sugar from a cart was held within the scope of the carter's authority to protect his employer's goods, but the position would have been different if, say, the carter had fired a shot at the boy: such an act would be so excessive as to take it altogether outside the class of act he was authorised to perform. The employer's liability for misguided enthusiasm is not without its limits. As to the other point, the cases on theft by employees illustrate the imposition of liability even though the wrongdoer's purpose is to benefit himself. The same may be true of fraud committed by the employee. In *Lloyd* v. *Grace, Smith & Co.*[47] a solicitor was liable where his managing clerk tricked the plaintiff into making over her property to him.[48] Cases of fraudulent misrepresentation need, however, to be treated with some care because the essence of the plaintiff's case is that he has reasonably relied on the servant's statement within the scope of his authority. This authority may be actual or ostensible (*i.e.* arising from the employer presenting the employee as having an

---

[45] [1976] 1 W.L.R. 141.
[46] [1927] 1 K.B. 236.
[47] [1912] A.C. 716.
[48] It is interesting that Lord Macnaghten adverted to the possibility of the employer's insuring against such infidelity and regarded that as mitigating the hardship to employers of a rule of liability.

authority greater than he actually has) but it must in some sense have been conferred by the employer, so that the employee's own assertion that he has authority, however convincing it may be to the outside world, is not a sufficient basis for his employer to be liable. Grace, Smith & Co. were liable because their clerk had authority to deal with conveyancing business and perverting such a transaction for his own benefit was an improper way of doing what he was authorised to do. Had he been someone who was not authorised to deal directly with clients at all the result would have been different even though Mrs. Lloyd's mistake in relying on him might have been just as reasonable.

In those cases where the employer is involved in liability because of the negligence of his independent contractor it is not enough that the act might be said to be in the course of the contractor's employment, for the employer is not liable for negligence which is "collateral" to the task for which the contractor is employed. The employer is not, therefore, liable for the negligence of the contractor in bringing material to the site but he is if the end product of the contractor's work is dangerous and causes harm. More difficult is an act of negligence in the very act of carrying out the work itself but which does not affect the completed work. It has been suggested that if the negligence involves the very risk which is the justification for the imposition of the non-delegable duty in the first place then it is not collateral but this very sensible approach is unfortunately inconsistent with one of the principal English cases.[49]

---

[49] *Padbury* v. *Holliday & Greenwood* (1912) 28 T.L.R. 492. Compare *Holliday* v. *National Telephone Co.* [1899] 2 Q.B. 392.

CHAPTER THREE

Negligence

> "You must take reasonable care to avoid acts or omissions which you can reasonably foresee would be likely to injure your neighbour. Who, then, in law is my neighbour? The answer seems to be—persons who are so closely and directly affected by my act that I ought reasonably to have them in my contemplation as being so affected when I am directing my mind to the acts or omissions which are called in question."

These words are from the speech of Lord Atkin in *Donoghue* v. *Stevenson*,[1] a case on appeal from Scotland in which it was alleged that the plaintiff had been poisoned by the defendant's negligence in allowing a snail to get into an opaque bottle of ginger beer manufactured by him and consumed by the plaintiff. The statement must be the most influential in any decision on any subject in the history of the common law in England. Negligence is the unchallenged sovereign of torts both in terms of current importance and of potential but its origin as a unified concept lies no further back than *Donoghue* v. *Stevenson*. Of course there had been many cases before 1932 in which a defendant had been held liable on the ground that his conduct was negligent, but the cases were looked at as a series of disparate situations in which liability was imposed, not as examples of a broader theme.

Negligence as a tort[2] occurs when the defendant (1) owes a "duty of care" to the plaintiff, (2) breaks that duty by failing to come up to the standard of care required by law and (3) thereby

---

[1] [1932] A.C. 562.
[2] The point has already been made that negligence may be an element in other torts.

causes some legally recognised damage to the plaintiff. The second and third aspects produce most of the disputes in court but it is the first that gives rise to the most difficult conceptual problems and it is the "heart" of an understanding of this tort and its place in the law.

A. THE DUTY OF CARE

Return for a moment to Lord Atkin's words in *Donoghue* v. *Stevenson* and it will be obvious that as a sole determinant of the existence of a legal duty of care not to cause harm it is too wide. One trader, far from being under a duty of care not to cause harm to his competitors, is allowed to run his business as efficiently as he can (provided he uses only lawful means) so as to take away as much of their trade as possible. Such "harm" is not negligent, it is deliberate, but far from being legally penalised he is positively encouraged to compete. So extreme and so obvious is this example that it may be objected that it does not invalidate a general statement which was clearly never formulated with the area of competition in mind. However, there are a fair number of other situations, perhaps not so obvious to the lay person, where it has been found necessary or desirable to deny or qualify the applicability of the "Atkinian formula." While it is true that it applies pretty much without exception to physical damage caused by acts its scope is much more restricted where the defendant has failed to act so as to prevent damage (despite Lord Atkin's reference to omissions) or where the damage is purely financial in nature. If D negligently destroys X's factory it is certainly foreseeable that the workers there may suffer loss of income through being laid off but the defendant is not liable to them for that. In such cases the courts have concluded, for reasons not necessarily to do with foreseeability, that the law of negligence should not extend the defendant's liability so far. The duty of care question is in fact two questions. The first is, "Is this a case of the *type* to which the law of negligence is applicable?" Only if the answer to that question is in the affirmative do we get to the second question, "Was a duty owed to *this* plaintiff?" or, to put it another way, "Was it foreseeable that this plaintiff would be harmed by the defendant's act?" These rather straightforward ideas have, however, been much obscured by the way the law in this area has developed since 1932.

There is no doubt that *Donoghue* v. *Stevenson* was a "type" case, that is to say the real issue was not whether it was foreseeable that negligence on Mr. Stevenson's production line might cause harm to Mrs. Donoghue but whether manufacturers (or at least manufacturers of foodstuffs) were to be brought within the law of negligence in relation to harm caused by their products.[3] Before *Donoghue* v. *Stevenson* the existence of a contract of sale between the manufacturer and the retailer was regarded as preventing the application of the law of torts as between manufacturer and consumer.[4] Now the famous "neighbour" passage comes at a point in Lord Atkin's speech which shows that he intended it to have at least some bearing on the first or general question, though he can hardly have intended it as a sufficient test for all cases. In the years following *Donoghue* v. *Stevenson*, however, the courts not infrequently confirmed previous decisions denying the application of negligence law in particular areas and, while it could no longer be denied that negligence was a tort in its own right, the prevailing attitude continued to be that duties of care existed in situations where they had been recognised by previous authorities and that, while the list of duties could certainly be extended, it required a positive decision by the courts to do so, with the burden on the plaintiff to show good reason why the law should be extended. Thus the immunity in negligence of the builder of a defective house (something which might be thought to bear at least some resemblance to a defective manufactured product) survived *Donoghue* v. *Stevenson* by 40 years. The neighbour formula was not regarded as having any real part to play in deciding the question whether the law of negligence should apply in situations where it had not been applied before.

This "conservative" view was challenged by several members of the House of Lords in 1970 in *Home Office* v. *Dorset Yacht Co.*[5] but the real change came in *Anns* v. *Merton London Borough*[6] in which the House unanimously concurred in a passage in the speech of Lord Wilberforce which must be quoted in full:

> "The position has now been reached that in order to establish that a duty of care arises in a particular situation, it is not necessary to bring the facts of that situation within those of previous situations in which a duty of care has been held to exist. Rather the question has to be approached in two stages. First, one has to ask whether, as between the alleged wrongdoer and the person who has suffered damage

---

[3] In many cases, negligence liability of the manufacturer is in practice now eclipsed by the strict liability under the Consumer Protection Act 1987 (Chap. 6) but it remains for those cases to which the statute does not apply.

[4] A friend had bought the ginger beer from the retailer and given it to the plaintiff. Had the plaintiff bought it she would have had a claim under section 14 of the Sale of Goods Act against the retailer.

[5] [1970] A.C. 1004.

[6] [1978] A.C. 728.

there is a sufficient relationship of proximity or neighbour-hood such that, in the reasonable contemplation of the former, carelessness on his part may be likely to cause damage to the latter—in which case a prima facie duty of care arises. Secondly, if the first question is answered affirmatively, it is necessary to consider whether there are any considerations which ought to negative, or to reduce or limit the scope of the duty or the class of person to whom it is owed or the damages to which a breach of it may give rise."

Anns was a case in which the House of Lords confirmed the validity of some radical developments affecting liability for defective premises and for the negligent exercise of statutory powers but it seems unlikely that the Wilberforce two-stage approach to the duty of care was thought by any of the judges to be particularly revolutionary. Nonetheless, the result of it has been a greater amount of upheaval and uncertainty in the law of negligence than at any time since 1932. The issue is of course irrelevant in the vast majority of cases coming before the courts, in which the existence of a duty of care has been established time out of mind: no one in a "running down" action would open by arguing that drivers owed a duty of care to pedestrians, for the point would be regarded as too obvious to be worth disputing. But in novel situations or in cases where a duty had previously been denied the potential of the Wilberforce approach was considerable. One view, that which at first strongly prevailed, was that the formula made foreseeability of harm the sole test of the existence of a prima facie duty of care. (Attempts have been made to show that this was not so, but the words used by Lord Wilberforce suggest strongly that this view was correct and that "proximity or neighbourhood" were meant to include no further factors). Once that hurdle had been passed liability followed unless the court was satisfied that the countervailing factors were sufficiently powerful to rebut it at the second stage. Some judges took this as an invitation to reassess well-established lines of authority denying the existence of a duty. Further, while Lord Wilberforce clearly contemplated that there would continue to be cases in which a duty of care was rejected, the formula seemed to look at both foreseeability of harm and the countervailing considerations in terms of the detailed facts of the individual case. Were there to be no more predictable and generally applicable bars to recovery? Were judges to be given a form of discretion to pronounce "duty or no duty" according to what they conceived to be the justice of the case? Whether or not Lord Wilberforce meant to create such a state of affairs (and it is most unlikely that he did) a reaction has set in. The emphasis on foreseeability at the first stage has been greatly lessened and a rather different meaning given to the superficially synonymous concept of "proximity."

The leading case is the Privy Council's decision in *Yuen Kun Yeu* v. *Att.-Gen. of Hong Kong*[7] though there were earlier indications in the House of Lords of the way the wind was blowing. The defendant (represented for the purposes of the action by the Attorney-General) was the Commissioner of Deposit-Taking Companies and his function was to license and register such bodies. The plaintiffs invested sums of money in a registered deposit-taking company which failed because, they alleged, it had been run fraudulently. They thereupon brought an action for negligence against the defendant alleging that he should have known how the company was being run and should either not have registered it or revoked its registration. The Privy Council upheld the Hong Kong courts in striking out this claim as disclosing no cause of action. Their Lordships pointed out that the case was based upon failure by the defendant to protect the plaintiffs against the wrongdoing of a third party, that the law had traditionally required some sort of "special relationship" either with the victim or with the wrongdoer in order to raise such a duty of protection[8] and that this was absent on the facts. The defendant had neither the resources nor the authority for detailed day-to-day supervision of the defaulting company and the plaintiffs were simply a few among the many inhabitants of Hong Kong who might choose to invest their money in institutions subject to the defendant's powers. Accordingly, there was insufficient "proximity" between the parties and it was unnecessary to rely as such on arguments of public policy, for example that the defendant's general performance of his functions for the public benefit might be adversely affected by the threat of claims against him. A little earlier the Court of Appeal in *Hill* v. *Chief Constable of West Yorkshire*[9] had dismissed a claim against the police based on alleged negligent failure to prevent a murder by apprehending the offender, who had already committed 12 similar crimes. The court had to some extent relied on the possible inhibiting effect on the police service of the imposition of liability but the Privy Council remarked that the case could simply have been decided on the basis of lack of proximity between the police and the victim. "Proximity" has accordingly become a term of art which includes foreseeability

---

[7] [1987] 2 All E.R. 705.
[8] See further, p. 48, *post*.
[9] [1987] 2 W.L.R. 1126. The decision was affirmed by the H.L.: [1988] 2 W.L.R. 1049.

but is by no means confined to it since it seems to include at least some of those other factors which a court takes into account in deciding whether it is *just* that a duty of care should be imposed. If so, one might think that we may as well abandon the two-stage test altogether, since the second stage has been merged into the first, but it seems that this is not entirely so and that one must still proceed to the second stage in "rare" cases. Such a case might be that in which an action is brought against a barrister alleging negligence in the conduct of a case in court. If a barrister fails to conduct a case with due care and skill it is obvious that the client may suffer. However, the barrister is in a peculiar position because he owes a duty (though not a tort duty) to the court as well as to his client. For example, the ethics of his profession oblige him to draw the court's attention to precedents of which he is aware even though they go against his client's case and he must not give his active assistance to the presentation of cases which he knows to be false. It is argued that if he were to face the prospect of liability for negligence to his client there is a risk that he would lean in favour of his client rather than towards his duty to the court. Further, since proof by the client that he has suffered loss as a result of the negligence would require proof that had it not occurred the outcome of the case would have been different, the court trying the negligence action would need to engage in the task of determining the hypothetical outcome of the first trial. For these reasons it is clear law that there is no duty of care.[10] Yet the relationship between barrister and client is so close that it would be strange to deny that there was proximity between them. Hence the need to fall back to a second stage. Another case where it would be preferable to deny a duty at the second stage would be that where the plaintiff's conduct deprived him of the protection of the law, as where he was jointly involved with the defendant in the commission of a crime.

The reader may by now be asking whether all this subtlety, these fine shifts of emphasis and degree are of much practical importance. At one level, the answer is "no." Expressions like "proximity" and "foreseeability" are so vague that they are unlikely to constrain a trial judge in coming to a decision on the question of duty. Further, it might not have been too difficult to come to exactly the same result in *Yuen Kun Yeu* via the two-stage approach as set out in *Anns*. The defendant had failed to protect the plaintiffs against wilful wrongdoing by a third party. Since the law has always shown great reluctance to impose a positive duty to protect others, was not that clear and consistent evidence of "considerations which ought to negative" the duty claimed by

---

[10] *Rondel* v. *Worsley* [1969] 1 A.C. 191.

the plaintiff? However, at another level there is more than a verbal quibble involved in the different approaches, for they reflect different trends in the law of negligence. Whatever *Anns* actually meant it was thought to put great emphasis on the close connection between foreseeability and the prima facie duty and it therefore pointed towards an expanding concept of liability, tolerant of exceptions, but requiring those exceptions to be justified by argument rather than by mere longevity. This expansionary trend was illustrated, in the post-*Anns* era, by some truly revolutionary decisions on economic loss. But there has been a reaction, perhaps prompted by a growing awareness of the burden of negligence liability insurance in some trades and professions. Subsequent cases have largely reversed the expansionary trend on economic loss and the line taken in *Yuen Kun Yeu* on the general approach to duty reflects this reaction by depriving foreseeability of its primary place and relegating it to a more subsidiary role among the factors which determine what a court will consider "just." The Privy Council commented that the issues in the appeal had "far reaching implications as regards the potential liability in negligence of a wide variety of regulatory agencies carried on under the aegis of central or local government and also to some extent by nongovernmental bodies. Such agencies are in modern times becoming an increasingly familiar feature of the financial, commercial, industrial and social scene."[11] It seems that in the new climate we should not look too much to the law of negligence to remedy the deficiencies of such bodies.

So, as we said at the outset, there are situations in which the law of negligence does not apply, notwithstanding that harm to the plaintiff is foreseeable. The question of duty or no duty is one of law but it is a question of law of a very different kind from, say, the question whether there is consideration to support an alleged contract or whether the crime of murder requires an intention to kill, for the factors at which the court will have to look may be moral, social or even political rather than narrowly legal, factors which are subsumed into the shorthand expression "policy." Doubts have sometimes been expressed whether judges are necessarily the best arbiters of such matters or whether the process of adversarial litigation is best suited to bring out the best balance of the competing considerations. A strong example is the speech of Lord Scarman in *McLoughlin* v. *O'Brian*,[12] dealing with

---

[11] The court must have had in mind the radically new regulatory provisions in the Financial Services Act 1986. But section 187 exempts most regulatory bodies from liability for negligence.

[12] [1983] 1 A.C. 410. Compare Lord Edmund Davies in the same case.

the extent of liability for shock caused by witnessing an accident or its aftermath:

> "The policy issue as to where to draw the line is not justiciable. The problem is one of social, economic and financial policy. The considerations relevant to a decision are not such as to be capable of being handled within the limits of the forensic process."

Nevertheless, it is submitted that this is not the way the courts actually operate and that matters of policy are regularly taken into account in marking the extent of liability, either more or less covertly under the guise of "proximity" or more openly by laying down seemingly arbitrary rules predicated upon a need to keep liability within acceptable bounds. Short of a truly comprehensive statutory code of law providing for every eventuality or the application of a blanket principle that all foreseeable loss is recoverable (the first an unattainable goal, the second an undesirable one) considerations of "policy" must be faced.

Just as the student of the law of contract could not hope to give a confident answer to a practical question without some knowledge of the law governing individual types of contract, so there is much to be said about the extent as well as the content of the duty of care in particular situations and relationships. Indeed, it is customary to treat some areas (for example the duty of an occupier of land or the giver of information or advice) as almost self-contained topics in their own right and they are outlined in the next chapter. A full review of duties of care would be beyond the scope of an introductory book, but it is necessary to look at a few controversial areas at greater length because they illustrate the way the courts have to balance competing factors and at the same time they help to mark out the place of torts in the structure of the law.

Failure to Act

The distinction between action and inaction is fundamental to the common law. Despite the reference to "omissions" in *Donoghue* v. *Stevenson* there is no doubt that a stranger may pass by someone who is in grave danger of drowning and whom he might rescue with only trifling inconvenience to himself and escape the attention of the law of torts (and, indeed, of the criminal law). This state of affairs is probably the result of a combination of factors rather than one single policy.

First, we may feel some doubt about causation in relation to a person who has taken no positive part in the creation of the danger. It is certainly true that we instinctively attribute causative effect to omissions in some circumstances. If a person makes a promise to feed my goldfish while I am away we would probably agree that his failure to carry out the promise "caused" the death of the goldfish and we might say the same even if there were no promise but he had regularly done so and then stopped. But suppose he has promised or done nothing in relation to the goldfish in the past, happens to notice that they need feeding but does nothing. Has he caused their death? If so, we may be forced into the position that every one of a large number of people who could have saved a starving person has caused his death. Secondly, some may think that although public morality would condemn the passer-by in our first example, and it would not be too difficult for the law to deal with him, there would be difficulties in drawing the line beyond that case. Are we to stop at physical danger? Or am I to be liable for failing to ward off a danger to my neighbour's house which I see developing while he is on holiday? Or for failing to tell him that a company in which I know he is buying shares is in financial difficulties? And where a large number of people could have helped are they all to be liable? Thirdly, some would take the view that the law has enough to do in righting positive wrongs without venturing into the task of compelling altruism. To require the defendant to act for another's benefit would on this view be regarded as an unwarranted intrusion into his liberty. I am not my brother's keeper.

There is, however, a good deal more to be said than to state a simple rule of non-liability. In the first place, an apparent omission is not treated as such when on a true analysis it is only part of a course of positive conduct: the careless driver cannot defend himself simply by asserting that he *failed* to hit the brakes. More difficult are those cases which are true exceptions to the general rule in that the defendant is, for the purposes of the law of torts, under a positive duty to act. Such a duty arises where there is a relationship between defendant and plaintiff which in the eyes of the law requires the former to protect or assist the latter, for example carrier and passenger and employer and employee. The most obvious of such relationships might be thought to be that of parent and child but it is surprisingly difficult to find a clear recognition of this and the High Court of Australia has actually denied it.[13] No doubt the lack of authority is to be explained partly because in many cases there might be little point in pursuing a suit against a parent who was uninsured but a more subtle factor may come in, too. If a third party is partly to blame for the accident a parental duty of care will enable him to claim

---

[13] *Hahn* v. *Conley* (1971) 126 C.L.R. 276.

contribution from the parent,[14] thereby facing the plaintiff's advisers with a choice between bankrupting the family or accepting a lower settlement. It is not, therefore, surprising (though it is paradoxical) that it should be easier to find an authority for a duty of protection by persons, such as school-teachers, occupying a quasi-parental position.

The relationship between the defendant and the *wrongdoer* may justify the imposition of a duty to protect the outside world against the wrongdoer. Normally, the law does not require A to take steps to protect B against wilful wrongdoing by C[15] even though A is or ought to be aware of the threat and could take effective steps to neutralise it. For example, an occupier is not required to take precautions to render his premises secure against entry by persons who may use it as a means of access to burgle his neighbour's premises[16]: to impose such a duty would impose a socially unacceptable burden upon A when B can take his own precautions to protect his property. Some judges may deny liability because the theft is a bare possibility rather than a reasonably foreseeable likelihood, others may state a rule more firmly[17] but the effect is the same. Where, however, A has control of C (for example when A is a gaoler and C is a dangerous prisoner whom he allows to escape) a duty to persons in the immediate vicinity may arise. Cases where prison authorities have been held liable in negligence for failing to take steps to prevent assaults upon a prisoner by a fellow inmate illustrate both this and the previous exception: the plaintiff is unable to protect himself by escape because of the constraint imposed upon him by the defendant and the actual wrongdoer is subject to rigorous control by the defendant. Similarly, a parent's control and powers of discipline of a young child would render him liable not only for the negligent act of giving him a gun[18] but also for failing to remove a gun the child had obtained from others. The law will not, however, impose an unreasonable standard. It is not negligence to allow a 13-year-old to have a catapult provided he has been warned about the risks of using it and appears to have

---

[14] See p. 25, *ante*.

[15] It is assumed that C is not A's servant acting within the scope of his employment. If he is, A is liable even though he is not at fault: see p. 29, *ante*.

[16] *Perl* v. *Camden London Borough* [1984] Q.B. 342.

[17] See *Smith* v. *Littlewoods* [1987] 2 W.L.R. 480 and compare the speeches of Lord Mackay and Lord Goff.

[18] In this case the relationship and the right of control are not decisive for the defendant has furnished the means for the wrong to be committed and a stranger would be just as liable as a parent. However a car dealer is not liable for selling a car to someone who is known to have a string of convictions for drunken driving; there must be a threat of harm more inevitable or immediate when the wrongdoer is an adult.

absorbed those warnings[19] and in modern conditions a court would probably recognise that a delinquent child may be so far beyond control that the parent's duty is limited to exhortation and, where practicable, to warning others.

The most difficult area of the law relating to omissions is where the defendant, without a prior duty to do so, has voluntarily embarked on assisting the plaintiff. Two situations present no difficulty. The first is where the defendant has by contract undertaken to render assistance. The second is where his clumsy efforts to assist cause positive harm—if, while trying to rescue someone in difficulties in a lake I crack his skull with the prow of my boat it should be irrelevant that I was under no duty to go to his aid in the first place. But suppose (a) he is wholly incapable of saving himself and (b) I simply fail to carry through the rescue operation I started? Am I liable? It is thought that the answer should be no, for while tort liability may certainly be based upon an undertaking followed by reliance (see, for example, liability for negligent misstatement) that reliance must be "detrimental," that is to say, the person relying must be in some way worse off as a result. This may be because he does not take other precautions of his own (a motorist relying on the apparently reliable signal of a passer-by when visibility is hampered by an obstruction) or because he is deprived of the assistance of others (as where a shopkeeper takes in a person who falls ill in a public place). But if there has been no alteration of position in reliance on the undertaking then all we have is the expectation raised and dashed by the unfulfilled promise—the province of contract, not tort. It may be that even on this view there are cases in which no specific undertaking by the defendant is necessary. If it is common knowledge that a public body inspects boats, or used cars, or buildings under construction with a view to increasing safety then a member of the public may plausibly say that he has relied on the authority in omitting to have his own survey done but, logically, an admission that he was unaware of the public body's policy should be fatal to his case. Two American cases illustrate this approach. In *Indian Towing Co.* v. *U.S.*[20] the coastguard authority placed a lighthouse in a channel and then failed to maintain it. Liability for a grounding was properly imposed because the absence of the light caused navigators to believe they were somewhere else in the channel. However, in the other case[21] seamen injured in a tanker explosion failed in an action against the coastguard authority for negligent inspection

---

[19] *Smith* v. *Leurs* (1945) 70 C.L.R. 256.
[20] 350 U.S. 61 (1955).
[21] *Patentas* v. *U.S.* 687 F (2d) 707 (1982).

of the vessel, since they produced neither evidence that they were aware of the inspection having taken place nor evidence that there were any alternative measures they could have taken.

In view of *Anns* v. *Merton* (see above p. 41) it cannot, however, be confidently stated that English law is so limited. In that case the House of Lords founded a duty of care upon negligence by a local authority in the exercise of a statutory power (not a statutory duty) of inspecting buildings under construction even though there was no evidence that the plaintiffs (tenants of the buildings) knew of the council's activities in that regard. Lord Salmon went so far as to say that knowledge or reliance was irrelevant. This decision must probably be taken as governing only negligence in the exercise of statutory powers by public bodies but even in this context it has provoked some dissent, for the majority of the High Court of Australia, dealing with similar legislation, declined to follow it in the absence of any evidence of reliance, even of the general type arising from knowledge of the authority's functions.[22]

A less controversial example of an exception to the general rule is that a defendant comes under a duty to take steps to render safe a dangerous situation he has created *without negligence*. The fact that it is his action or instrumentality that has created the danger is thought to be enough to distinguish him from the onlooker who is merely present. A similar idea no doubt lies behind the imposition of a duty on a landowner upon whose land a danger naturally arises and threatens his neighbours. Of course, the duty to remedy the innocently created danger does not extend to requiring the defendant to compensate for the initial consequences of the innocent act, for that would amount to strict liability.

Economic Loss

It would be going too far to say that the plaintiff cannot recover damages in negligence for economic loss but the circumstances in which he can do so are undoubtedly restricted. No aspect of the law of negligence has generated more comment and controversy, but it would be as well at the outset to define our terms lest the issue assume greater practical importance than it has. By economic loss we generally mean pure loss of money. We do not mean loss of a physical nature which has to be quantified in terms of money simply because money is, generally speaking, the only recompense the court can give. Nor do we mean loss of money which is a consequence of injury to the plaintiff's person or property. If P is injured by D's negligence and crippled for life he

---

[22] *Sutherland Shire Council* v. *Heyman* (1985) 60 A.L.R. 1.

is likely to recover a sum of damages made up of (a) loss of enjoyment of life (b) pain and suffering (c) expenses (d) loss of earnings. The last two items are likely considerably to exceed the other two. They are certainly economic in nature, but they are nevertheless recoverable because they flow from the physical injury. As a result of the same accident, X, P's business partner, may suffer severe financial loss upon P's withdrawal from the business but he cannot recover from D even though that loss was foreseeable, because it does not flow from any injury to X or his property.[23]

This restrictive approach is probably the result of several factors. It certainly seems unlikely that it is a historical relic of the time when only tangible property and land was of significance, for the modern law of negligence post-dates the creation of a highly developed system of contract and commercial law which gave full and sophisticated recognition to a wide variety of intangible assets. It may owe something to an instinctive feeling that if we were to draw up a scale of interests deserving legal protection then physical safety and tangible property should come higher on that scale than financial expectations. However, the dominant reason has been a recognition that the requirement of physical injury to the plaintiff or his property is a useful control factor upon the scope of liability and to remove it might be to open up a potentially very wide range of claimants seeking compensation for the consequences of a negligent act. In one of the early cases it was pointed out that if a mine were flooded and the law allowed recovery of economic loss then all the workers in the mine could claim compensation for their redundancy from the tortfeasor. Similarly, a manufacturer of a machine might be liable to an ultimate user, with whom he had no contract, if the machine failed to operate efficiently; and a building sub-contractor whose negligence caused late completion might be liable to an intended tenant whose expansion of his business activities had been delayed. It is true that the plaintiff can only succeed in negligence if he can show that the loss he has suffered should have been foreseen by the defendant and an accident involving widespread *physical* damage (for example, a fire in a city) may involve the court in very awkward questions of "drawing the line", but a change in the law on economic loss might greatly multiply those questions and make the range of liability (and hence the amount of insurance required) wholly

---

[23] At common law an employer had an action in tort for loss of his employee's services. This has been abolished in England but survives in some jurisdictions. Losses caused to family members by death are recoverable by statute: see Chap. 14.

unpredictable. To use a cliché popular in this area, "the floodgates of litigation would be open." It is, therefore, widely thought that it is better that the potentially numerous victims, who are in a better position to predict their likely losses (in many cases individually small, though large in aggregate), should insure themselves accordingly, rather than expose the defendant, in the famous words of an American judge, to "liability in an indeterminate amount for an indeterminate time to an indeterminate class." Under our system the dangers of a multiplicity of small claims may be exaggerated because most victims will probably conclude it is better to bear the loss rather than indulge in the risks of litigation, but if we were to embrace the American institution of the "class action" a relaxation of the economic loss rule might be very significant.

No difficulty is felt about the recovery of economic loss in contract precisely because the rule that one must be a party to the contract to sue upon it (or, in more generous jurisdictions, an "intended beneficiary" of the contract) automatically guards against the danger of wide-ranging liability. In any event, a party who has paid money for something ought surely to recover from his supplier when he "loses" that money by being supplied something valueless. If I buy a machine from you there is not merely a duty to see that it is safe but a warranty that it will work and be fit for the purpose for which it was sold. In fact, many of the leading cases on economic loss in tort have arisen in situations in which there is normally in principle a perfectly adequate contractual remedy and the plaintiff has only been hunting for a tort defendant because some accidental circumstance (an exemption clause or the insolvency of his supplier) has rendered that remedy inapplicable or valueless. For not dissimilar reasons more generosity is shown to plaintiffs where the defendant is a wilful wrongdoer. A fraudster who induces his victim to invest in worthless shares is liable for that loss and, if we adapt our example above of the injury of one of the partners to a business, D would be liable to X if he intentionally injured P with the purpose of causing loss to X. The intention to harm the plaintiff puts the floodgates argument out of court,[24] not to speak of the fact that we feel little need to protect the wilful wrongdoer from the consequences of his acts.

Even in negligence, however, there is no blanket rule of non-recovery. First, there is no doubt that there is liability for economic loss arising from negligent misstatements. The cynic

---

[24] But some decisions in this area equate "intention to harm the plaintiff" with "knowledge that the plaintiff will be harmed" which may not limit the range of liability in the same way: p. 195 *post*.

might conclude that this is so because economic loss is normally the only sort of loss caused by such negligence, but the real reason is that the necessary restriction of liability has been achieved by requiring a "special relationship" between plaintiff and defendant and denying that a duty may arise from mere foreseeability of reliance by unidentifiable persons.[25] The law relating to economic loss arising from negligent acts is harder to state, principally because of one decision. In *Junior Books* v. *Veitchi*[26] the defendants were nominated sub-contractors in charge of flooring in a building project. The flooring was negligently installed and, though not dangerous, required replacement. Rather than suing the main contractor on the building contract, the plaintiff, the building owner, proceeded straight against the sub-contractor in tort. The decision of the majority of the House of Lords in favour of the plaintiff could just about be explained, and has in some subsequent cases been explained, on the basis that the negligence of the defendants had damaged the plaintiff's property (the building) but the court quite clearly did not consider itself to be proceeding on this basis. The case was at first widely interpreted as doing away with any particular restriction on the recovery of economic loss but the way in which it has subsequently been treated in decisions of the House, of the Privy Council and of the Court of Appeal shows that it is a decision of much more limited importance, though its precise basis remains uncertain. Possibly it is to be explained on the basis that since the defendants had been nominated (chosen) by the plaintiffs to do the sub-contract work they had given, or must be treated as having given, a direct undertaking to the plaintiffs to use care in producing what was to become the plaintiff's property and the plaintiffs had relied upon that undertaking. In other words, the relationship was so close to contract[27] that it justified the recovery of what was in fact, if not, in name, a loss of a type normally only recoverable in contract. The case does *not* mean that a manufacturer is liable for economic loss to foreseeable consumers who have bought his product from an intermediary in the market.[28] In fact even a much closer relationship will not do if the requisite undertaking cannot be inferred from the facts. In *Simaan General Contracting* v. *Pilkington Glass* S instructed SG to construct a building. The curtain walling

---

[25] See p. 86, *post*.
[26] [1983] 1 A.C. 520. The case was an appeal from Scotland in the fiftieth anniversary year of *Donoghue* v. *Stevenson*.
[27] Though as a matter of law the sub-contractor's only contract was with the main contractor.
[28] *Muirhead* v. *I.T.S.* [1986] Q.B. 507. As to buildings, see further, p. 83, *post*.

was to be done by F and F was to obtain supplies of green glass from PG. This did not comply with contractual specifications so S withheld some money under his contract with SG. SG could not sue PG in tort because in no meaningful sense had they relied on PG—F obtained the glass from PG because S insisted on that.[29] In some other modern cases liability has been imposed where there was no risk of wide-ranging liability but where there was no reliance by the plaintiff on any undertaking by the defendant. In *Ross* v. *Caunters*[30] a solicitor was held liable to an intended beneficiary under a will who lost her legacy as a result of his negligence. The decision has, however, been firmly rejected by an Australian court in *Seale* v. *Perry*.[31] In another Australian case, the *Willemstad*[32] the High Court imposed liability where the defendants cut an oil pipeline belonging to a third party which they knew (or ought to have known) supplied oil only to the installation of the plaintiff across the bay, but this is difficult to distinguish from the later decision of the Privy Council denying recovery to a plaintiff who had chartered (*i.e.*, hired the use of) a vessel belonging to a third party which was damaged by the defendant.[33] In this case an argument based on the plaintiff's being an individual or a member of a small, ascertainable class was specifically rejected.

It is unlikely that the law will ever reach a state of complete stability in this area. Having shown signs in the early 1980s of experimenting with a more pragmatic, case-by-case approach based on "justice" and foreseeability, the English courts now seem to have swung back towards more mechanical rules producing predictable results. However, we cannot say that the fact that the nature of the plaintiff's loss is economic is always sufficient to enable us to reject his claim and the broader approach still lingers in those cases which impose liability upon the basis of close proximity and reliance, from which it may one day emerge to take up the attack again.

Mental Trauma

No less problematical an area is that of "nervous shock." At what point should the law recognise a legally compensable injury

---

[29] [1988] 1 All E.R. 791. There could, of course, be a chain of contractual claims (S-SG—F-PG) and the court's refusal to allow a tort action was largely based upon the danger of circumventing the terms of these contracts by so doing. Perhaps S could have sued PG in tort.

[30] [1980] Ch. 297.

[31] [1982] V.R. 193.

[32] (1976) 136 C.L.R. 529.

[33] *Candlewood Navigation* v. *Mitsui O.S.K.* [1986] A.C. 1.

along a spectrum from a fright to total mental collapse? Can we be sure that even acute depression is causatively linked with an incident produced by the defendant's negligence? And most serious of all, how do we limit the range of liability, since mental trauma may not be limited by those natural laws which tend to limit the physical consequences of a defendant's act: a road accident in Penzance cannot hurt someone in Carlisle but the news of the victim's injury may well cause mental trauma to his wife there. The caution and suspicion with which such cases were first treated has not been wholly shaken off. The courts have remained pretty faithful to the requirement that there is no liability unless there is "some recognisable psychiatric illness" (so that the plaintiff cannot found a case on mere distress or grief[34]) but there has been some liberalisation on the circumstances in which a duty will be regarded as owed. After a period in which the courts strove for fairly rigid rules to determine liability (for example, by requiring that the shock be caused by injury to a close relative of the plaintiff or that the plaintiff be a witness of the actual accident) at least some members of the House of Lords in *McLoughlin* v. *O'Brian* chose to rely on the broad principle of the foreseeable plaintiff.[35] Nevertheless, some of the old "rules" seem likely to survive as predictable patterns of decision-making within the foreseeability formula so that, for example, the witness of an ordinary highway accident is no more likely to recover damages now than when the House of Lords rejected such a claim in 1942.[36] It may well be medically correct to say that "the ordinary frequenter of the streets has sufficient fortitude to endure such incidents" but it is significant that the courts appear to have made no attempt to verify the statement: as was said above, the decision on foreseeability is less a conclusion based upon the weighing of data than a statement of policy as to how far responsibility should reach.

Duty to This Plaintiff

In most cases there are no issues of policy and the court can proceed straight to the question of whether the defendant owed a

---

[34] Distinguish the case where the plaintiff suffers some physical injury and damages for worry or distress may form an element of the award for "pain and suffering."

[35] [1983] 1 A.C. 410. It is not clear whether a majority took this view. Two judges certainly preferred to add another "rule," allowing recovery to a witness of the immediate aftermath.

[36] *Bourhill* v. *Young* [1943] A.C. 92. But in *Attia* v. *British Gas* [1987] 3 W.L.R. 1101 the C.A. said that there may be cases in which damages can be recovered for shock arising from damage to the plaintiff's property.

duty of care to the particular plaintiff, in other words whether the plaintiff was a person foreseeably likely to be affected by the defendant's conduct. The focus now is on "this case," not "cases of this type." There is far less law about this than about duty in the sense outlined above, and a respectable case can be made for saying that in this sense the concept is unnecessary. For example, suppose D is driving carefully along the road and suddenly a motor cyclist, P, appears unexpectedly from a side turning, is hit by D's vehicle and injured. We might say that D owed no duty to P because someone behaving as P did was not an eventuality that a reasonable driver should have contemplated,[37] but equally—and perhaps more naturally—we might simply say that D was not in breach of his duty, that is, he was not negligent at all. Alternatively, it may be that the defendant clearly ought to have had X in contemplation but his conduct, by some freak chance he could not have foreseen, causes injury to P. The law imposes a limit ("remoteness of damage") upon the extent of the defendant's liability by confining it to consequences which were reasonably foreseeable. Instead of saying that D owed no duty to P (which is generally what we do say) why do we not say that he is not liable to P because that is too remote a consequence of his negligence? As far as this case is concerned, the reason may be historical, for there was a time when the courts admitted as "non-remote" consequences those which were direct even though unforeseeable so that to decide such cases solely by reference to remoteness *might* have produced an unacceptably wide-ranging liability.[38] In the modern law the question of remoteness, like that of duty, is decided by reference to foreseeability, though in some cases the concept is applied in such a broad, even lax, manner as to make it doubtful if it would serve as an adequate test of the range of persons to whom the defendant's liability should extend. It has been suggested that duty, breach and remoteness could all be subsumed under one question of whether the risk was one which the defendant ought to have guarded against and as a matter of theory this may be correct. However, it would be "wrong" in the sense that it would not reflect the common patterns of overt judicial reasoning. Furthermore, even if we reduced the law to one question of risk we should then probably be obliged, for purposes of manageable exposition, to break it down into something like the present tripartite decision, which

---

[37] It is assumed that P's conduct is very foolish indeed: some degree of care against the thoughtlessness or incompetence of others is obviously a necessary element of careful driving.

[38] But "directness" was so malleable and imprecise a concept that it would probably have allowed a court to reach what conclusion it chose.

reflects three broad types of issue: was the plaintiff likely to be affected? (duty); was the way in which the defendant acted likely to cause damage? (breach); was the damage suffered by that plaintiff the sort which should reasonably have been foreseen? (remoteness).

The classic illustration of the requirement that a duty be owed to the particular plaintiff is the famous New York case of *Palsgraf* v. *Long Island Rail Road*[39] in which the plaintiff's statement of claim alleged that the defendants jostled X, 30 feet away from her, that X as a result dropped a package which exploded and that the blast knocked over a set of heavy scales which fell on the plaintiff. If (as seems unlikely) the events did happen this way, there was nothing in the circumstances surrounding the jostling of X which should have led the defendants to expect that the plaintiff would be physically affected by their actions. She was the unforeseeable victim of the defendants' undoubted negligence towards X.

The issue in *Palsgraf* is essentially factual in the sense that it is a matter of degree, judgment and "opinion" and it is certainly not susceptible of any scientific formula. In some cases, however, the court may manipulate the foreseeability formula so as to operate a more or less covert policy, though the point is usually less obvious than in those situations, considered in the previous section, where the court must decide whether the law of negligence is to apply at all in a particular field of activity. For example, blind persons are pretty uncommon but it was held in *Haley* v. *LEB*[40] that a street works undertaker should take steps to guard against the special risk to them presented by excavations in the pavement; and persons who take high risks to rescue others are also readily deemed to be within the proper contemplation of defendants who negligently create situations of danger, provided their conduct is not "wanton" or "foolhardy."[41] It may well be (courts do not go in for statistical analysis of such matters) that burglars and petty thieves are more common than either blind men or rescuers but it does not seem likely that a householder would be liable to a burglar who injured himself by tripping over a defective paving stone: a court that was reluctant to face the policy issue by denying liability on grounds of illegality (the scope of which is problematical in tort) would be likely to decide the issue by simply declaring that he was unforeseeable. Changes in what is perceived to be desirable policy may bring whole categories of plaintiffs in from the cold even though they were previously excluded as unforeseeable. An Irish court in a

---

[39] 162 N.E. 99 (1928).
[40] [1965] A.C. 778.
[41] The rescuer also escapes the defence of *volenti*: see p. 77, *post*.

decision in 1891 that would probably have been widely concurred in denied any liability for pre-natal injuries. Before the issue was squarely raised in England, Parliament passed comprehensive legislation on the point in the Congenital Disabilities (Civil Liability) Act 1976 but it seems probable that our courts would have followed the lead of other common law jurisdictions and imposed liability. The older view was largely based on difficulties of proof of causation, which have been reduced, though by no means eliminated, by advances in medical science.

B. BREACH OF DUTY

We have already noted[42] that the standard of care demanded by the law of negligence is nearly always an objective one, that of the hypothetical "reasonable man" in that situation. It has been said that the whole theory of negligence presupposes some uniform standard of behaviour even though that is a standard to which none of us can conform through every moment of life. Even the reasonable man, it seems, has forgivable lapses (for example, he may be overcome by unexpected physical illness or may take the "wrong" decision in a dire emergency) but if he has entered a trade or profession he cannot say that he lacks the experience to cope with the situation, even though we must all learn somehow. The result is that a junior doctor on his first day on the wards must come up to the standard of a hypothetical competent doctor of that rank, for the patient's legitimate expectations of competent treatment cannot vary as he is moved from the hands of Doctor A, the new recruit, to those of Doctor B, who has been in post for five years, and then back to Doctor A. If that were the law the plaintiff could only recover if he could show that the employer of the doctors was in some way at fault in selecting or supervising them, but could not the employer reply that he, too, was effectively compelled to employ inexperienced as well as experienced staff and to leave some things to the judgment of each category? All this is certainly not to say that there is one standard of competence for all doctors, for a junior houseman is not expected to show the expertise in cardiology of a senior consultant in that specialism and if a crisis is thrust upon him by circumstances beyond his control he will satisfy the legal standard by doing the best that can be done by a person of his training. He should, however, be able to recognise when he is getting out of his depth so as to call on more expert assistance when that is available.

[42] See p. 16, *ante.*

To say that the standard is that of this personification of the law, the reasonable man, does not of course answer the question of what that paragon would or would not have done in the circumstances of the particular case and the law of negligence is certainly not a highway code of "dos" and "don'ts" for particular activities. There has, however, been enough judicial analysis of the idea of reasonable care to give us a few more pointers to the decision in an individual case, even though the final outcome may be unpredictable. The fundamental point is that in order to determine whether conduct is negligent there must be a balancing of risks against the cost (in a broad sense) of precautions. There has been one famous attempt to express this in an algebraic formula[43] ("If the probability [of injury] be called P; the injury L; and the burden [of adequate precautions] B; liability depends upon whether B is less than L multiplied by P; *i.e.* whether B is less than PL") and this has been described as a test based on "economic efficiency." However, the author of the formula himself recognised that it is little more than a description of how courts reason because it is rarely possible to assign precise mathematical values to all the elements and in any case some of them involve value judgments on which there may be wide differences of opinion. In commerce or government a cost-benefit analysis may be undertaken by assigning values based on statistical averages to certain types of loss. Thus a highway authority may decide to make a road improvement costing £X000 if the "cost" of not doing so (probably based upon official figures assigning costs to broad categories of accidents) is £Y000 over N years. Though courts may occasionally hear such evidence (usually when the plaintiff can show that a precaution is absurdly cheap or a defendant that it is outrageously expensive) litigants are not usually in a position to produce such data. Even as a description, however, the formula is deficient in treating the burden of precautions as a unit, whereas in fact it consists of two elements: the cost of the precautions and the "utility" of the object being pursued by the defendant. If, for example, the plaintiff is injured by an accident occurring during a police chase of a dangerous criminal the court is likely (though it may not say so in as many words) to strike a balance between the demands of society in respect of the apprehension of offenders and in respect of the safety of road users. Without for a moment suggesting that "anything goes" in the pursuit of crime it is fair to assume that a judge might give more

[43] Learned Hand J. in *U.S.* v. *Carroll Towing Co.* 159 F 2d 169 (1947).

leeway to risks taken to apprehend a murderer or a robber than a pickpocket or a speeding motorist. In *Watt* v. *Herts C.C.*[44] it was held that a risk to a fire officer in an emergency could be justified when perhaps the same risk could not be run if the defendants had been pursuing "the ordinary commercial end to make profit." No doubt the fireman may to some extent be said to be paid to run risks and may have a pension or disability scheme which takes account of them (though this certainly does not mean that he is "outside the pale" of negligence in performing his duty.)[45] The justice of the result is not so clear where the victim is a bystander. Should we call for sacrifice from those injured for the public good or (as is to some extent the case under French administrative law) compensate them even though there has been no fault since we all benefit from the state function which injured them?

A defendant who follows the normal custom and practice in a trade or profession is likely to escape liability. The burden is upon the plaintiff to particularise what it is that is wrong with the defendant's conduct and if the defendant is only doing what everyone else does it is not surprising that the burden should be a heavy one, especially when the practice in question is that of a profession. A good modern illustration in the context of protection against noise is *Thompson* v. *Smiths Shiprepairers*[46] where the court held that the employer must keep up to date but the law "should be slow to blame him for not ploughing a lone furrow." Nevertheless, there is a line beyond which even universal practice is negligence and this is sometimes, if rarely, crossed, as it was in *Lloyds Bank* v. *Savory*[47] where the House of Lords held that a bank was negligent even though it might be following the custom of all other bankers in collecting cheques. Failure to follow general practice is not of itself negligence (otherwise there could be no advances in anything) but it may throw upon the defendant the burden of justifying his actions.

If an accident suggests that steps can be taken to prevent its recurrence and they are taken, that is not an admission of negligence, that is, the defendant is not accepting that such steps *should* have been taken in the light of the then available knowledge. Nevertheless, the fact that the steps can easily be taken is some evidence that they ought to have been taken and it is sometimes argued that the law acts as a disincentive to an immediate response to an accident. Insurers, however, deny that

[44] [1954] 1 W.L.R. 835.
[45] See *Ogwo* v. *Taylor* [1987] 2 W.L.R. 988.
[46] [1984] Q.B. 405.
[47] [1933] A.C. 201.

tactical considerations relating to pending litigation would influence a decision on remedial measures.

In many trades and activities there are statutory standards and regulations of greater or lesser precision. Sometimes failure to comply with statutory standards may amount to the independent tort of breach of statutory duty[48] but where this is not so, what is the relevance of the statutory standard for negligence? In the first place, non-compliance may be evidence from which a court may infer a failure to take reasonable care, but it is not obliged to do so. There are circumstances in which exceeding the speed limit would not amount to civil negligence[49] despite the apparently odd conclusion that a reasonable man may choose not to obey the criminal law. Secondly, compliance with the statutory standard will be evidence that the defendant has taken reasonable care but will not necessarily in all cases absolve him: to adapt our earlier example, it would clearly be negligent to drive at 29 m.p.h. in a crowded shopping street and when the legislature enacted the 30 m.p.h. limit it meant to set a minimum standard of general application, not to prescribe that driving at such a speed was always and in all conditions acceptable to the law. Indeed, this is implicit in the criminal law in the existence of "non-specific" crimes such as careless driving. There may, however, be some areas (particularly regulations governing permissible amounts of toxic substances incorporated in goods) where the legislature must be taken to have laid down an absolute standard so that compliance will automatically insulate the defendant from the law of negligence. Any other approach would render the statutory standard of little use as a guide to behaviour and substitute the judgment of the court for the (presumably expert) judgment of the legislature.

C. REMOTENESS OF DAMAGE ("PROXIMATE CAUSE")

We have already seen that wherever the law of torts requires proof of damage (and it generally does) that damage must have been caused in whole or in part by the defendant's wrong. That is a necessary condition of his liability. But it is not enough that it is so caused by him because the chain of "factual" causation is infinitely long. Suppose P while on holiday goes to visit an amusement park. On the way he is involved in a minor collision caused by D's negligence and this delays him for an hour. At the park he slips on a discarded ice-cream and hurts himself. Mere commonsense attributes responsibility to (a) the person who

---

[48] See Chap. 5.
[49] But as to Canadian and American law see p. 94, *post*.

dropped the ice-cream and perhaps (b) to the occupiers of the park for failing to clear it up. Nobody would attribute responsibility to D, though it is a fact that but for the delay caused by D, P would not have slipped because there would, an hour earlier, have been no discarded ice-cream there. We might express our reason for not attributing responsibility to D in various ways: that the fall was not within the risk created by D, that the fall was "too remote" from it, that it was not foreseeable when D caused the collision or that he had not "substantially caused" the fall but only made a small contribution to setting the scene for it. If the court speaks in terms of causation it is not the "but for" causation we have met before, because we are not denying that the defendant's act was factually linked with the harm, we are merely saying that the link is not one on which we are willing to base legal responsibility. Under the Factories Act 1961 every dangerous part of machinery must be securely fenced "while in motion or in use." This may be contravened without any fault on the part of the employer and gives rise to civil liability. Now suppose that the plaintiff is operating the machine and wilfully interferes with the fence in flagrant disregard of safety instructions so that he is drawn into the machine and injured while it is operating. Contributory negligence by the plaintiff is generally not a complete defence but only a ground for reducing damages but in the situation outlined the court may conclude that the sole effective cause of the injury is the plaintiff's own fault, thereby denying liability altogether, even though there has been a contravention of the Act. Such causation is sometimes called "legal causation"[50] because it is concerned with picking out from a number of factual causes one or more to which the law will attach responsibility. In terminology which is still sometimes used, a factual cause is a *"causa sine qua non"* (a necessary cause) while a legal cause is a *"causa causans"* (an effective cause). Causation in this sense is not a wholly different concept from that of remoteness of damage but another way of expressing the same idea. In a case where the defendant is held not liable it may be a question of taste whether we say this is because some other cause was in law the cause of the plaintiff's injury or that the injury was too remote a consequence of the defendant's breach of duty. In some cases, one formulation or the other may look more natural. For example, it is common to speak of the intervening act of a third party after the defendant's wrong as "breaking the chain of causation." The use of two apparently different concepts may at first confuse the student, but it is perhaps no bad thing that in some cases we speak in the language

---

[50] The terminology of the U.S. Restatement of Torts, 2d, s.431.

of causation because it contributes to saving us from a tempting fallacy, that because the law has adopted foreseeability as the basic test of remoteness (which is true) then a defendant is liable for all the foreseeable consequences of his negligence (which is untrue). Whichever formula we adopt, we are dealing with something which is even less scientific and predictable than cause in fact and in which policy plays a large part.

The Foreseeability "Test"

Most decisions on remoteness of damage in the modern history of the common law are referable to two broad competing principles. One is that the defendant is liable if the harm suffered by the plaintiff is a "direct" consequence of the defendant's wrong. The other is that the defendant is liable to the plaintiff for the "foreseeable" consequences of his wrong. Under either test it is assumed that the plaintiff was owed a duty by the defendant, *i.e.* that *some* harm to the plaintiff should have been foreseen by the defendant. The first is exemplified by the famous decision in *Re Polemis*[51] where the defendants were held liable for the destruction of the plaintiffs' ship by a fire started by the dropping of a plank into a hold full of petrol, notwithstanding the (rather surprising) finding of fact by the arbitrators that a fire could not reasonably have been anticipated. This test has been ousted in England and the Commonwealth by the Privy Council's decision in *The Wagon Mound*.[52] The defendants negligently spilled fuel oil into Sydney harbour. This spread and fouled the plaintiffs' wharf, causing foreseeable but very minor damage. Two days later molten metal from welding operations on the wharf set fire to cotton waste floating on the oil, this acted as a "wick" and the wharf was destroyed in the resulting blaze. On the basis of a finding of fact that the ignition of oil floating on water was not foreseeable[53] the Privy Council allowed an appeal by the defendants. Much has been said about the competing merits of the two "rules." The court clearly considered it both logical and just that since foreseeability was undoubtedly the test for the existence of a duty so it must apply to determine the extent of the defendant's responsibility.

[51] [1921] 3 K.B. 560.
[52] [1961] A.C. 388.
[53] Again a rather surprising conclusion, but the plaintiffs did not argue that the fire was foreseeable because they would then have been met by the defence of their own contributory negligence in welding. In *The Wagon Mound (No. 2)* [1967] 1 A.C. 617, involving different plaintiffs and different evidence, the fire was held foreseeable.

"To hold [D] liable for consequences, however unforeseeable, of a careless act, if, but only if, he is at the same time
liable for some other damage however trivial, appears
neither logical nor just. This becomes more clear if it is
supposed that similar unforeseeable damage is suffered by
[P] and [X] but other foreseeable damage, for which [D] is
liable, by [P] only. A system of law which would hold [D]
liable to [P] but not to [X] for the similar damage suffered by
each of them could not easily be defended."

On the other hand, it must be pointed out that P has suffered
the damage through no fault of his own, whereas D has, *ex
hypothesi*, created a situation in which he should have foreseen some harm to P. As between them, therefore, it is arguable
that it should be D who bears the cost even of unforeseeable
harm.

The Privy Council also laid stress on the difficulty of
determining what was a direct consequence and it is certainly
true that the case law provided little guidance on the meaning of
"directness." It was certainly *not* being used in the sense in which
it is used in the trespass torts[54] for that would render the
defendant's responsibility too narrow. Nor was it the case that
the appearance of some new, intervening factor necessarily
rendered the harm indirect: it could hardly have been the law that
the defendant was liable for the spread of a fire set when a wind
was blowing but not liable if the wind arose two minutes later. It
must, however, be said that if the concept of directness is subject
to criticism on the ground of uncertainty its successor is hardly
less flexible and imprecise.

What, then, do we mean by "foreseeability" in this context?
The first point is one that is not expressly mentioned in judicial
opinions but which may, nonetheless, have had a big influence
on the results of cases. As a matter of principle the question of
remoteness in negligence is probably to be determined by asking
what a reasonable man in the defendant's position ought to have
foreseen when he did the act in question. However, since the
court is determining the question *ex post facto* a natural way of
phrasing the enquiry is "was this an unforeseeable consequence
of the defendant's act?" and this points towards liability unless
the consequence is very unusual indeed. If one were to ask a
group of people what were the foreseeable consequences of
negligently taking a bend too fast they would probably suggest
the obvious risks of collision with another vehicle coming the
other way or running off the road. If, however, it were suggested

[54] See Chap. 8.

to them, they would probably agree that it was not at all far-fetched that one of the passengers should be struck by another vehicle while attempting to render assistance at the scene of the crash. In truth, the law does not limit the consequences to what the hypothetical reasonable man *would* have contemplated before the collision. An extreme example of such "deemed foresight" is the Canadian case of *Falkenham* v. *Zwicker*.[55] D negligently crashed into P's fence. As a result some metal fence staples were ejected from the fence and injured cows which ate them when placed in the field some time later. The judge commented:

> "Damage to the plaintiff's wire fence . . . is what a reasonable person would anticipate. It is common knowledge that wire on pasture fences is usually held by means of staples. Breaking of the fence, as was done in this instance, indicates a reasonable foreseeability of staples being ejected and eventually damaging the cattle that used this pasture."

The plaintiff is further aided by a judicial tendency to describe the foreseeable risk in broad terms, for the "likelihood" of an event is in inverse proportion to the detail with which it is described, just as it is more likely that you will meet "a man" at the corner rather than someone with fair hair, blue eyes and weighing 150 lbs. Most people would probably agree that if an employee were sent on a long trip across northern England in an unheated van in bad winter conditions he might come to some harm from the cold; they might well demur at the suggestion that he would suffer frostbite. Yet in *Bradford* v. *Robinson Rentals*[56] liability was imposed on such facts, the foreseeable risk being injury from cold. The other interpretation of the decision probably amounts to the same thing in different words: as long as the damage is of the kind foreseeable it does not matter that it is much greater in extent than the defendant could have contemplated. Commonly contrasted with this case is *Tremain* v. *Pike*[57] where Weill's disease (an extremely rare condition caused by contact with rats' urine) was regarded as "different in kind" from more obvious dangers connected with rats like bites or food contamination. Neither decision can be said to be "right" or "wrong," though the *Bradford* case is probably more in line with the general run of decisions in England and elsewhere. In reality, the court is making a judgment, perhaps instinctive, about the acceptable limits of responsibility and then expressing it in the language of foreseeability.

---

[55] (1978) 93 D.L.R. (3d) 289.
[56] [1967] 1 W.L.R. 337.
[57] [1969] 1 W.L.R. 1556.

Yet further assistance comes to the plaintiff from an important qualification of the foreseeability principle: if the plaintiff is more susceptible than the average man to serious injury the defendant must bear the extra cost because he "takes his victim as he finds him." In the example usually given, a plaintiff with a thin skull recovers damages for a fracture even though the blow would only have bruised a normal man. A dramatic illustration of this is *Meah* v. *McCreamer*[58] where head injuries received in a road accident caused the plaintiff to lose his inhibitions and display to a much exaggerated degree aggressive tendencies which were already a part of his personality. These manifested themselves in two rapes for which he was sentenced to life imprisonment. The defendant driver who was responsible for the head injuries was held liable to pay the plaintiff damages in respect of this imprisonment. It is important to note that in committing these rapes the plaintiff was not acting like an automaton: he was sane enough to be convicted in the criminal proceedings and, subsequently, to be held liable in tort to both of his victims, he having become "claimworthy" by reason of his judgment against the defendant. It is obvious that the defendant driver could not have been liable to the rape victims for they would have been completely unforeseeable victims of his act—he owed them no duty.[59] Not so obvious is the result of *Meah* v. *McCreamer (No. 2)*[60] where the judge denied the plaintiff a right of indemnity against the driver in respect of the damages he had had to pay his victims: if the imprisonment was not too remote, why was the civil suit by the victims? Perhaps policy rather than logic dictated the result, for most people would find it revolting that the plaintiff should recover a large sum of damages and, in effect, wholly escape the financial consequences of his criminal acts by throwing that burden on the defendant's insurers.[61]

It may be that the thin skull rule is only part of a wider principle that the defendant is liable for any natural, physical sequel of the injury without reference to foreseeability. Suppose that after an injury the plaintiff succumbs to a viral infection. As a practical matter it may be impossible to decide whether the death was

---

[58] [1985] 1 All E.R. 367.
[59] See p. 57, *ante*.
[60] [1986] 1 All E.R. 943. But in the first case the defendant does not seem to have contested the remoteness issue.
[61] A good example of a consequence being expressly excluded on policy grounds is *Pritchard* v. *J. H. Cobden* [1987] 2 W.L.R. 627 where the C.A. rejected a claim for the financial consequences of a divorce which had been brought about by the plaintiff's injuries. The investigation of such cases would involve difficulty and expense, might involve much speculation and, given the ease of divorce, might lead to abuse.

attributable to the plaintiff's pre-existing condition, to the weakness caused by the accident or to the unusual virulence of the virus, but the defendant should certainly be liable.[62] In the great majority of cases it may be possible to achieve this result simply by saying that the matter is one of the *extent*, not of the *kind* of the injury or that while death from the virus was unusual it was not so far-fetched as to be unforeseeable.[63]

Whether or not the "thin skull" gives rise to an independent legal doctrine, the plaintiff must establish the initial duty and breach in the normal way, so that if *no* harm was foreseeable to a normal person the plaintiff loses notwithstanding his susceptibility. Further, his weakness may affect the measure of damages because all or part of the damage he has in fact suffered might have occurred anyway. In *Meah* v. *McCreamer* a discount was made for the fact that the plaintiff's underlying personality traits might anyway have led to some periods of imprisonment. The proposition that you take your victim as you find him cuts both ways and to some extent meets the criticism that might be made of these cases, namely, that the defendant's act is only the trigger rather than the substantial cause of the harm. Even where there is no pre-existing weakness it is necessary to make a discount for the "vicissitudes of life" which might anyway have laid the plaintiff low[64] but a contingency is likely to have a much greater effect if it can be shown to involve a pre-existing weakness in the plaintiff. For example, the remote possibility that the plaintiff might have suffered imprisonment would not be brought into account unless, as in *Meah* v. *McCreamer*, a foundation was laid for it by giving evidence of criminal tendencies.

The courts have shown themselves less ready to apply the thin skull principle to matters other than personal injury. It is by no means clear that it applies to damage to property,[65] though even if it does not it is certain that one need not foresee the physical extent of the damage: if a manufacturer fails to warn of the danger of washing chemical ampoules in water he is liable even though the explosion is greater than might be expected because of the proximity of other ampoules. Nor does the principle apply to loss caused by a pre-existing weakness in the plaintiff's financial

---

[62] At the time of writing, a claim is pending where P was injured by D in a road accident and received a blood transfusion from which she contracted the HIV antigen (potential AIDS).

[63] Indeed, there may be a temptation to conclude that either the harm was foreseeable or, if it was not, it *must* have been attributable to the plaintiff's pre-existing susceptibility.

[64] See p. 211, *post*.

[65] A standard illustration in discussions is the haemophilic horse. If it does apply, was *Re Polemis* rightly decided?

position, at least if the famous case of *Liesbosch Dredger* v. *Edison S.S.*[66] is still law. The plaintiffs had been too poor to buy a replacement for their sunk dredger so they hired a substitute, incurring higher overall costs than they would have done in purchasing a replacement. This extra cost was denied by the House of Lords. The decision was probably intended to lay down a complete bar to recovery for financial loss attributable to the plaintiff's impecuniosity but in the last few years the courts have been moving towards allowing recovery where the extra cost was foreseeable to the defendant. Foreseeability still seems, however, to be a necessary pre-condition to recovery. Even at its height of authority the *Liesbosch* did not limit all aspects of the defendant's responsibility for the financial as opposed to the physical consequences of his negligence. It has never been seriously questioned that if the plaintiff had a very high income his damages for loss of earnings are to be based upon that income even though he was dressed like an old tramp when the defendant ran him down. Equally, if I collide with your battered old car and crush the valuable antique you were transporting in it I have to pay the value of the antique, not the value of the "foreseeable" or "average" contents of an old car, whatever that may be. We may say that here we are concerned with the *valuation* of non-remote consequences, whereas remoteness is concerned with the prior question of whether the defendant should be liable for those consequences at all; but could we not express the *Liesbosch* situation in valuation terms, *viz.* the financial cost to the plaintiffs of the destruction of their vessel? It seems that the law has not produced a coherent policy in this area.

Intervening Forces

An intervening, unforeseeable, natural event may make the damage too remote: if P is injured in a road accident caused by D and then, while lying at the roadside awaiting treatment, he is crushed by an unexpected landslip, D is not liable for his death and the amount of damages he has to pay in respect of the injuries is limited because their consequences do not extend beyond the death. However, as we have seen, infection or natural deterioration in the plaintiff's medical condition would not be regarded as insulating the defendant in this way. There is a good deal more case law in relation to intervening human conduct.

At one time the intervening conduct of the plaintiff saved the defendant from liability because "contributory negligence" was a complete defence. Now that the courts have power to make a

---

[66] [1933] A.C. 449.

reduction in damages on account of the plaintiff's want of care for his own safety it would be a rare case in which it deprived him of his damages altogether.[67] Where it is the conduct of a *third party* which is in issue we must first note that there is an analytical distinction, not always observed in practice, between duty and remoteness. If the defendant has not himself inflicted any direct harm upon the plaintiff but has brought about a situation in which a third party inflicts the harm the question is whether the defendant owed and was in breach of any duty in respect of that harm.[68] We are now considering the case where the defendant has already inflicted damage upon the plaintiff and in doing so has created the opportunity for a third party to do further damage. Not surprisingly, the results in the "remoteness" cases parallel those in the "duty" cases. It is not unusual for *negligence* by a third party to be held foreseeable (for example in a multiple collision case) and the law probably now is that this would extend to damage caused by negligent medical treatment of the initial injury.[69] As Professor Prosser put it, "It would be an undue compliment to the medical profession to say that bad surgery is no part of the risk of a broken leg." No doubt, however, the courts would reserve the right to say that really crass treatment broke the chain of causation. The doctor himself would of course be liable for the harm done by him, whether or not the defendant is. In seeking to extend a defendant's responsibility to embrace the acts of others we are normally concerned with maximising the number of persons whom the plaintiff can sue and against whom he can recover an *enforceable* judgment. Since judgments against doctors are (at least in England) bound to be satisfied the extension of the initial wrongdoer's liability may not be very important to the plaintiff but it may not be without significance from the point of view of the doctor for it may enable him in effect to reduce his final liability by recovering a contribution.

Wilful misconduct by a third party is much less likely to lead to liability and it is not enough that it is foreseeable. In *Lamb* v. *Camden London Borough*[70] the defendants negligently damaged the plaintiff's house so that it had to be left unoccupied for a long period. Squatters moved in, an event which was foreseeable but not likely, and did a great deal more damage, for which the Court of Appeal held the defendants were not liable. Recognising that a

---

[67] See p. 74, *post*.
[68] See p. 48, *ante*.
[69] So held by the High Court of Australia in *Mahony* v. *Kruschich* (1985) 59 A.L.R. 722. The matter is put tentatively in the text because *Hogan* v. *Bentinck West Hartley Collieries* [1949] 1 All E.R. 588, a Workman's Compensation case, might be thought to the contrary.
[70] [1981] Q.B. 625.

higher degree of likelihood than mere foreseeability was necessary in such cases, Oliver L.J. remarked that "there may... be circumstances in which the court would require a degree of likelihood amounting almost to inevitability before it fixes a defendant with responsibility for the act of a third party over whom he has and can have no control." As in the "duty" cases there is a policy which holds it unfair to saddle a careless wrongdoer with responsibility for the wilful acts of others.[71] The courts have also no doubt been influenced by the fact that most of the cases have concerned property loss, where insurance is common.[72]

Remoteness of damage is not of course confined to negligence cases, though there is curiously little authority for some torts. It will be mentioned at various points later in this book.

D. PROOF OF NEGLIGENCE

The burden of proof of negligence is upon the plaintiff,[73] who must prove what the defendant did or did not do, that this caused the plaintiff's loss and that it amounted to negligence in law. We have already dealt with the second element. As to the third it is often said that it is a matter of fact but if it is, it is clearly of a different nature from the issue of what the defendant did, for it involves the court applying a legal standard to facts. However, in former times the question of "negligence or no negligence" was essentially one for the jury and this is reflected in the modern law in the fact that an appeal court will not lightly interfere with the trial judge's assessment of the defendant's conduct unless there is some error of principle.

As to the first matter, that is likely to take up far more of the time of the practising trial lawyer than consideration of abstract issues of law but the facts of cases are so infinitely various that little can be said about it here. In any event, the proof of facts by direct testimony, real evidence or inference is not inherently different in a tort case from any other type of action. Tort has, however, developed a "doctrine" (the quotation marks are used advisedly) for the situation where the plaintiff cannot produce any direct evidence of what the defendant did: *res ipsa loquitur*. In truth this maxim probably does no more than provide a label for certain recurrent conclusions of common sense and its

---

[71] Watkins L.J. in *Lamb* relies heavily on an "instinctive" approach.
[72] But it does not seem likely that the plaintiff in *Lamb* was insured: she was legally aided and the house had been empty so long the usual cover would have lapsed.
[73] There is a statutory exception or quasi-exception in s.11 of the Civil Evidence Act 1968, p. 6, *ante*.

identification by a Latin name does more harm than good, but it has certainly attracted a good deal of case law and we must look at it.

Res ipsa loquitur[74] means that an inference of negligence is raised against the defendant by reason of the happening of certain events. As an American judge laconically remarked in a bizarre early product liability action, "we can imagine no reason why, with ordinary care, human toes could not be left out of chewing tobacco, and if toes are found in chewing tobacco, it seems to us that somebody has been very careless."[75] It is commonly said that two conditions must be met to entitle the plaintiff to rely upon the maxim. First, the thing causing the damage must be under the control of the defendant or his servants. Thus in one case it was applied where a barrel rolled out of the storeroom above the defendant's shop and struck the plaintiff, who was passing by. But where, in an American case, the plaintiff was hit by an armchair dropped from an unidentified window of the defendant's hotel on VJ day, it was rejected, for the guest, not the hotel management, was in effective control of the contents of the room from time to time.[76] The second requirement is that the accident must be such as in the ordinary course of things could not happen without negligence (or worse). This condition was certainly satisfied in the hotel case, though the circumstances were such that they did not point to negligence on the part of the *defendants*. No hard and fast tests can be laid down, for it is clear that the inference to be drawn will vary so much from one case to another and may change as an activity becomes more common and more familiar. For example, there was probably a time when the court would have refused to apply the doctrine to aircraft flight but the fact that air travel is nowadays the safest means of transportation would justify its application. Similarly it can be applied to medicine and surgery. As it was put in one case, the plaintiff should be able to say, "I went into hospital to be cured of two stiff fingers, I have come out with four stiff fingers, and my hand is useless. That should not have happened if due care had been used. Explain it if you can."

The real difficulties of *res ipsa loquitur* arise when we try to determine its procedural effect. Logically, once it has been brought into play by satisfaction of the above conditions, it may

---

[74] "The event speaks for itself" thought not quite a literal translation, is probably the most accurate.

[75] *Pillars* v. *R. J. Reynolds Tobacco Co.* 78 So. 365 (1918).

[76] Of course, if such conduct were at all common the hotel might be required so to design its premises as to prevent things being thrown from windows, but that is another issue.

have one of three effects, bearing in mind that the civil standard of proof is the balance of probabilities, "more likely than not." First, it may *justify* the finder of fact in coming to a decision in favour of the plaintiff but in no way compel him to do so: the maxim merely expresses the inference that may be drawn from certain sorts of circumstantial evidence and the strength of that inference is one for the fact-finder's judgment. On this view, subject to a point made below, a decision for the defendant is unappealable. Though this is in some ways the most attractive view of the maxim's effect is must be admitted that it is more suitable for a system of trial by jury, in which the judge in deciding that the maxim applies is in effect saying that there is sufficient evidence to go to the jury; there is something odd, in a non-jury trial, in the idea of the judge deciding that the maxim applies (*i.e.* that the accident is one which could not normally happen without negligence) and then, in the absence of countervailing evidence, finding for the defendant. The second possible effect is that the maxim creates a *presumption* of negligence. The effect of this would be that if the defendant came forward with no evidence of an innocent explanation the finder of fact would be *required* to find for the plaintiff. If, however, the defendant does adduce evidence, then the weight of that may or may not rebut the initial inference of negligence raised by the maxim. But even in this situation the ultimate issue is whether the whole of the evidence justifies the conclusion that it is more likely than not that the defendant was negligent. It is as if the initial application of the maxim tipped the scales in the plaintiff's favour and the defendant's evidence is argued to have the effect of tipping them back into a neutral position. Thirdly, the application of the maxim may create a situation in which the ultimate onus of proof is shifted to the defendant and he is required to produce an explanation which makes it more likely than not that there was no negligence on his part. On this view, if the court is left in doubt on the totality of the evidence the plaintiff wins.

The overwhelming weight of authority in the United States (where trial by jury is very common) is that the effect of *res ipsa loquitur* is the first of the above, and the law is the same in Australia. To this must be added one qualification, that there are some cases in which the circumstantial evidence of the accident's happening shouts negligence so loudly that in the absence of rebutting evidence a verdict for the defendant would be perverse. An example might be a head-on collision of two trains belonging to the same company. In such a case the practical effect of the maxim would be the same as that under the second explanation, though not because it raised a genuine presumption, simply because inferences from circumstantial evidence may sometimes be as overwhelming as the weight of direct testimony. The present stance of the English courts is rather unclear and dicta can certainly be found to the effect that the maxim has the effect of reversing the legal burden of proof but there are others denying that it raises any special rule of law. It is probably now too late to bury the maxim and to recognise that there are simply varying inferences to be drawn from circumstantial evidence from one case to another, but questions of the formal burden of proof are rarely important in trial by judge alone.

Sometimes the onus of proof is truly reversed by statute or some rule of common law. For example, legislation in Ontario requires a driver in collision with a pedestrian to prove that he was not negligent, and at common law, a bailee, though he is only liable, in the absence of a special contract, for negligence, must show that the loss of or damage to goods in his care was not attributable to fault on his part.

E. CONTRIBUTORY NEGLIGENCE AND ASSUMPTION OF RISK

Contributory negligence may be applicable to some torts other than negligence but that is its main sphere of operation and it is conveniently dealt with here. By speaking of contributory negligence we in England[77] mean that the accident is partly caused by the negligence of the defendant and partly by the failure of the plaintiff to take such care for his own safety as is reasonable in the circumstances. At common law the plaintiff's fault was a complete defence, perhaps because of an unwillingness to recognise that an event was capable of having more than one cause. This rule was mitigated first by a certain generosity in some areas in assessing the plaintiff's conduct and secondly by the rule of "last opportunity," but, fortunately, legislative intervention has made it unnecessary to explore this obscure doctrine.

The English law is now contained in the Law Reform (Contributory Negligence) Act 1945, which is fairly typical of legislation throughout the Commonwealth.[78] The Act provides that "where any person suffers damage as the result partly of his

---

[77] The reader should take great care with U.S. authorities here. Not only does the law differ widely from state to state, but the terminology also differs. The expression "contributory negligence" is there normally used to describe the position where the plaintiff's fault forms a complete defence. Where a reduced award can be made in his favour, as in England, Americans speak of "comparative negligence."

[78] Ontario led the way in 1924.

own fault and partly of the fault of any other person or persons, a claim in respect of that damage shall not be defeated by reason of the fault of the person suffering the damage, but the damages recoverable in respect thereof shall be reduced to such extent as the court thinks just and equitable having regard to the claimant's share in the responsibility for the damage." "Fault" means "negligence, breach of statutory duty or other act or omission which gives rise to liability in tort or would, apart from [the] Act, give rise to the defence of contributory negligence." The Act does not define what amounts to contributory negligence nor the circumstances where it is relevant but is concerned with the *consequences* of a finding of contributory negligence. With the qualification that the courts will probably now not strain so hard to avoid a finding of fault on the part of the plaintiff, the pre-1945 authorities therefore remain relevant.

The first point is that the plaintiff's fault must have had a causal connection with the damage he has suffered and the burden of proof of this lies upon the defendant. Thus in *Owens* v. *Brimmell*[79] no reduction was made for the plaintiff's failure to wear a seat belt where on the evidence it was not possible to determine whether the plaintiff had been thrown against part of the car or the car had been forced back on him. Nor is proof even of a factual causal connection enough if the injury which occurs is not within the risk created by the failure to take care. Driving at excessive speed would amount to contributory negligence in respect of a collision but not where the plaintiff's injuries were caused by his car being crushed by a tree falling from the defendant's land. In other words, the concept of remoteness of damage is as applicable to the plaintiff's fault as to the defendant's. It also follows that notwithstanding the 1945 Act a court may still come to the conclusion that although the defendant "set the scene" for the accident, the plaintiff's own fault is so great that it is the sole effective cause of his injuries and provides a complete defence. The defendant does not have to establish that the plaintiff owed him any "duty of care" but the point is hardly of significance for the circumstances of the case must be such that the plaintiff should anticipate some risk of injury to himself and hence the need to take precautions against it. This anticipation may, however, be general and it is not necessary that the plaintiff should believe himself to be in imminent danger from some act of the defendant. This is illustrated by the English rule whereby failure to wear a seat belt normally amounts to contributory

[79] [1977] Q.B. 859.

negligence.[80] The standard required of the plaintiff is normally the objective one of the reasonable, prudent person, though notwithstanding the 1945 Act the courts still seem to show more willingness to make allowance for disabilities than is the case where they are concerned with a defendant's fault. Even the prudent, reasonable person may make the wrong choice when in the "agony of the moment" produced by a sudden emergency without a finding of contributory negligence being made against him, and while the same is no doubt true of a defendant who is faced with an emergency, the courts may in practice require rather more of him in the way of anticipation of the emergency. The formulae of liability-creating negligence and contributory negligence are fundamentally the same but their application may lead to differing results.

In reducing damages under the Act the court is directed to do what is "just and equitable," which gives the judge a wide discretion which will not be interfered with on appeal unless he has failed to take the proper considerations into account or his decision is manifestly unreasonable. In practice the courts take into account the relative causative force of the conduct of both parties *and* their comparative blameworthiness. In the context of failure to wear a seat belt the practice is to make a 25 per cent. reduction where the injuries would have been entirely prevented by wearing a seat belt and a 15 per cent. reduction if they would have been less severe. It is not clear that such a standard formula is wholly consistent with the discretion conferred by the Act but it certainly provides a welcome element of predictability and consistency for a regularly recurring factual situation.

The fact that the 1945 Act is concerned with the consequences of contributory negligence and not the scope of the doctrine gives rise to some uncertainty. It is clear from the wording that it applies to strict statutory duties and it seems that it also applies to the strict liability arising at common law under *Rylands* v. *Fletcher*. There is some authority in England that it would apply to intentional trespass to the person, though the contrary Australian view is historically more soundly based—contributory negligence would not have been a defence to such a claim at common law. More serious in practice is the question of whether the Act applies to the breach of a contractual duty to take care (it

---

[80] There is a wide variation in this from one jurisdiction to another. Apart from widely held doubts about the efficacy of seat belts in certain types of accident, courts may be influenced by the fact that in this area above all others the defendant is likely to carry liability insurance whereas the plaintiff will have to bear his own loss so far as it is attributable to his fault. The problem provides a neat illustration of the perennial tension in tort law between compensation and loss-spreading on the one hand and the morality of fault on the other.

clearly does not if the contract duty is strict). The plaintiff can sometimes frame his claim in respect of negligent conduct as tort or breach of contract in the alternative.[81] Since the fault of the plaintiff does not, at common law, affect the defendant's liability for breach of contract unless it is sufficient to break the chain of causation and amounts to the sole legal cause it is important to know whether the plaintiff can gain an advantage by framing the claim as contract. The present law in England is that the Act applies if the claim, though framed in contract, could equally well be framed in tort, but it does not apply where there is a purely contractual duty to take care which would not found a tort claim.[81a] From a policy point of view there is much to be said for allowing the courts a power to reduce damages in contract cases. Indeed, why should it not apply even where the contract duty is strict, as where the plaintiff relies on goods being unmerchantable but he has contributed to his loss by misusing them?

Consent negatives liability for what would otherwise be an intentional tort.[82] Closely related is the defence of assumption of risk or, as it is often called, *volenti non fit injuria*. This means that the plaintiff has expressly or impliedly agreed to run the risk without compensation of the defendant's negligence if it occurs. Cases where the plaintiff has contracted to excuse the defendant from liability or has taken advantage of a licence to use the defendant's property subject to such a condition are probably better regarded as being based on an independent defence but there is now quite rigorous statutory control in this area. Provided the defendant is engaged in business (which is widely defined so as to include professional and governmental activities) section 2 of the Unfair Contract Terms Act 1977 invalidates any attempt to exclude or restrict liability for negligence causing death or personal injury and attempts to exclude or restrict liability for other types of damage are made subject to a test of "reasonableness." The Act does not abolish the common law defence of assumption of risk, but merely provides that his agreement to the condition is not of itself to be taken as indicating his voluntary acceptance of the risk. Hence, a participant in a motor race would not be barred by a term in the contract by which he entered purporting to exclude the liability of the organiser for the condition of the premises; but he could not sue another participant on the ground that he did not drive like the reasonable man on the public highway—unless he seriously infringes the rules or is reckless he is allowed to go "all out" to win and his

[81] For example, a fare-paying passenger.
[81a] *Forsikringsaktieselskapet Vesta* v. *Butcher* [1988] 3 W.L.R. 565.
[82] See p. 158, *post*.

fellow participants (and even the spectators) are taken to assent to the risks of that. As this example shows, assumption of risk may be (indeed, usually is) implied from the plaintiff's conduct.

At one time the defence was readily applied in employment cases where the worker was aware of shortcomings in his employer's safety system but continued in the employment, but there was a change of judicial attitude towards the end of the last century and thereafter so such emphasis was placed upon the proposition that knowledge of a risk was not necessarily to be taken as assent to it that the defence is virtually dead in this area. In fact, the notion of willingness to run a risk is so vague that the courts have enormous scope to apply or reject the test as they choose. A good example is the refusal to apply the defence in cases involving passengers who knowingly continue in a vehicle with a drunken driver[83] or even in respect of a claim by a driving instructor against his pupil,[84] though the latter decision may owe something to a prior conversation between the parties about insurance cover. To modern thinking, assumption of risk, with its complete rejection of the claim, is too harsh for such cases when there is available the more flexible method of reducing the plaintiff's damages for contributory negligence. Indeed, the spread of legislation like the 1945 Act may be the largest single influence on the decline of the assumption of risk defence.

Rather different in their motivation are the "rescue" cases. As was remarked in a famous American case, "danger invites rescue" and the defence of assumption of risk has received short shrift where the plaintiff has been injured while responding to an emergency created by the defendant's negligence,[85] even where the plaintiff has carefully weighed the risks of his action. His heroism leads the court to ignore the fact that he has knowingly faced the prospect that he may suffer damage from his action and even if his conduct is rash it will probably be treated as a case of contributory negligence rather than exposed to the full consequences of the defence of assumption of risk. Nevertheless, the defence is not a dead letter and it is quite likely to be applied where the plaintiff embarks on a foolhardy common venture with the defendant, as in the Canadian case where a group including the plaintiff took turns to drive with the defendant over a series of

---

[83] *Dann v. Hamilton* [1939] 1 K.B. 509; *Car and General Insurance Corpn. v. Seymour* [1956] S.C.R. 322 (Sup.Ct. of Canada).

[84] *Nettleship v. Weston* [1972] 2 Q.B. 691.

[85] In most cases the defendant has put a third party in danger, but he is liable even if he has put himself in danger. The argument that the plaintiff's intervention broke the chain of causation is no more likely to succeed than is that about assumption of risk.

sharp hills in an effort to make the car take off,[86] or where two employees agreed to contravene safety regulations, thereby putting their employer, the defendant, in breach of a statutory duty.[87] To allow recovery in such cases would sever all connection with a fault-based system of liability.

---

[86] *Deskau* v. *Dziama* (1973) 36 D.L.R. (3d) 36.
[87] *I.C.I.* v. *Shatwell* [1965] A.C. 656.

CHAPTER FOUR

Some Special Categories of Negligence

Just as the general law of contract is supplemented by many detailed rules applicable to particular contracts, so the general law of negligence has developed special features when regularly applied to particular factual contexts. Some of these are no more than propositions derived from commonly recurring facts and are of concern to the practitioner rather than the student, but there are some areas which are sufficiently distinctive to merit, indeed to require, a degree of separate treatment.

Occupiers' Liability

Historically, this is not part of the law of negligence at all, the principles having been developed by the mid-nineteenth century, well before the generalisation of the law in *Donoghue* v. *Stevenson*, and these principles continue to prevail in large parts of the common law world. In England, however, the law was remodelled along the lines of the general law of negligence in the Occupiers' Liability Act 1957. The mere fact that the law is in statutory form demands a degree of separate treatment but the similarities to negligence are so great that we are justified in regarding it as a category of that tort rather than a branch of the law in its own right.

Occupiers' liability concerns liability for damage to others on the occupier's premises. At common law most entrants were classed as "invitees" (those in whose entry the occupier had some material interest, for example, a customer in a shop) or "licensees" (persons who were on the premises with the occupier's permission but without any community of interest with him) the duty owed to the first category being higher than the duty owed to the second. Both were assimilated by the 1957 Act into a new class of "visitors," to whom is owed the "common duty of care," which the Act defines as "a duty to take such care as is reasonable to see that the visitor will be reasonably safe in using the premises for the purposes for which he is invited or permitted to be there." This is the sort of language one would use if one were attempting to express the content of *Donoghue* v. *Stevenson* in the context of liability for premises and the essential similarity of the Act and negligence is demonstrated by the fate of the "activity duty." Before the Act the courts had developed a doctrine whereby the special rules governing the different classes of entrant were relevant to the state of the premises but not to current activities thereon, these being governed by general negligence law. Whether or not the Act was intended to abolish the activity duty one hears nothing of it these days because (apart perhaps from the point of view of pleading) it can have no significance in view of the fact that its content is likely to be the same as the duty imposed by the Act.

The Act specifically draws attention to two points that may be relevant in determining whether the common duty of care has been fulfilled, *viz.*, that an occupier must be prepared for children to be less careful than adults and that he may expect a person to appreciate and guard against any special risks ordinarily incident to his job—you do not have to give the window cleaner advice on the safe angle at which to prop up his ladder. It is doubtful if these statutory "examples" achieve very much since they merely express what would otherwise be implied. It is further provided that a warning is not of itself a defence unless it is enough to make the visitor reasonably safe and that an occupier will generally fulfil his duty by entrusting work to an apparently competent contractor and taking such steps (if any) as are reasonable to satisfy himself that the work has been properly done. Although these provisions also follow the general law of negligence it was probably necessary to insert them to prevent the "carry over" of apparently contrary decisions in the pre-Act case law.

Liability to contractual entrants (for example, hotel guests or cinema patrons) turns primarily on the terms of the contract but since contracts are often silent on the point the Act provides that if recourse to an implied term is needed then it is that the common duty of care shall apply. Although under the Act as passed the occupier had virtually unlimited power to exclude his liability to visitors by contract or even by notice this has largely been taken away by section 2 of the Unfair Contract Terms Act 1977. The other main class of entrant is the trespasser. The 1957 Act did not apply at all to a trespasser and the common law imposed upon the occupier only a duty not to cause him injury deliberately or recklessly.[1] As a result of the decision in *B.R.B.* v. *Herrington*[2] the common law adopted a new standard of "common humanity," which was quickly taken up by courts in Australia and Canada. It is not easy to state precisely how this differs from a duty to take reasonable care but it probably requires a higher degree of likelihood of harm and makes more allowance for the particular circumstances and resources of the occupier, which are normally excluded from the calculation by the standard of the reasonable man. Fundamentally, however, the duty is so flexible that a court has a good deal of leeway in moulding it to a "just" result. Now, however, English law is found in section 1 of the Occupiers' Liability Act 1984, under which a trespasser is owed a duty if the occupier:

(a) is aware of the danger or has reasonable grounds to believe that it exists;

(b) knows or has reasonable grounds to believe that the [trespasser] is in the vicinity of the danger concerned or that he may come into the vicinity of the danger, and

(c) the risk is one against which, in all the circumstances of the case, he may reasonably be expected to offer the [trespasser] some protection.

This formulation is virtually tantamount to saying that the ordinary duty of reasonable care applies to trespassers, the circumstances of the trespass being a factor of varying weight in framing the content of the duty. As the Act indicates, prominent warning notices may in many situations be enough to discharge the occupier's duty though it will probably be held that something more, such as a reasonably effective barrier, is required to protect youthful trespassers. No doubt it is still the law[3] that the primary obligation for protection of young children rests upon their parents not those who happen to have attractive scrap-yards or building sites in the vicinity, but experience unfortunately shows that they cannot be entitled in all circumstances to expect that parents will fulfil this duty. Indeed, this area illustrates most graphically the criticism of the law of negligence that it gives very little advance guidance on how to frame one's conduct so as to avoid liability.

---

[1] Moderate force might, of course, be *lawfully* used to expel a trespasser and if this resulted in some accidental injury there would be no tort. This is still the law.

[2] [1972] A.C. 877.

[3] *Phipps* v. *Rochester Corporation* [1955] 1 Q.B. 450.

The duty under the occupiers' liability legislation is imposed upon the "occupier." A non-occupier who by his action creates a danger on the land of another is no doubt liable at common law but it is only the occupier who is under a positive duty to act to remedy dangers due to the state of the premises. The courts tend to approach the question of who is an occupier in a rather circular manner by saying that a person is an occupier for tort purposes (and this is all we are concerned with, for the word may have a different meaning in other legislation) if he has sufficient control of the premises to justify the duties of an occupier being imposed on him. A landlord who has let the premises is not an occupier (though he has a statutory duty to visitors if he has powers of entry and repair)[4]; a tenant or a squatter is. A servant is not generally an occupier of his employer's business premises even though he has day-to-day control or supervision, rather the employer occupies through him, though no hard and fast rule can be laid down: for example, the manager of a public-house may be an occupier along with his employer, the brewery. In applying the control test the court may be influenced by the fact that a person in the defendant's position is likely to have the means, whether from insurance or other sources, to meet claims against him. Hence a main contractor is readily treated as occupier of a building site though he has no form of interest in the land and in *Harris* v. *Birkenhead Corpn.*[5] a local authority which had served notice of entry under a compulsory purchase order was treated as an occupier even though it had in no sense taken physical control of the premises.

Liability of Vendors of Defective Premises

The law of occupiers' liability is straightforward, but few areas of tort have fallen into greater confusion than the liability of those who build and sell premises. The first point is that since buildings are generally bought not given away we must take into account the law of contract. The principle of *caveat emptor* (let the buyer satisfy himself as to the quality of what he is buying) was much more tenacious with buildings than with goods and the only circumstances in which the common law implied any warranty of fitness was when there was a contract for the sale of a house yet to be built or completed by the vendor. Section 1 of the Defective Premises Act 1972 imposes upon persons who take on work in connection with the provision of a dwelling a non-excludable duty to ensure that it will be fit for habitation when completed.

---

[4] See Defective Premises Act 1972, s.4.
[5] [1976] 1 W.L.R. 279.

The limitation period is six years from completion. The Act is not, however, applicable where the dwelling is covered (as are nearly all new houses) by the "N.H.B.C." scheme of insurance against structural defects during the first 10 years after completion. The plaintiff is likely to rely on the law of torts if (a) the premises are not a dwelling, in which case neither the Act nor the N.H.B.C. scheme applies or (b) when the time limit under those has expired. The fact that the plaintiff is a second purchaser and not in privity of contract with the builder is not a problem: the duty under the Act is owed to subsequent purchasers and the benefit of the N.H.B.C. scheme is assignable.

Originally, the vendor of a building was treated as immune from tort liability for negligence even though he was also the builder and had created the defect in question by shoddy workmanship. This immunity was formally abolished by section 3 of the Defective Premises Act, though the courts had brought about the same result in a series of decisions more or less contemporaneous with the Act. It is now clear that if a building collapses as a result of negligent construction and injures the purchaser, or his family, or anyone else likely to be foreseeably affected thereby the builder is liable, which is perfectly proper and uncontroversial. The problem is that this is not what has happened in the cases. Rather, the plaintiff has been complaining that his building is defective and needs repairs. Is not that rather like the situation of a person who buys shoddy goods on the repair of which he is constantly having to spend money? Except in very unusual circumstances it is clear law that the tort of negligence is not meant to afford protection in such a case[6] but the point was largely ignored in many building cases. However, the decision of the House of Lords in *D. & F. Estates* v. *Church Commissioners*[7] marked a move some way back towards orthodoxy. It was held in that case that even if the main contractors for a block of flats had been vicariously liable in tort for plastering sub-contractors (which they were not) no claim could have been brought in negligence by owners or occupiers of a flat in respect of the cost of replacing badly applied plaster: to have held otherwise would in effect have been to create, via the tort action, a transmissible warranty of fitness, a matter for contract law. However, buildings cannot be entirely equated with chattels because it is suggested in the case that where, for example, a building suffers cracking as a result of defective foundations it may be proper to treat the component parts of the building as independent units. In this way, negligence in

---

[6] See p. 53 *ante*.
[7] [1988] 3 W.L.R. 368.

constructing the foundations of the building results in damage to "other property" of the plaintiff (the rest of the building) which gives at least a semblance of according with ordinary tort principles. A potential source of confusion, however, still remains in the earlier decision of the House in *Anns* v. *Merton London Borough*[8] where a broader principle seems to have been laid down whereby even though no actual damage has been suffered a claim may be made in respect of the cost of repairs necessary to avert imminent danger to life or health. It must, however, be recognised that *Anns* was primarily about the duty of a local authority with statutory powers of inspection of dwellings and that broader principle probably has no application to the common law negligence liability of the builder.

The muddled state of the law on defective premises has only been tolerable because the N.H.B.C. scheme and, on a smaller scale, the Defective Premises Act, do directly give the redress required to purchasers of dwellings which are unfit for their purpose. One further statutory provision will strengthen the building owner's position, namely section 38 of the Building Act 1984, which will impose liability for failure to comply with the statutory Building Regulations. We are, however, still waiting for this to be implemented (despite a previous incarnation in a statute of 1974!) and the Act is regrettably unclear as to the nature of the damage covered by it.

The tort problems thrown up by leasehold premises have been less acute. The short leaseholder is less likely to suffer economic loss from structural defects and statute imposes certain ongoing obligations on the landlord to keep the structure and main services of dwellings in repair. Where the landlord has a duty (or even a power) to repair the premises this creates a statutory duty of care for the benefit of persons who might be expected to suffer personal injury or property damage from defects in the premises.[9] A long lease may be indistinguishable in practice from an outright sale and a builder-lessor is subject to the same liability as a builder-vendor. A lessor who has not created the defect is not liable in tort (though he may be in contract or by statute) but nor is a vendor in such a case.

Negligent Statements

The common law has approached with caution the possibility of imposing liability for loss caused by statements. There are two main reasons for this: first, while the consequences of physical

---

[8] [1978] A.C. 728.
[9] Defective Premises Act 1972, s.4.

acts tend to be contained by the natural law of inertia, "words have wings" for common experience tells us that they will be repeated; secondly, words are much more likely than deeds to give rise only to financial loss and this occupies a lower scale on the law's priorities than physical harm.[10]

It is particularly important in this area to put tort liability in the general legal context. A contractual warranty[11] may be either a pure promise ("I will deliver the car on the 1st June") or a guarantee as to a present fact ("the car has done 30,000 miles"). In either event it gives rise to liability in damages, in many cases without any requirement of fault, for the content of the defendant's contractual duty is a matter of the interpretation of his promise. Thus in *Esso* v. *Mardon*[12] the defendants' estimate of the throughput of a filling station was held to be a warranty that they had exercised care, but had they used slightly different language, it would have been a warranty that that throughput would be achieved. If a statement is not part of the contract but induces it to be made it is a "representation." As such, it always gives rise to a right to rescind the contract and gives rise to a right to damages under the Misrepresentation Act 1967 if the maker is unable to show that he had good reason to believe it to be true. An inaccurate statement may be made within a contractual context in a rather different way, that is to say it may be made in performance of an ongoing duty, as where my solicitor advises me on how I should effect a land purchase or my broker advises me on a share transaction. Such professional negligence has always been regarded as actionable in contract and in most cases it mattered little whether or not there was liability in tort. However, a plaintiff may suffer from an inaccurate statement made wholly outside any contract or negotiations for a contract and then his only refuge[13] is the law of torts.

If the statement is made fraudulently (that is, the maker knows it to be untrue or is indifferent whether it is true or false) and was intended to be acted upon by the recipient it has since the late eighteenth century been actionable as deceit. This remains the law[14] but fraud is a serious charge to make and not easily proved even in a civil court. It was not until the decision of the House of Lords in *Hedley Byrne* v. *Heller & Partners*[15] that liability was

---

[10] See p. 50, *ante.*
[11] Using the word in its more general sense of "contract term" rather than the narrow sense of the Sale of Goods Act 1979.
[12] [1975] Q.B. 801.
[13] But there is an equitable right to compensation where there is a breach of duty in a fiduciary relationship: *Nocton* v. *Ashburton* [1914] A.C. 932.
[14] See Chap. 13.
[15] [1964] A.C. 465.

formally extended to negligent statements. The plaintiffs, advertising agents, made enquiries of the defendant bank about the financial stability of a client company with a view to incurring liability on advertising contracts for the company. It is not clear that the defendants' reply would have amounted to breach of a duty of care but the action failed because the reply had been accompanied by a clear, express disclaimer of responsibility. What is important, however, is the decisive recognition by the House of Lords that such a situation *could* give rise to a duty.

There is no doubt that a liability for every (literally) foreseeable reliance on words would be intolerable and for this reason the House of Lords in *Hedley, Byrne* intended to create a category of liability which was to some extent separate from the general law of negligence, which at that time was concerned overwhelmingly with liability for physical harm caused by negligent acts. The early 1980s saw a more liberal attitude towards the duty of care which might in due course have assimilated *Hedley, Byrne* entirely within the formula of *Donoghue* v. *Stevenson* but as we have seen the English courts have taken a clear decision to restrict the advance of negligence and the formulae chosen to achieve this ("proximity," the "close and direct relationship") have some similarity to the terms used in negligent misstatement cases. Perhaps in due course we shall end up with one, very far-reaching liability for acts causing physical damage and another, much more restricted, covering economic loss and into which *Hedley, Byrne* can be subsumed, but for the time being it seems justifiable to continue to give this area special treatment. The two major problems raised by the misstatement cases are, first, in what circumstances does a duty arise, and, secondly, how far does the duty extend beyond the direct recipient of the information or advice?

As to the first question, English courts find themselves in the rather peculiar position that the majority of the Privy Council (which is the House of Lords sitting as a Commonwealth appeal court) in *Mutual Life* v. *Evatt*[16] held that the duty of care caught only those who were in the business of giving advice about the matter in question or held themselves out as possessing equivalent expertise or (probably) had a financial interest in the matter. The bank in *Hedley, Byrne* no doubt fell within the first group, but the defendant insurance company in *Mutual Life* was held not to be under a duty when it made statements to an intending investor in an associated company. *Mutual Life* does not bind any English court, has been treated here with less respect than is customarily accorded to Privy Council decisions

---

[16] [1971] A.C. 793.

and may not even represent English law—though in the English cases which have criticised it the same result would probably have been reached if it had been applied. Most courts in Canada seem to have rejected it[17] and it was criticised in the High Court of Australia in an appeal from the same jurisdiction that had given rise to it.[18] In its defence, however, it may be said that not only does it accord fairly closely with the formulation in the American *Restatement*[19] but it may be easier to apply than a vague test of "reasonable reliance" and have the effect of confining liability to those who as a practical matter are in a position to cover themselves by insurance. However, the principal reason given by the Privy Council for confining liability to the "professional" adviser, namely, that it is only by reference to the professional adviser that a standard of care can be set, is suspect. As the minority pointed out, it is perfectly possible to have a flexible standard which varies according to what the recipient can reasonably expect of the adviser. Suppose a first-year law student consults his tutor (whose field is criminal law) about investing a windfall in the Cayman Islands. The tutor is presumably not in the business of advising about offshore tax havens and it may be that the law should deny the student the right to any more than an *honest* answer (though many would think it better that the adviser should say nothing at all). But suppose instead that the student, wishing to make a home-made will, were to enquire whether it needed to be witnessed and the tutor were to answer, "NO." He is no more in the business of giving advice about wills than about offshore investments but *Mutual Life* may deny a duty no matter how simple the question and how crass the response.[20] On the view of the minority in *Mutual Life*, however, it may be possible to say that an incorrect answer to so straightforward an enquiry could be regarded as negligent in anyone who had received a legal education.

On the whole it would be better to assume that *Mutual Life* did not put rigid fetters on *Hedley, Byrne* and the *indicia* of a duty situation must therefore be sought in the latter case and its subsequent development by the courts. The key—though an imprecise one—is to be found in the idea of the "special relationship." In *Hedley, Byrne* itself this was expressed in various ways but all had in common that the duty arose from a voluntary

---

[17] See Linden, *Canadian Tort Law*, 3rd ed.
[18] *Shaddock* v. *Paramatta City Council* (1981) 36 A.L.R. 385.
[19] Torts, 2d, s.552.
[20] This might of course turn upon the willingness of the court to give a liberal interpretation to the alternative head of "holding out."

undertaking of responsibility by the defendant,[21] though this could, and indeed usually would, be implied from the circumstances in which the statement was made rather than expressed as a promise. Accordingly, no liability arises from advice given on a "social occasion" and it will not be easy to establish a duty where a "snap" or "off the cuff" response is given, for in such a case it may not be reasonable for the recipient to assume that the speaker is undertaking responsibility.[22] In cases like *Hedley, Byrne* it is possible to accept the voluntary undertaking analysis because the defendant is under no obligation to speak: he may give an unqualified response, he may remain silent or he may answer disclaiming responsibility.[23] However, there are a number of Commonwealth authorities (which might be followed here) where liability has been imposed upon a public authority responding to an enquiry which it has been under a legal duty to answer. Indeed, the Court of Appeal in *Ministry of Housing* v. *Sharp*[24] found the defendants liable when their negligent conduct of a land charges search caused the plaintiff to lose his rights over a piece of land. This case is not a straight application of *Hedley, Byrne* for it was not the plaintiff but a third person, a prospective purchaser of the land, who enquired and thereby caused to be issued the certificate which destroyed the plaintiff's rights, but the point for our purposes is that the court was not dissuaded from imposing liability by the fact that there was a duty to speak.

Can the defendant be liable to someone other than the enquirer but into whose possession the information or advice comes and who relies upon it? Over 100 years ago it was held that while promoters could be liable to a person who applied for an initial allotment of shares in response to a fraudulent prospectus they were not liable to a person into whose hands the prospectus came and who, on the faith of it, bought already-allotted shares on the market. While this may still be the common law of fraud on such facts it would be wrong to assume that a defendant's liability in negligence extends only to the person who made the direct enquiry of him. First, it may be clear that the enquirer is acting on

---

[21] Hence Lord Devlin's "equivalent to contract" and the view that the case is closer to contract than to tort.

[22] But judicial opinions can differ. In *Howard Marine* v. *Ogden* [1978] Q.B. 574 one judge thought there was no duty under *Hedley, Byrne*, the second thought there probably was not and the third thought there was a duty and it had been broken.

[23] It has been controversial whether the disclaimer is subject to judicial control under the Unfair Contract Terms Act 1977. The point is under appeal to the House of Lords.

[24] [1970] 2 Q.B. 223.

behalf of a third party and if so the fact that the third party is unidentified does not matter. This was so in *Hedley Byrne* where the enquiry was made on behalf of the plaintiffs by their bank. Secondly, the plaintiff may be one of an "identifiable class" of persons to whom it is foreseeable that the information may be passed on. On this basis a building society surveyor has been held liable to a house purchaser for errors in his report,[25] an accountant liable to an investor in a company in respect of a report which he knew would be used generally to attract loans and investments[26] and a public weigher engaged by a seller of beans to weigh them preparatory to sale has been held liable to the buyer of the beans.[27] But the "class" is hard to define. Is an accountant to be liable where a takeover bidder relies upon a routine audit report in making his bid? He may not have any particular transaction in mind, but it is common knowledge that such reports are exhibited for many purposes to persons outside the company. According to the Court of Appeal of New Zealand the answer is "yes"[28] but the English Court of Appeal, influenced by the current restrictive attitude to the expansion of negligence, has answered in the negative.[29] The implications of the application in such cases of the usual foreseeability formula may be illustrated by the extraordinary case of *Jaillet* v. *Cashman* where the defendant's "ticker tape" service negligently published a story that the United States Supreme Court had handed down a ruling that would have made dividends taxable income, thereby causing loss to the plaintiff.[30] The decision that the defendants incurred no liability is consistent with Denning L.J.'s famous example in *Candler* v. *Crane, Christmas*[31] to the effect that a careless marine hydrographer would not be liable for the loss of an ocean liner on the reef which he omitted to include in his chart. It will be observed that in this example liability is denied even though the loss is physical, something around which the law is usually readier to cast its protection. There is no very intellectually satisfying explanation of why liability does not extend to these cases and one can only repeat the famous words of Cardozo C.J. in *Ultramares Corpn.* v. *Touche*[32] a case denying

---

[25] *Yianni* v. *Edwin Evans* [1982] Q.B. 438.

[26] *Haig* v. *Bamford* (1977) 72 D.L.R. (3d) 68 (Sup.Ct. of Canada).

[27] *Glanzer* v. *Shepard* 135 N.E. 275 (1922).

[28] *Scott Group Ltd.* v. *McFarlane* [1978] 1 N.Z.L.R. 553. The plaintiff in fact failed to prove any case.

[29] *Caparo Industries* v. *Dickman* [1988] N.L.J. 289. But the auditor may be liable to shareholders.

[30] 139 N.E. 714 (1923). The reporters assumed that a dissenting judgment (read first) was that of the court.

[31] [1951] 2 K.B. 164.

[32] 174 N.E. 441 (1931).

liability where a lender had advanced loans on the faith of the balance sheet certified by the defendants: "If liability for negligence exists, a thoughtless slip or blunder, the failure to detect a theft or forgery beneath the cover of deceptive entries, may expose accountants to a liability in an indeterminate amount for an indeterminate time to an indeterminate class. The hazards of a business conducted on these terms are so extreme as to enkindle doubt whether a flaw may not exist in the implication of a duty that exposes to these consequences." While this remains undeniably true, it must be added that the scale of modern business is such that even a duty confined to a single identifiable enquirer may lead to just these results. Unless *Hedley Byrne* is held firmly in check, we may be reaching the stage when accountants and lawyers cannot practise without the protection of corporate status, statutory limitation of liability or at least a wide power to disclaim responsibility.

Negligence and Public Law

Public bodies other than the Crown (which has the additional legal source of the prerogative) act exclusively under statutory powers. The statute may provide a defence to what would otherwise be a legal wrong, a point which is of considerable importance in relation to the tort of nuisance. It is not likely that Parliament will in express terms authorise someone to be negligent but it must be recognised that the grant of statutory authority to carry on an activity will have some impact upon the application of the law of negligence, which has grown up largely as a system for governing private rights between subjects. Decisions like those to liberalise the system of custody for young offenders[33] or to institute a plan for the development of an area of a city may have an effect upon a very wide range of persons and cause serious foreseeable damage to the interests of some of them but not only are the courts an unsuitable forum for debating the wisdom or unwisdom of these decisions, there is something inherently unsuitable in the negligence formula as a means of resolving what are essentially political matters of risk and resource allocation. As Lord Diplock put it in *Home Office* v. *Dorset Yacht Co.*:

> "Parliament has entrusted to the department or authority charged with the administration of the statute the exclusive right to determine the particular means within the limits laid down by the statute by which its purpose can best be

---

[33] *Home Office* v. *Dorset Yacht Co.* [1970] A.C. 1004.

fulfilled. It is not the function of the court, for which it would be ill-suited, to substitute its own view of the appropriate means for that of the department or authority by granting a remedy by way of a civil action at law to a private citizen adversely affected by the way in which its discretion has been exercised. Its function is confined in the first instance to deciding whether the act or omission complained of fell within the statutory limits imposed upon the department's or authority's discretion."[34]

Accordingly, the plaintiff's first (and difficult) task is to show that the discretionary decision is *ultra vires* (not within the powers given), usually by demonstrating that no sensible authority could have arrived at that decision or that the authority was activated by improper motives, for example bias. Improper motives are much the most likely grounds of attack in practice and if that can be shown a person who has suffered damage may be able to sue for the tort of "misfeasance in a public office"[35] even though the invalidity of the decision does not itself give rise to a claim for damages. It may be that in rare cases where an authority has come to an *ultra vires* decision in good faith but after crassly misinterpreting its powers an action for negligence could lie at the suit of someone who has suffered damage thereby,[36] but the law of negligence does not apply to a public officer or body deciding whether a payment should be made from public funds—the remedies are the statutory right of appeal (if any) and judicial review.[37]

To be contrasted with matters of policy with which the court will not generally interfere are so-called "operational" matters, which are more likely to be subjected to the ordinary duty of care. In *Anns* v. *Merton L.B.C.*[38] the plaintiffs' case, had the matter come to trial, would probably not have been that the council was devoting insufficient resources to inspection of houses under construction but that the council's inspector had failed to do his job properly. Similarly a claim based upon the increased risk to neighbours of running an "open" custody centre for young

---

[34] *Ibid.* at p. 1059.

[35] See *Dunlop* v. *Woollahra M.C.* [1982] A.C. 158.

[36] But see *Rowling* v. *Takaro Properties*, below. The authority might, of course, commit some independently tortious act such as trespass or conversion as a consequence of its erroneous decision, in which event negligence would be irrelevant: the act is wrongful without lawful authority.

[37] *Jones* v. *D.o.E.* [1988] 2 W.L.R. 493. Even where there is a right to damages, the plaintiff may be required to proceed by way of judicial review under R.S.C.Ord. 53 if his rights derive from "public law." This puts him at a procedural disadvantage. See *Cocks* v. *Thanet D.C.* [1983] 2 A.C. 286.

[38] See p. 50, *ante*.

offenders would be doomed to failure, but the same obstacles would not lie in the way of an allegation that the custodians had gone to sleep on the job. Though widely adopted in cases since *Anns* v. *Merton* this distinction between the "policy" and the "operational" must be substantially qualified. In the first place, it is not possible in practice to achieve a tidy division between non-justiciable areas of discretion and those which are "merely" operational. A hypothetical illustration may be based on *Rigby* v. *Chief Constable of Northants.*[39] A chief constable issues a set of guidelines for handling "siege" situations, that is to say, where armed persons barricade themselves in property and threaten violence. Presumably, the fundamental decision whether the normal policy should be a "passive" approach involving cordoning off the area and putting psychological pressure on the offender or one involving more active steps to ferret him out is discretionary and unassailable unless manifestly absurd for the normal run of cases. At the other extreme, mishandling of a CS cartridge by an untrained officer so as to start a fire is presumably "operational." But what of a decision to use existing stocks of CS cartridges after a new model has come on the market, which substantially reduces fire risks? Or a decision by a senior officer to use gas at a time when there is no fire appliance at the scene to deal with any fire which may arise? Is there any real difference between these decisions and the first, clear policy one except that, in the case of one of them, it is made on the spot rather than "back at base"?

Secondly, while true policy decisions are non-justiciable it does not follow that a duty of care is automatically to be imposed on persons whose conduct is capable of being described as operational. This point is made by the Privy Council in the difficult case of *Rowling* v. *Takaro Properties*[40] in which it was unnecessary finally to determine whether a duty of care existed because the defendant, the New Zealand Finance Minister, was not in breach of any duty, his view of his powers in relation to the issue of shares to a foreign company being tenable (albeit, as it turned out, incorrect). The trial judge had been disposed to regard the decision in question as "operational" but even if this were correct the Privy Council was of the view that there were still considerations of which militated against the imposition of liability.[41] One was the danger of "overkill" for "once it became known that liability in negligence may be imposed on the ground

---

[39] [1985] 1 W.L.R. 1242.
[40] [1988] 2 W.L.R. 418.
[41] As to such considerations in the decision whether to impose a duty of care, see p. 45, *ante*.

that a minister has misconstrued a statute and so acted *ultra vires*, the cautious civil servant may go to extreme lengths in ensuring that legal advice, or even the opinion of the court, is obtained before decisions are taken, thereby leading to unnecessary delay in a considerable number of cases."

Thirdly, the adoption of the policy/operational distinction tends to obscure the fact that the ordinary law of negligence already has built in to it a good deal of latitude for "discretion." It is trite law, for instance, that due allowance must be made for the "agony of the moment," the dilemma presented to a defendant who finds himself in an emergency not of his own making; that the risks inherent in a course of conduct must be weighed in the balance against the gains likely to be produced thereby; and that in the field of professional negligence the court will not stigmatise as negligent a practice approved by a significant proportion of the profession even though it is disapproved by others. In *Dorset Yacht* it could have been held that "it is not negligence to keep an open Borstal" without reference to the doctrine of *ultra vires*, as, indeed, seems to have been the view of some of the judges. No doubt it is the great importance of discretion in the activities of a public authority which has led the courts to emphasise it in these cases. It may also be significant that the policy/operational distinction is most prominent in two cases (*Dorset Yacht* and *Anns*) concerned with the exercise of statutory powers which were the foundation of duties of care inapplicable to private persons. The distinction may be less relevant where a public authority is being sued for negligence in carrying on an activity (for example, the occupation of land) which others may also carry on without statutory authority. Limited resources are no more an excuse for a local authority which allows its premises to fall into disrepair than for you or me.

CHAPTER FIVE

Breach of Statutory Duty

The legislature sometimes creates a duty expressly remediable by an action for damages. Whether or not one considers these in a book on torts is to some extent a matter of convenience and history rather than strict logic. This book contains a fairly extended account of the Occupiers' Liability Act and the Consumer Protection Act but not of the Data Protection Act. The first two are primarily concerned with civil liability and modify the law in areas where the common law of tort previously operated under different rules. The last is primarily regulatory and while it does give rise to some liabilities which may properly be described as tortious these are comparatively minor aspects of the Act. This chapter, however, is not concerned with the rules of statutory liability governing certain areas of tort but with the principles upon which depend the *implication* of civil rights of action from statutes which are primarily criminal or regulatory in their function.

It should be said at the outset that in some common law jurisdictions much of the material in this chapter would not be so classified. The prevailing American view with regard to state legislation (federal legislation is subject to rather different considerations) is that violation of the statute is conclusive evidence of negligence in a civil action. Thus suppose the speed limit on a street is 30 m.p.h. but D is travelling at 35 m.p.h. The street is wide and straight, the visibility is good and it is strongly arguable that driving at 35 m.p.h. is not negligence as understood by the common law. Nevertheless, according to this doctrine the legislature has pre-empted this issue and has set a precise and mechanical standard by reference to which civil, as well as criminal, responsibility is to be measured—violation of the statute, as they say, is negligence *per se*. In some states this doctrine is modified so that the violation is prima facie, but not conclusive, evidence of negligence: if the defendant is able to show that the violation was truly beyond his control he will escape civil liability even if such an excuse would not be a defence to a criminal charge. Under both variations, however, the source of the liability is not the statute but the common law duty of care and the statute merely "concretises" and gives rigid and predictable form to what constitutes breach of that duty. Naturally, this doctrine is inapplicable if the statute deals with an area where there is no common law duty of care (for example, matters of constitutional and civil rights): if the statute is to have any effect in this case it must itself be treated as giving rise to a civil action. In other words, where statute operates in a situation already governed by the common law there is no separate tort of breach of the statute; where statute is concerned with matters on which the common law is silent, there is.

In contrast, Anglo-Australian common law[1] treats breach of statutory duty as a tort in its own right in all cases, even where there already exists a common law duty. It would, however, be quite wrong to think that *any* breach of a penal statute gives rise to a civil action for damages and since the legislation is normally silent on the matter the great difficulty is to know when such an action is to be implied: whatever principle one extracts from the cases, there are other decisions which will seem wholly inconsistent with that principle. For example, the proposition that the statute gives rise to a civil action if it was passed for the benefit of an identifiable class of persons rather than for the benefit of the public as a whole might explain cases where statutes governing factory machinery, safety of school premises or the housing of homeless persons have been held civilly actionable; but it is then hard to see why the crime of harassment of residential tenants has been held to fall outside this category. Indeed, as Atkin L.J. forcefully pointed out in *Phillips* v. *Britannia Hygienic Laundry*[2] the very basis of the "class" approach is suspect, for it "would be strange if a less important duty, which is owed to a section of the public, may be enforced by an action, while a more important duty owed to the public at large cannot." In the same case Bankes L.J. referred with approval to the proposition that when the statute is silent as to the consequences

---

[1] Canada, which formerly took this line, moved towards the U.S. position in *R.* v. *Saskatchewan Wheat Pool* (1983) 143 D.L.R. (3d) 9 (Sup.Ct. of Canada), though the doctrine there laid down has features of its own.
[2] [1923] 2 K.B. 832.

of violation a civil action is to be implied, but where a remedy (including a criminal penalty) is prescribed it is to be presumed that this is the only legal consequence intended. Yet in a case in the nineteenth century which established that a civil action arose from breach of factory safety legislation not only was there a penalty provided but there was provision for that penalty to be paid to the victim. It is, therefore, all the more remarkable that the court should have concluded that a further civil remedy was to be superimposed on this.

For the purposes of an introduction it must suffice to say very broadly that the English courts have consistently held that industrial safety legislation gives rise to a civil action but have tended to reject the inference with other types of statute, most notably those dealing with road safety.[3] Unfortunately, one cannot therefore extend beyond the employment context in which it was spoken the generalisation of Dixon J. in the High Court of Australia[4] that in the absence of an expressed contrary legislative intention a duty "to take measures for the safety of others seems to be regarded as involving a correlative private right, although the sanction is penal, because it protects an interest recognised by the general principles of the common law." It would, however, be wrong to dismiss the action for breach of statutory duty as *solely* confined to the employment relationship. Courts have recently held that an action for damages may lie at the suit of performers whose live concerts are wrongfully recorded contrary to statute,[5] or for breach of the competition provisions of the EEC Treaty[6] and it has long been established that an action for breach of statutory duty lies where the owner of a vehicle allows an uninsured person to drive it.[7] In the majority of cases the search for a concealed legislative intention is a search for something which is simply not there, for it is not likely that Parliament adverted to the matter at all. No doubt the legislative draftsman did but chose to leave the matter to the courts to work out. The point is made clearly in an American case rejecting a civil right of action for violation of a child-neglect statute:

"When neither the statute nor the common law authorizes an action and the statute does not expressly deny it, the court

---

[3] With the rather curious exception of the Pedestrian Crossing Regulations!

[4] *O'Connor* v. *S. P. Bray* (1937) 56 C.L.R. 464.

[5] *Rickless* v. *United Artists* [1988] Q.B. 40.

[6] *Garden Cottage Foods* v. *Milk Marketing Board* [1984] A.C. 130.

[7] *Monk* v. *Warbey* [1935] 1 K.B. 75. This may be seen as not introducing a novel liability but buttressing the law of negligence by ensuring a claimworthy defendant.

should recognize that it is being asked to bring into existence a new type of tort liability on the basis of its own appraisal of the policy considerations involved. If a court decides to create a cause of action... the interest which is invaded derives its protection solely from the court although the legislative action in branding the act or omission as culpable is taken into consideration by the court in deciding whether a common law action should be established. If a civil cause of action based upon a statute is established by the court, it is because the court, not the legislature, believes it is necessary and desirable to further vindicate the right or to further enforce the duty created by statute."[8]

Even where the statute does not give rise to a civil cause of action it is not, of course, irrelevant for where it lays down detailed rules for conduct it is evidence, and sometimes very strong evidence, of what should be required as reasonable care. Indeed, even non-statutory norms, such as those contained in the Highway Code, may be similarly persuasive. In these cases English law therefore approaches the American theory of negligence *per se* but in the last resort the statute is not controlling. The court may reject the statutory standard as unsuitable (slightly exceeding the speed limit in good conditions) or deny civil liability on the facts even when it does provide a suitable standard. For example, suppose a statute requires tyres to have a minimum tread depth of one millimetre. It is highly likely that a defendant involved in an accident to which his bald tyres have contributed would be held negligent and that the court would rely on the statute as evidence of a minimum standard. But let us say that the defendant has checked his tyres before a 200-mile trip and found them to have three millimetres of tread. As a result of a latent defect in the manufacture of one of the tyres it has worn below the statutory minimum before the end of the journey and an accident occurs. Proof of this would certainly exculpate the defendant from civil liability for negligence even if it provided no defence to a criminal prosecution.

Where a civil law duty does arise from a statute its scope and effect must, of course, depend on the wording of the statute in question, but a general principle applicable to all cases is that the harm suffered must be of a type the legislation was intended to prevent. In *Gorris* v. *Scott*[9] the defendant failed to comply with an Act requiring the penning of livestock being carried aboard ship but this did not avail the plaintiff when his sheep were washed

---

[8] *Burnette* v. *Wahl* 588 P 2d 1105 (1978).
[9] (1874) L.R. 9 Exch. 125.

overboard, for the clear purpose of the statute was to prevent the spread of disease by overcrowding, not loss by drowning. Had the plaintiff alleged negligence, then the statute, in so far as it prescribed the nature of the pens required, might have been of some persuasive value on what was required to keep beasts confined. No doubt, English courts would have come to similar conclusions adverse to the plaintiff as did American courts[10] where a child, sold fireworks in breach of a statute, was poisoned by eating them; where rat poison, laid down in a restaurant in contravention of a public health ordinance, exploded; or where a straying cow was killed by a train unlawfully being run on a Sunday. The reader will observe that the issue is very similar to that of remoteness of damage (we might express it as "what was the risk governed by the statute?") and the court should not therefore be astute to define the statutory purpose too narrowly. For example, the obvious risk envisaged by a statute requiring lift shafts to be guarded is that of persons falling down the shaft; but an American court was correct to construe the statute as also covering damage caused by objects falling down the shaft.[11]

Another aspect of the same issue is the requirement that the plaintiff be a person for whose benefit the duty exists. Some factory legislation is expressed to apply only to regulate the safety of "persons employed" in the factory and claims by persons who were merely lawful visitors have failed. In other cases, however, the legislation operates "geographically" rather than by reference to employment.

Relationship between Common Law Negligence and Statutory Duty

A statutory duty may be to take reasonable care, in which event it adds nothing of substance to the equivalent duty of care at common law. In many cases, however, the plaintiff relies upon a statutory duty because it gives rise to a stricter form of liability. The best known example is section 14 of the Factories Act 1961, which requires every dangerous part of machinery to be securely fenced while it is in motion or in use. There is no question here of negligence and liability cannot be avoided if the fence breaks because of some latent defect or even if the effect of a secure fence would be to render the machinery unusable, but it should not be

---

[10] The requirement that the harm be of a type intended to be prevented by the statute is applicable even under the negligence *per se* theory so American cases may be used for comparison.

[11] *De Haan* v. *Rockwood Sprinkler Co.* 179 N.E. 764 (1932). See also *Grant* v. *N.C.B.* [1958] A.C. 649.

thought that such legislation represents a coherent exercise in compensation without fault for employment injuries, for the statute contains a wide variety of duties of varying strictness.[12] This is because it has been drafted primarily as a protective safety code backed by penal sanctions and the draftsman will have had to bear in mind engineering and other considerations which have no obvious relevance to compensation. For example, section 14 has been interpreted as requiring a fence "to keep the worker out, not to keep the machine or its product in"[13] but there is no very good reason why a worker who is drawn into a machine should receive hundreds of thousands of pounds in damages whereas one hit by an exploding machine should not. From a regulatory point of view, however, it may be unreasonable or even impracticable to impose upon the employer a duty to install the sort of massive construction which would be necessary to contain an explosion of the machine. The apparent anomalies have been created not by the legislation but by the courts' using a legal device designed for one purpose for the wholly different purpose of compensation.

There is no reason why the plaintiff should not bring concurrent claims for negligence and breach of statutory duty and in industrial cases it is common to do so.[14] If the statutory duty is strict he may succeed on it where his action in negligence would fail. It is also perfectly possible for the negligence claim to succeed where the statutory claim fails because the statute has been complied with: Parliament is not to be taken to have covered the whole ground in the statutory requirement. Thus in the case where it was established that the fencing requirements did not extend to keeping the machine in, it was expressly recognised that if a machine had a history of ejecting parts of itself or of the material being worked that might require the employer to take other steps to protect the workers from

---

[12] A duty to take steps "so far as practicable" may be somewhere between strict liability and negligence.

[13] *Close* v. *S.C.O.W.* [1962] A.C. 367.

[14] The classic formulation of the employer's duty of care is in *Wilsons Clyde Coal* v. *English* [1938] A.C. 57, namely the duty to provide a competent staff, adequate material and equipment and a proper system and effective supervision, though it must be stressed that these three heads are only a convenient way of breaking down what is a single, all-embracing duty of care. Since the abolition of "common employment" it is possible to decide many cases simply by saying that the employer is vicariously liable for the negligence of another worker: see p. 30 *ante*.

injury.[15] One should, however, guard against the tendency to assume that because the circumstances come close to but do not amount to infringement of the statute then the "near miss" is automatically negligence. If statute requires that persons working two metres above the ground must have a working platform one metre wide it does not necessarily mean that a person working at 1.9 metres requires such a platform (or even one 0.95 metres wide). Nonetheless, the statement in one decision[16] that the statute was not even *relevant* is hard to understand for it is clear that even statutes which have no direct civil sanction may be of persuasive (though not controlling) value.

For the most part, the remaining elements of a case of breach of statutory duty are likely to be similar to an action for negligence. The plaintiff must show that his damage was caused in the factual sense by the breach and that it is not too remote. His damages may be reduced (or even wholly extinguished in an extreme case) by his contributory negligence. The defence of assumption of risk cannot, however, be raised in an action for breach of statutory duty against an employer, though this rule dates from an era when assumption of risk was more readily implied than it is now and might well have largely nullified the statutory protection conferred by Parliament. However, the defence is applicable where two employees of equal status agree to contravene statutory regulations. In such a case there is a technical violation by the employer which is wholly vicarious but it would not be possible to dismiss the claim on the ground that the injury was wholly caused by the fault of either of the plaintiffs.[17]

---

[15] Though an employer's duty to take care for his workers' safety cannot be fulfilled by delegation (p. 34 *ante*) he was not, at common law, liable for latent production or design defects attributable to the negligence of the manufacturer of his equipment. Under the Employers' Liability (Defective Equipment) Act 1969 he now is. This is of importance in a case where the worker cannot effectively sue the manufacturer, but his task in that respect is eased by the Consumer Protection Act 1987 (Chap. 6).

[16] *Chipchase* v. *British Titan Products* [1956] 1 Q.B. 545.

[17] *I.C.I.* v. *Shatwell* [1965] A.C. 656.

CHAPTER SIX

Strict Liability

There are many critics of tort law who assert that much of it is an outdated and inefficient vehicle for the compensation of accidental losses, particularly in relation to personal injuries and death, and that we need a system (probably a state system though possibly one based on some form of loss insurance) of compensation which steers by the principle of the needs of the victim rather than the circumstances in which the loss was suffered. This is considered further in the final chapter but such proposals are making slow progress and may succumb to the effects of economic cycles. In any case, a state compensation system is unlikely ever to apply to property damage. Given that we are likely to retain for the foreseeable future a major role for tort, what should be its guiding principle? The choice is essentially between reliance on a criterion of fault ("negligence") or its abandonment in favour of non-fault or "strict" liability. Of course, such a division is a gross over-simplification. First, there is the point made in Chapter 2 that a particular tort may have different requirements for different elements: libel is in some respects a tort of strict liability but in other respects it requires a malicious intention to injure. Secondly, the very terms fault and strict liability may be misleading in practice. Mere momentary inadvertence to which most of us would succumb may be legal negligence leading to hundreds of thousands of pounds in damages even though it would not attract moral condemnation[1]

[1] This is particularly true of professional negligence and of cases where the court chooses to reject common practice as the measure of due care. See, *e.g. Helling v. Carey* 519 P. 2d 981 (1974) where an American court stigmatised as negligent the practice of the whole ophthalmology profession.

but on the other hand there are few, if any, forms of tort liability which are truly strict in the sense that they offer no excuse whatever for circumstances beyond the defendant's control. Nevertheless, over-simplification as our simple distinction may be, it does reflect the truth that some areas of tort are stricter than others. Since liability based upon fault may be thought to have at least some connection with generally shared moral values and therefore to be the "natural" position for the law to adopt,[2] what are the arguments for a stricter liability?

A system of strict liability may reduce the issues to be determined in litigation (and hence the cost of the process) and increase the numbers of persons who receive the "full" compensation which the tort system approaches more nearly than social security. The first point must, however, be heavily qualified because in many cases under the present law there is either no difficulty in establishing the facts relating to the defendant's conduct or liability is readily admitted but the matter is bitterly fought on questions of causation and quantum of damages, both of which would continue to be relevant to any strict liability tort system that could be devised. In any event, there is likely to be strong opposition to a system of strict liability unless it makes provision for reduction of damages on account of the plaintiff's contributory negligence and this may produce almost as many disputed issues of fact as the present fault-based system.[3] Further, even if it is true that a system of strict liability is cheaper to administer on a case by case basis, American experience with strict products liability indicates a risk that it may lead to an increase in the overall level of litigation. As to the full compensation point, it cannot be assumed (though it often is by critics of the tort system) that increasing the range and quantum of compensation is necessarily an unqualified good for it may impose an excessive burden (either by way of damages awarded and their effect on insurance rates or by way of the costs necessary to prevent injuries) upon the persons carrying out the activity in question. Injury by accident is a misfortune like disease and unemployment and it is unlikely that there will be any society willing to compensate all misfortune so generously as to restore all victims to their prior financial position. Whether the victims of accidents or of particular types of accidents are

[2] This proposition may be challenged on historical grounds in that some areas of tort have seen a shift from a stricter liability towards fault (see p. 132 *post*) but this trend is probably more concerned with burden of proof than with substance: it is unlikely ever to have been the law that a man acts at his peril.

[3] But a non-common law system, France, legislated in 1985 for a form of strict liability for road traffic accidents in which damages are not generally reduced for contributory negligence.

deserving of special treatment above the "floor" level of social security is a matter of values and politics upon which there are widely differing views.

Another argument advanced in favour of strict liability is that an activity should bear its own costs, including the cost of harms caused by it (in economists' jargon the costs should be "internalized"), no doubt on the basis that he who gets the benefit should also bear the burden. Under this theory the costs of unavoidable accidents are not, as under the law of negligence, left to lie where they fall but are shifted back on to the person conducting the activity. He in turn will no doubt pass them on in his prices to his customers so far as the market will allow him to do so, thereby achieving the desired goal of "loss distribution." Alternatively, if his competitors' prices will not allow him to pass on the cost he will improve his safety procedures or be driven out of business and the other desirable goal of accident prevention thereby served. There are two objections to this approach. First, it is not necessarily the most efficient way of ordering affairs. It may well in some cases be cheaper for, say, an owner of property to cover a risk by loss insurance than to pass it across to the person causing the harm. In this sense a rule of no-liability is the most efficient. The present law may be regarded as an awkward attempt to "tame" efficiency with a degree of moral responsibility but strict liability would be more inefficient still. Unfortunately, efficiency arguments tend to be conducted in a rather rarefied atmosphere in which it is *assumed* that this or that is the cheapest way of proceeding, but in real life we rarely have the data to proceed in this way. The second objection is that any general rule of strict liability raises serious problems of causation. Suppose a cyclist is blown off course by the slipstream of a passing juggernaut and falls into a drainage ditch, where he drowns. Now under the present law we would simply ask whether the driver of the juggernaut was negligent and if he was attribute sole responsibility to him (and his employer). It is just about possible that an issue might be raised about whether having an unfenced, deep ditch in that proximity to the highway amounted to negligence but that seems unlikely. If, however, we say that an activity should carry its own costs the picture starts to look different. No doubt we would still say that the death was one of the costs of long-distance road haulage, but is it also attributable to land drainage, to the highway system and to the activity of cycling? And if the last, why not to manufacturing cycles or the goods being carried in the lorry? Such an endless regression is obviously wholly impractical and any strict liability system is likely to adopt, expressly or by implication, some test of "dominant" or "effective" cause or to limit its reach by reference to an additional requirement of abnormality. Thus product manufacturers are not strictly liable under the Consumer Protection Act 1987 for injuries caused by their products but for injuries caused by *defects* in their products. If one cannot design a lawnmower that will cut grass but not cut off toes one is entitled to market it without risk of liability if it is well made in accordance with generally recognised standards of design. No doubt, in 99 per cent. of the cases where the plaintiff's action against a lawnmower manufacturer would fail we would be able to say that the accident was not "attributable" to lawnmower manufacture because it was entirely his own fault but in law the manufacturer escapes liability for the more fundamental reason that his product is not defective.

Though strict liability has attracted much attention from theorists it seems unlikely that any common law system will adopt it as a general replacement for liability based upon negligence. It may, however, make advances in particular areas as a result of legislation, as has recently happened here with product liability. The present law seems like an almost random collection of isolated instances of liability without fault, some based on the common law and of respectable antiquity (though in some cases modified by statute) others being modern statutory creations. The law has certainly not been designed as a coherent whole according to a plan, though some have discerned in it the shadow of a theme of responsibility for an increased or unusual risk. One of the main sources of strict duties is industrial safety legislation, particularly the Factories Act 1961. This has been briefly mentioned in Chapter 5 but is not pursued here because it would be too detailed for an introductory book and in any case the strictness of the legislation varies considerably from one section to another.

A. STRICT LIABILITY FOR DEFECTIVE PRODUCTS

Since March 1, 1988 the English law of "products liability" has been transformed by Part I of the Consumer Protection Act 1987. The origin of the Act is a European Community Directive which reached its final form in 1985 and with which this country was, of course, obliged to conform by virtue of its treaty obligations. The preamble to the Directive speaks of liability without fault on the part of the producer as being "the sole means of adequately solving the problem, peculiar to our age of increasing technicality, of a fair apportionment of the risks inherent in modern technological production" and as a result of the Directive the law will, subject to certain permitted variations, be the same throughout the European Community. The fundamental principles of the Directive have been found in U.S. law for the best part of two decades and other common law jurisdictions may follow a similar path. The new law must, however, be set in its context, for it co-exists with older forms of liability.

Since most goods are acquired under contracts of sale or similar contracts such as hire-purchase the primary law governing defects in them is the law of contract in the shape of the Sale of Goods Act 1979. There are implied into the contract terms (often unexcludable) that goods are "merchantable" and reasonably fit for their purpose, and these undertakings on the part of the seller are truly strict so that if the goods are defective not even the utmost care provides a defence. However, because this liability is contractual it operates only for and against contracting parties. This means that where the seller and manufacturer are different persons, as they usually are, only the seller is liable on the contract, though he may be able to seek an indemnity against the manufacturer under *his* contract of sale with him. Similarly, only the buyer may sue on the contract of sale and this is so not only where the goods simply fail to work but where they cause personal injury or damage to property. If P's new car crashes as a result of a latent defect, injuring P and members of his family, only P can sue under the Sale of Goods Act.

The contractual liability of the seller is, however, supplemented by the law of negligence, under which the manufacturer is regarded as owing a duty of care to "ultimate consumers" of his goods even though he has no contract with them. This is, of course, the principle of law directly established in *Donoghue* v. *Stevenson* before that case became the launching point for the extension and rationalisation of the tort of negligence. The seller, too, may be liable in negligence, though where the defect is not easily discoverable (for example, poison in canned foodstuffs or a design defect in the braking system of a car) he will probably not be in breach. Negligence liability is in some respects wider than that imposed by the Consumer Protection Act 1987 so that it will continue to be of importance here, as well as in those jurisdictions which have not enacted strict liability. It extends to assemblers and repairers as defendants and in favour of any persons who are foreseeably harmed by the goods—in one case a pedestrian who was injured by a piece of a lorry wheel coming adrift. In *Donoghue* v. *Stevenson* itself the duty was said to arise only if there was "no reasonable possibility of intermediate examination" but the modern cases treat this not as a separate requirement but as a factor in determining whether the damage was foreseeable. If an intermediary is required to carry out a detailed examination which would have revealed the defect the manufacturer will not be liable, but a mere possibility of inspection will not normally protect him. As to proof, the burden is upon the plaintiff but, despite a curious reluctance in the English case law to admit that *res ipsa loquitur* applies, it is clear that in a suitable situation the court is entitled to draw the inference of negligence from the mere happening of the accident and the defendant does not necessarily escape by showing that he has the most up-to-date production system, for that is quite consistent with some act of negligence in the operation of the system. Because the liability is in tort it extends to personal injury and property damage but not to mere deficiencies in value in operation or economic loss. In *Muirhead* v. *I.T.S.*[4] the defendants' negligence in manufacturing aeration pumps caused the death of a consignment of the plaintiff's lobsters. The plaintiff recovered damages in respect of this, but not in respect of the cost of the pumps nor the profits that could have been made from other consignments had the pumps operated as they should have.

What follows is no more than an outline of the product liability provisions of the Consumer Protection Act 1987. As with all statute law, there is no substitute for the statutory words themselves. Several provisions of the Act raise difficult questions of interpretation which will, sooner or later, have to be answered by the courts but it is unusual in one respect. Since it was passed in order to comply with the 1985 E.C. Directive the Act provides that its purpose is to give effect to the Directive and "it shall be construed accordingly," which may mean that an English court will have to have regard to the decisions of other member states on *their* versions of the Act.

The Act imposes liability on the producer of a "product," which means goods and electricity, though the definition is wide enough to cover fixtures in buildings and even component parts of the building itself. The Directive certainly intended to include moveables incorporated into immovables. If, on the other hand, a building collapses not from a defect in a component part but as a result of a deficiency in its design or construction the Act does not apply. Though the person liable will usually be the manufacturer the Act extends liability to others in certain cases. Thus a person who "won or abstracted" the product or subjected it to certain processes is equated with a manufacturer, though no liability is imposed on the producer of agricultural or fishery products who has not subjected them to an "industrial" process. An "own-brander" is liable if he holds himself out as the producer and the Act also imposes liability upon the person who first imports the product into a member state from outside the E.C. The *seller* of

---

[4] [1986] Q.B. 507. See the general discussion of economic loss at p. 50 *ante*.

goods is not liable under the Act,[5] though he will be where he fails to comply with the plaintiff's request to identify the source of the goods. Where more than one person is liable there may be joint and several liability so that if Company A manufactures the brake mechanism of a car assembled by Company B and the mechanism is defective causing injury to P, *both* are liable to the plaintiff, though Company B may of course have a contractual right of indemnity against Company A and the Civil Liability (Contribution) Act[6] will apply. Since many products are imported and/or made up of components from different countries there will be some complex conflict of laws issues involving the jurisdiction of the English courts and the choice of law to be applied but this is beyond the scope of an introduction.

The Act is more restrictive than the common law in relation to the damage to which it applies. It extends only to personal injury (including death) and to damage to property intended for private use. As well, therefore, as excluding economic loss (as does the common law) the Act excludes damage to business property, such as the lobsters in *Muirhead* v. *I.T.S.* A further exclusion is damage to the product itself caused by failure of a defective component (for example, a car which is burned out due to defective wiring), though this sort of case may well fall within *Donoghue* v. *Stevenson*.

The core of the Act is the concept of a "defect" in the product for it is this which leads to liability if a causative link can be shown between it and the plaintiff's loss. The Act provides that there is a defect "if the safety of the product is not such as persons generally are entitled to expect." This is expanded by section 3(2), which says that

> "[in] determining . . . what persons generally are entitled to expect . . . all the circumstances shall be taken into account, including—
> (a) the manner in which, and purposes for which, the product has been marketed, its get-up, the use of any mark in relation to the product and any instructions for, or warnings with respect to, doing or refraining from doing anything with or in relation to the product;
> (b) what might reasonably be expected to be done with or in relation to the product; and
> (c) the time when the product was supplied by its producer to another;

---

[5] Hence a seller of U.S. goods would be wise to buy them from an intermediary in Europe rather than buying them directly from the manufacturer, to avoid being caught as importer.
[6] See p. 25, *ante.*

and nothing . . . shall require a defect to be inferred from the fact alone that the safety of a product which is supplied after that time is greater than the safety of the product in question."

Though the Act speaks of "persons generally," it is what those persons are *entitled* to expect that is in issue and it is thought therefore that it requires the court to engage in some form of weighing of the benefits which come from using the product in its present form against the risks associated with it, indeed that the very idea of "defect" *demands* an exercise of this nature: a fine carving knife is not defective because the fitter it is for its purpose of carving the more dangerous it may be to the user. It might be argued that if a manufacturer has taken all possible care in his production then the end result, even if flawed, is what persons are entitled to expect, for the flaw is unpreventable—but that is a form of negligence and would render the legislation pointless, especially bearing in mind that it is up to the plaintiff to prove a defect. It is thought, therefore, that where the product is not as it was designed to be, what is sometimes known as a production defect (the situation where "something breaks") the courts will allow the plaintiff to succeed simply on proof of the dangerous flaw and resulting damage.

Where the product operates exactly as it was designed to do and the danger is a known risk attached to it there is no real difference between the Act and negligence, for the court will need to be satisfied that the product as marketed has risks which outweigh its utility or that there are other, feasible and safer methods of achieving the same result.[7] For example, in *Griffiths* v. *Peter Conway*[8] the plaintiff suffered skin trouble from contact with the collar of a tweed coat bought from the defendants. This was attributable to her abnormal sensitivity, of which the defendant had no knowledge, and her action for breach of the contractual warranty of fitness for purpose failed. Exactly the same result would have followed had she sued the manufacturer under *Donoghue* v. *Stevenson* for it is not negligent to market something which carries a risk of injury only to a tiny proportion of the population. Similarly, it is thought that the coat is not defective under the Act. This is not to say that in some circumstances the manufacturer might not have to incorporate a prominent warning if the side effect could be very serious or if a significant proportion of the population might be affected—but there is

---

[7] This may involve technical matters in presenting which the plaintiff may be at a comparative disadvantage.

[8] [1939] 1 All E.R. 685.

something bizarre in the notion of a tweed coat carrying a health warning.

A third class of case is where the product has an inherent danger which is not scientifically discoverable at the time (for example, a drug with unknown side effects). Such a product seems to be defective under the Act, but the manufacturer may have a defence under section 4(1)(*e*), which is considered below.

The fact that the safety of a product is to be judged when it is put on the market and not in the light of subsequent improvements and discoveries is only elementary justice, but the statute clearly uses "product" to mean the individual article in respect of which the action is brought, not the "model" or "the line." Hence if the manufacturer goes on producing to an old design after his competitors have introduced safety improvements he can no longer claim to be judged on the old, unimproved standard.

Even when a defect has been established the liability is by no means absolute for the defendant may establish a number of defences. Those likely to be the most important are (1) that the defect did not exist when he put the product into circulation, (2) that the defect was attributable to the design of a subsequent product in which his product was incorporated or to his compliance with instructions given by the producer of that subsequent product and (3) the controversial "state of the art" or "development risks" defence found in section 4(1)(*e*)—

> "that the state of scientific and technical knowledge at the [time when the producer put the product into circulation] was not such that a producer of products of the same description as the product in question might be expected to have discovered the defect if it had existed in his products while they were under his control."

It is just possible that this paragraph does not accurately reflect the equivalent provision of the EC Directive (Art. 7(*e*)) which speaks of knowledge "such as to *enable*" the existence of the defect to be discovered, for what *can* be done is arguably different from what *may be expected* to be done.[9] This aside, it is possible to read section 4(1)(*e*) as covering even the practically untraceable production flaw, and if that is right we have little more than *Donoghue* v. *Stevenson* with a reversed burden of proof. What, however, section 4(1)(*e*) certainly *is* aimed at is the inherent danger which cannot be detected during the development of the

---

[9] Though there is no clear dividing line between the two. Many things which are possible would be regarded as impossible in practice. The European Commission has formally challenged s.4(1)(*e*).

product. Pharmaceuticals provide the best known examples of this[10] and it is ironic that the defence should be included when it was the thalidomide disaster which was one of the mainsprings of the campaign for change in product liability law. The argument for the defence (which is optional under the Directive, has not been adopted by some other member states and is subject to review in 1995) is that cases of this sort involve "catastrophe" risks which are effectively uninsurable and liability for which would very seriously inhibit product development. On the other hand it must be pointed out that the needs of the victim are the same whether or not the defect was discoverable and that the law of contract does not allow any such defence to claims in respect of merchantable quality or fitness for purpose. One way of dealing with the problem is to remove the defence but have a global limit on a producer's liability for identical items having the same defect. The Directive allows this (the limit is 70 million E.C.U.) but it raises formidable practical problems and has not been adopted by the Act.

Liability under Part I of the Consumer Protection Act is assimilated to the general law of torts for ancillary matters like contributory negligence and the application of fatal accident legislation. Exclusion of liability by contract or notice is banned, though it is necessary to distinguish between a notice excluding liability and one which warns of a danger and thereby makes an otherwise dangerous product safe. A special feature of the Act is that there is superimposed upon the general law governing time limits on the bringing of claims[11] a "cut-off" limit of 10 years from the time when the product was put into circulation. At that point any existing claim is extinguished unless proceedings have been commenced and no further claim can arise. This does not, however, affect the law of negligence. If a defective product is made in 1988 but does not cause injury until 1999 a claim for negligence is available, for no cause of action arises until the damage has been done.

---

[10] In the United States some cases on cigarettes raise this issue, though their holdings are in conflict. It might be thought that the fact that the risks of smoking have been known to consumers as well as manufacturers for many years would bar any new cases, but the ingenuity of plaintiffs' lawyers knows no bounds and some recent litigation has been founded on the theory that the addictive properties of cigarettes exclude the consent defence.

[11] See Chap. 14.

B. OTHER CATEGORIES OF STRICT LIABILITY

Liability for Animals

Animals are things, property, but they are sentient and mobile things with wills of their own. One or two legal systems embraced personal "liability" of the animal, but not its master[12] and one would have expected that developing legal systems would have produced special rules for animals because they must in an agricultural society have been a significant cause of accidents and damage. What, however, is remarkable is the way that these special rules have survived in widely disparate legal systems to produce a stricter than normal responsibility long after animals have been eclipsed in the annals of disaster by aircraft, motor cars and railway trains.[13] Indeed the current English law, the Animals Act 1971, is unmistakably no more than a revision and "fine-tuning" of the common law doctrines which can be traced back six hundred years. A student from Western Australia, where the common law still applies, would get a very fair idea of the general structure of his law from a reading of the English Act, though he would be misled on points of detail.

Strict liability is imposed on the keeper of an animal belonging to a "dangerous species" (and danger here includes danger to property, for example such as might be presented by Colorado beetles). If the species is commonly domesticated here it cannot be regarded as dangerous but it is not decisive that it is domesticated abroad. Thus camels and elephants are within this category[14] even though they are widely used as beasts of burden in other parts of the word. Liability is truly strict in that even the unforeseeable, malicious act of a third party does not excuse the keeper, though damages may be reduced or even extinguished on the ground of the plaintiff's own fault. It is not likely that many people will dissent from the proposition that he who chooses to keep a tiger should bear the risk of harms done by it. Perhaps rather more controversial is the other form of strict liability, that for an animal which does not belong to a dangerous species but which has individual dangerous characteristics which are known to the keeper. In the early law this was probably conceived of as a form of fault liability. A man who kept a dog could assume that

---

[12] See Exodus, Ch. 21, v. 28; XII Tables, Tab. VII.L.1.
[13] See, *e.g.* French C.C. art. 1385; German C.C. § 833.
[14] Camels are dangerous because they bite. Was it right to apply the Act to injuries caused by falling off a camel? *Tutin* v. *Chipperfield Promotions* (1980) 130 N.L.J. 807.

the dog was harmless because that is the common experience. Once, however, the dog had displayed vicious characteristics then he was automatically blameworthy for keeping the animal with this knowledge (*scienter retinuit* as the old plea said). Nothing less than an attack was enough to put the owner on his guard but once there had been an attack he was in breach of his duty if he failed to destroy the animal. The modern law of negligence is more subtle: it is wider in that a duty is imposed on the defendant who *ought* to have known of the danger but it is also narrower because the duty would not be broken if the owner had taken all reasonable precautions. The old *scienter* rule was left isolated as a separate rule of strict liability arising from knowledge of a past event and existing in parallel with the law of negligence. It is preserved by the Act (though the drafting has been described by a court as "remarkably opaque") and some would question whether it was really worth the effort or whether it does much more for the plaintiff than the law of negligence supplemented by *res ipsa loquitur*. On the other hand, it does relieve the plaintiff of any concern with the carefulness or otherwise of the defendant's conduct once knowledge has been established. The common law is modified to some degree by the Act: this liability is no longer confined to injury by attack but extends to "skittishness" and unpredictability, a point of some importance in relation to horses.

Another form of common law strict liability preserved by the Act is "cattle trespass" (now rather more clumsily called "liability for straying livestock"). This extends only to damage to the land and property on it and is coupled with a right of detention as security for damages. Its rationale is not the concept of special or unusual risk but the provision of a simple rule for the settlement of small claims without recourse to litigation.

As is implicit in what has been said above, underneath all this statutory liability lies the law of negligence, which applies to keepers of animals as much as to keepers of other property[15] and a claim for negligence may be combined with one based on the statute.

Dangerous Things: the Rule in Rylands v. Fletcher

The rule in *Rylands* v. *Fletcher* is often regarded as English law's broadest attempt at a principle of strict liability for accidental

---

[15] At common law there was an exception in the form of a rule that an occupier of land owed no duty to prevent his animals causing accidents by straying on to the highway. This was abolished by section 8 of the Act (though it still applies in parts of Australia). Of course, the abolition of the common law rule does not mean that the owner of sheep on unfenced moorland is automatically or even presumptively negligent.

harms. The case[16] involved flooding of the plaintiff's mine as a result of inadequate measures to stop up shafts on the defendant's land in the vicinity of a reservoir being built for him. Giving judgment for the plaintiff, Blackburn J. enunciated what has come to be known as "the rule" as follows:

> "[A] person who, for his own purposes, brings on his land and collects and keeps there anything likely to do mischief if it escapes must keep it in at his peril, and if he does not do so he is *prima facie* answerable for all the damage which is the natural consequence of its escape. He can excuse himself by showing that the escape was owing to the plaintiff's default; or perhaps that the escape was the consequence of *vis major*, or the act of God."

The effect of the decision of the House of Lords on appeal has been treated as adding a further requirement to the rule, namely that the use of the land in question must be "non-natural." In fact, Lord Cairns L.C. seems not to have intended this to be an additional requirement so much as an alternative basis of strict liability.

In its latest American incarnation (sections 519 and 520 of the *Restatement of Torts*, 2d) *Rylands* v. *Fletcher* has become a principle of strict liability for "abnormally dangerous" activities. Some of the strands of history which were pulled together in the original judgment might support this interpretation but others would not: cattle trespass and overflowing privies hardly seem the stuff of the "ultra-hazardous." On balance, *Rylands* v. *Fletcher*, at least in England, has less of the characteristics of liability designed to cope with catastrophe risks than of a liability for some cases of nuisance, the law governing the competing rights of adjacent landowners. On this basis the House of Lords was right in *Read* v. *Lyons*[17] to deny liability under the rule for injuries suffered by a munitions worker in an explosion, for a nuisance necessarily involves some sort of "escape" (even if intangible) from land occupied by the defendant. Such a requirement of escape would, of course, make little sense if the rule rested on the ultra-hazardous activity.[18] Yet the "nuisance" approach has by no means been consistently followed for where there has been an escape damages have been recovered for personal injuries by persons who lack the fundamental qualification to sue for nuisance, which is to be the occupier of the property invaded. We should be near the mark if we said that the law has never really

---

[16] (1866) L.R. 1 Ex 265; (1868) L.R. 3 H.L. 330.
[17] [1947] A.C. 156.
[18] Though the consent of the plaintiff might be relevant even under this.

made up its mind what purpose this "rule" is to serve. In England, however, the tendency in modern times has been to cut down the scope of the rule and to insist on a general requirement of negligence. The principal vehicles of this have been the requirement of non-natural user and the defence of act of a third party.

Given some of Blackburn J.'s illustrations in *Rylands* v. *Fletcher* "non-natural" may have been intended quite literally as covering the accumulation of anything brought on to the land, but at least since the decision in *Rickards* v. *Lothian*[19] it has been given the different meaning of a "special use bringing with it increased danger to others . . . not merely the ordinary use of the land or such use as is proper for the general benefit of the community." This formulation, especially the last part, gives a court which is hostile to *Rylands* v. *Fletcher* a pretty free hand to reject the rule. In *Read* v. *Lyons*, for example, some members of the House of Lords doubted, *obiter*, whether the manufacture of high explosive shells in time of war could constitute a non-natural use and there are dicta which doubt the applicability of the rule to public authorities carrying out statutory functions (though in many cases the rule would be impliedly excluded by the terms of the authorising statute). No doubt one may feel that to impose strict liability upon such public benefactors is unfair, but that conclusion is wholly inconsistent with a loss-spreading philosophy, public authorities being in a better position than anyone, by reason of their monopoly or quasi-monopoly positions, to spread loss over the community at large. If we put public authorities on one side, what the case law amounts to is the acceptance of a rather imprecise distinction between common risks and those which, by reason of the quantity or place or method of accumulation by the defendant go well beyond those one normally finds. Each of us must put up with a certain amount of risk generated by his neighbour's activities because that is the price of his own freedom of action, but there comes a point when this "reciprocity" of risk is exceeded. Hence the storage of large quantities of inflammable paint has been held within the rule but it is not applicable to a fire in a domestic grate. Similarly, the rule applies to a reservoir but not to a domestic cistern. Where the activity is carried on by large numbers of people it escapes the rule even though it is very dangerous: where bursting reservoirs have slain their scores the motor car has slain its tens of thousands but the rule applies to the former and not the latter, motoring is "natural."[20] One reason for the difficulty in

---

[19] [1913] A.C. 263.
[20] Compare *Haddock* v. *Thwale*, Uncommon Law, 124.

reconciling all the cases is the simple fact that the passage of time and technical developments make commonplace what was formerly unusual. Even in 1919 it is surprising that an English court should have regarded the keeping in a domestic garage of a motor car with petrol in the tank as within the rule, but today the proposition would be likely to be treated as humorous. Again, geographical conditions may dictate different answers so that for example a Texas court held to be outside the rule the use of large pools for the collection of polluted water from oil drilling.[21]

The strictness of a liability depends on the defences available to it and a multitude of defences can turn what is strict in name into fault-based in fact. If the escape takes place as a result of a natural event or state of affairs the defendant may call up the defence of act of God, though it has not figured prominently in the decided cases. It seems to signify something more than a mere plea of no negligence for, speaking of wind, the judge in one case[22] said that "before wind can amount to an act of God . . . the wind must not merely be exceptionally strong, but must be of such exceptional strength that no one could reasonably be expected to anticipate or provide against it." Dicta in some cases seem more favourable to the defence, but the modern trend is against it. It is not easy to see why the law retains this long-stop which is consistent with neither a loss-spreading nor an exceptional risks philosophy, though that may merely show that the common law rarely wholeheartedly embraces any particular theory of liability. The same criticism may be made of the defence of act of a third party or "act of a stranger" and this is probably more often successful than act of God. Neither the defendant's servants nor his independent contractors are strangers for this purpose. The flood in *Rylands* v. *Fletcher* was in fact attributable to the negligence of the defendant's contractor and attempts have been made to explain the case as nothing more than an instance of vicarious liability for an independent contractor but while the decision certainly could have been given on that basis, there is no doubt that the judges intended to lay down another principle. Nor, probably, do we class as strangers persons on the occupier's land with his permission and over whom he may reasonably be expected to have some degree of control, though the state of the case law makes it hard to be precise. There is also some doubt about the nature of the acts by the stranger required to bring this defence into operation. One view is that the defence applies only if the act is "intentional" or "malicious," but it seems better to say that *any* act, whether it be deliberate interference with the

---

[21] *Turner* v. *Big Lake Oil Co.* 96 SW 2d 221 (1936).
[22] *Cushing* v. *Walker & Sons* [1941] 2 All E.R. 693.

dangerous thing or conduct which inadvertently affects it, will do but that the defendant is still liable if he should have foreseen and guarded against it, and the onus on this issue is on him. The significance of the distinction between wilful interference and mere negligence by the third party is then simply that the latter may in the particular circumstances be more foreseeable to the defendant than the former. An illustration is *Northwestern Utilities* v. *London Guarantee & Accident Co.*[23] where the defendants' gas main caused a fire after having been fractured by excavations carried out by the City of Edmonton. In finding for the plaintiffs the Privy Council said:

> "In truth, the gravamen of the charge against the [defendants] . . . is that though they had the tremendous responsibility of carrying this highly inflammable gas under the streets of a city, they did nothing at all. . . . If they did not know of the City works, their system of inspection must have been very deficient. If they did know they should have been on their guard: they might have ascertained what work was being done and carefully investigated the position, or they might have examined the pipes likely to be affected so as to satisfy themselves that the bed on which they lay was not being disturbed."

This is an onerous duty but it is nevertheless the case that once the act of a third party is involved the strict liability disappears and the duty is a form of negligence. This contrasts with the position under the Animals Act 1971 which provides no such defence.

Statutory authority has already been mentioned. Though everything turns on the wording of the particular statute, the upshot of the case law is to exclude the rule whether the authority is mandatory or merely permissive, though in the latter case the presence of a clause preserving liability for "nuisance" is taken to show an intention to retain the rule. The other defences to the rule need comparatively little attention. It is a defence that the plaintiff's own act is the effective cause of his loss and the Law Reform (Contributory Negligence) Act probably applies where his fault is only a partial cause. Consent to run the risk of the accumulation is also a defence and this may be inferred where the plaintiff has the use of the premises where the thing is collected and benefits from it, though this is sometimes spoken of as a separate defence of "common benefit." However, most of the cases could have been (and nowadays would be) decided on the simpler ground that the activity was a natural use of the land.

---

[23] [1936] A.C. 108.

The legislature has saved us from the difficulties and uncertainties which would arise in the application of *Rylands* v. *Fletcher* to some risks by enacting specific legislation. For example there is strict liability for damage caused by marine oil pollution, poisonous wastes and ionising radiations (in the last case so strict as virtually to deserve the name absolute). Details of these matters are outside the scope of an introductory book.

A few words need to be said about liability for fire, if only because the law appears, for historical reasons, to be more complicated than it is. The effect of judicial interpretation of section 86 of the Fires Prevention (Metropolis) Act 1774 (which, somewhat surprisingly, applies to the whole of England, to New Zealand and to most of Australia) is that fire is governed by the ordinary law of negligence, though no doubt it will often require a high degree of care in dealing with it. If ever there was a stricter liability or one requiring the defendant to discharge the burden of proof of no negligence it has gone. The defendant's liability is not, however, confined to the case where he has started the fire, for if a fire is started on his property by the act of nature or a third party he is required to take steps to extinguish it for the protection of his neighbour.[24] The statute of 1774 does not exclude the rule in *Rylands* v. *Fletcher* so that if a fire starts from the accumulation of a dangerous thing the liability will be strict. An example is *Mason* v. *Levy Auto Parts*[25] where the defendants stored large quantities of petrol, acetylene and paint on the boundary of their land. Strictly in such a case there is no escape of the "thing" but of its product, the fire, but this makes no difference to the result.

[24] See p. 125.
[25] [1967] 2 Q.B. 530.

CHAPTER SEVEN

Nuisance

The Nature of Private Nuisance

The law of nuisance is a source of much difficulty and confusion. Professor Prosser remarked[1] that "there is perhaps no more impenetrable jungle in the entire law than that which surrounds the word 'nuisance'.... Few terms have afforded so excellent an illustration of the familiar tendency of the courts to seize upon a catchword as a substitute for any analysis of a problem; the defendant's interference with the plaintiff's interests is characterised as a 'nuisance' and there is nothing more to be said." Perhaps the root of the difficulty is that nuisance applies to a much more diverse range of circumstances than most torts: one might almost say that it was less a tort in its own right than the application of the law of torts to the protection of rights in and over land. Another source of confusion is the distinction between public and private nuisance. This chapter concentrates mainly upon the latter; the former, though certainly part of the law of torts, is largely concerned with the maintenance of public rights. It will be briefly outlined at the end of this chapter but until then it may be assumed that "nuisance" means private nuisance.

A definition of private nuisance which has received judicial approval from time to time is Sir Percy Winfield's: "unlawful interference with a person's use or enjoyment of land, or some right over, or in connection with it." This should, however, be read as not including intentional direct interference by entering

[1] Torts, 5th ed., p. 616.

118

the land or depositing something tangible on it for then the proper cause of action is trespass, which is better from the plaintiff's point of view because, unlike nuisance, it involves no balancing of the relative interests of neighbours—I have a *right* not to be subjected to trespass.

In some cases there is a good deal of overlap with the law of negligence, so much so that it may be a matter of indifference whether the case is described as one of nuisance, or one of negligence. In *Leakey* v. *National Trust*,[2] where the defendants had failed to take steps to prevent a mound on their land from slipping onto the plaintiff's property the statement of claim described the action as being founded on "nuisance." The defendants contended that since the plaintiffs were asserting that the defendants were under a duty to take reasonable care to prevent the landslip the claim was properly described as negligence. Megaw L.J. replied that (a) the plaintiffs' assertion was a proper way to formulate a claim for nuisance on such facts and (b) even if the claim were more properly regarded as sounding in negligence the omission of that word from the statement of claim did not, under the modern system of pleading, render it defective. In other cases, however, the very language of negligence may be inapt. If my neighbour is keeping an excessive number of pigs in close proximity to my house it would sound odd to say that he is in breach of a duty of care not to allow the smell of the piggery to cause me harm—much more natural to say that he is unreasonably interfering with my enjoyment of my land.

Two other points are helpful in recognising the true field of operation of nuisance. First, a nuisance generally (perhaps always) involves something on-going, a "state of affairs." If the defendant, driving his car down a common drive, loses control and finds himself involuntarily parked in his neighbour's flower bed it is unlikely that any court would classify his neighbour's claim as nuisance.[3] This does not, however, mean that an isolated event may not give rise to a claim for nuisance, for the isolated event may be the manifestation of a continuing state of affairs which in reality constitutes the nuisance. If the rule in *Rylands* v. *Fletcher* is properly regarded as a variety of nuisance then it is exceptional in admitting of liability for an isolated escape without any pre-existing fault on the defendant's part. This takes us on to the second point, which is that the remedy most often sought for nuisance is not damages but an injunction. Even where the plaintiff does claim damages for harm which has already taken

---

[2] [1980] Q.B. 485.
[3] It is probably trespass: p. 155, *post*.

place he is likely to be primarily concerned with getting the activity stopped. Indeed, the plaintiff may be awarded an injunction even though he has not yet suffered any harm, provided it is threatened. Nuisance is more about prevention and less about compensation than most branches of the law of torts.

Returning to our definition, not all interferences with the enjoyment of land are nuisances. First, the concept of interference with enjoyment, though somewhat nebulous, is not without its limits. The courts have (probably wisely) refrained from extending nuisance to what might be called aesthetic matters and the plaintiff whose tranquillity and solitude is taken away by the development of a supermarket at the bottom of his garden is left without remedy (even though there may be a dramatic effect on the value of his property) except, as sometimes happens with public works, where statute provides some form of *ad hoc* compensation. The plaintiff is unlikely to win a claim on the basis that the defendant is "lowering the tone" of the neighbourhood unless he can point to some sort of emanation such as noise or smells or obstruction, though in *Laws* v. *Florinplace* an interlocutory injunction[4] was granted against the operation of a sex shop. In any event an interference with enjoyment will only constitute a legal wrong if it is unreasonable. Attempts to frame a definition of what is "unreasonable" are likely to end in circularity so that even the *Restatement of Torts* says that interference is unreasonable if it is "severe and greater than the plaintiff should have to bear without compensation." It is often truly said that the matter can only be decided after all the circumstances of the case have been weighed, but the student need not wholly despair for certain themes recur in the decided cases and will be found helpful in deciding new ones. However, before we look at some of these we should say a word about the difference between "reasonableness" here and in the law of negligence. In the latter, the court is concerned with deciding whether the defendant displayed the care and skill which a reasonable man would use in the circumstances and if he did he escapes liability no matter how serious the effect upon the plaintiff of what he has done. But in the overwhelming majority of nuisance cases the central issue is not the conduct of the defendant but whether the degree of interference with the plaintiff's property rights is sufficiently great to call for legal intervention. If, therefore, the stench from my neighbour's piggery goes beyond the bounds of what I should have to tolerate

---

[4] [1981] 1 All E.R. 659. On an application for an interlocutory injunction the plaintiff need not satisfy the court that there *is* a nuisance, merely that there is a triable issue.

there is a nuisance even though the defendant is taking all reasonable, or even all humanly possible, steps to keep it to a minimum. Despite what is sometimes said this is not a "strict" liability, for the defendant is deliberately interfering with the plaintiff's rights and claiming (albeit perhaps, with regret) that he is entitled to do so as a legitimate part of his activities. The fact that in this situation a defendant who has used "due care" may be enjoined from continuing with his activity does not necessarily mean that a defendant who has used due care is liable in *damages* when an apparently safe activity suddenly goes unforeseeably wrong and inflicts damage on a neighbour. In this case, unless the case falls under *Rylands* v. *Fletcher*, negligence is probably required, though it must be admitted that the law is not particularly clear.[5]

Reasonableness in nuisance therefore goes primarily to the nature and gravity of the interference. It is, however, also relevant in a slightly different sense in relation to the defendant's motive. Suppose that P and D live in adjoining semi-detached houses with thin walls. D has three very young children who cry at night and this is audible to some degree in P's house. This is not a nuisance, for children (even crying children) are a necessary party of the continuation of human kind and the inconveniences arising from their upbringing are, up to a point, things we must all bear. It by no means follows that D could with impunity make the same amount of noise playing his gramophone in the small hours, still less that he could do so out of spite towards his neighbour. Nuisance is the law of give and take: each of us must put up with a moderate amount of inconvenience caused by others as the price of being able to inflict some inconvenience upon others in the conduct of our own activities.[6]

This takes us to the first of the commonly recurring themes referred to above. The reverse of the proposition that we must put up with the reasonable activities of others is that we cannot devote our own land to an unusually delicate use and then complain about it when it is deleteriously affected to a greater degree than would normally be the case by our neighbour's activities. In an American case[7] the defendant floodlit his premises, which produced in the immediate vicinity a light

---

[5] The decision in *Wringe* v. *Cohen* [1940] 1 K.B. 229 governing premises on the highway may be an exception, for it imposes liability for want of repair except where it is due to the act of a trespasser or a secret, unobservable process of nature. But these defences seem to make the substance of the matter very close to negligence.

[6] At least this is the theory of it. No doubt it would be received cynically by the small householder next door to a large industrial plant!

[7] *Amphitheatres Inc.* v. *Portland Meadows* 198 P. 2d 847 (1948).

intensity equivalent to that of a full moon. The plaintiff failed in a nuisance action when the quality of the pictures in his drive-in cinema screen was degraded by this light. The same is true where the plaintiff complains of personal annoyance or discomfort because he is personally hypersensitive to what the defendant is doing. The whole matter is to be considered, according to an old case, "according to plain and sober and simple notions, not merely according to elegant or dainty modes and habits of living" and while the mode of expression may be quaint, the thesis is as valid as ever, though its application may change with time. It is now over 20 years since an English judge doubted (the point was not directly in issue) whether "occasional... recurrent and severe" interference with domestic television reception could be a nuisance.[8] Even if this is still the law it was certainly not intended to imply that recreational activities are wholly outside the protection of the law of nuisance.

An important consideration in many nuisance cases has been the nature of the locality in which the activity is carried on for, as an American judge graphically put it, "a nuisance may be merely a right thing in the wrong place, like a pig in the parlor instead of the barnyard." In modern conditions, however, the applicability of the "locality" point is somewhat reduced by the requirement of planning permission for any change of use of land, which has the effect of "zoning" areas as residential, industrial and so on. While in England the grant of planning permission does not amount to statutory authority for the purposes of tort and does not of itself legalise what would otherwise be a nuisance the very existence of planning control will tend to reduce the risk of grossly unsuitable land uses and hence the number of cases in which the plaintiff's claim will rest principally upon the unsuitability of the locality. In any event, there is the authority of the House of Lords, albeit rather long ago, to the effect that the defendant cannot set up the suitability of the locality if the plaintiff complains of physical damage to his property—in the case in question, poisoning of vegetation by copper smelting fumes.[9] From an environmental viewpoint this is a not unattractive rule, but it does seem to lead to the result that A, who has to paint his exterior woodwork more frequently than the average because of acid fumes emitted from the defendant's factory may recover whereas B, whose property is substantially reduced in value because of noise, is at risk of the court holding that the noise is not excessive for the area. From the point of view of an individual plaintiff, it cannot be assumed that

---

[8] *Bridlington Relay* v. *Y.E.B.* [1965] Ch. 436.
[9] *St. Helens Smelting Co.* v. *Tipping* (1865) 11 H.L.C. 642.

nuisances involving physical damage are automatically "worse" than others.

Duration is also an important consideration in deciding whether an interference amounts to a nuisance. The same quantity of noise or dust which would be unreasonable in a residential area if continued over a long period by a manufacturing process may be justifiable if produced by demolition and reconstruction work on the plaintiff's property; the plaintiff has no right to require that his neighbour's property be kept in its present condition in perpetuity. A person doing such work must take reasonable steps to keep the inconvenience to a minimum (for example, pile-driving might have to be suspended at night) but this does not mean that he must conduct his operations as slowly (and expensively) as possible for, as always, there must be a balancing of the respective interests of the adjoining landowners.

The plaintiff may move in next door to an activity which is already affecting his land.[10] It would seem hard on the defendant that the plaintiff should be able to complain of nuisance, but that is the law, even where the prior absence of residential property meant that the activity was once entirely inoffensive. The point is illustrated by *Miller* v. *Jackson*,[11] a claim for nuisance by a plaintiff who acquired a new house on the edge of a village cricket field which had been in use for nearly 70 years. The case evoked a characteristically vigorous dissent from Lord Denning M.R. but though the majority of the court applied the traditional rule that "coming to the nuisance" is no defence, the unhappiness of one of them with it is perhaps reflected in his joining with Lord Denning in denying an injunction. On the other hand, the reach of the rule must not be exaggerated, for except in cases of physical damage to property the court must take account of the nature of the locality in which the activity is carried on. A person who moves into an industrial area cannot expect the clean air of Devon.

How far is the public interest to be taken into account in a case of nuisance? After all, the grant of an injunction may have the effect of closing an industrial plant or public service and inflicting loss upon the public as a whole far greater than the value of the plaintiff's property preserved thereby. The point is relevant at two stages: first, as to whether there is a nuisance at all; secondly as to whether an injunction should be granted. On the first

---

[10] An extreme example is the American case of *Spur Industries* v. *Del E. Webb Development Co.* 494 P. 2d 700 (1972). Cattle feed lot producing 450 tons of wet manure a day. "Sun City" developed by plaintiffs nearby.

[11] [1977] Q.B. 966.

question we may confidently say that "public benefit" does not of itself justify an interference substantial enough to qualify as a nuisance. On the other hand, an element of what may be regarded as "public interest" is probably a more or less concealed element in the overall notion of reasonableness (which is, of course, determined by the court) though it may be expressed by referring to a "natural" or "proper" use of the defendant's property. That the point has not arisen more often or more clearly is probably attributable to the long-established practice in England of obtaining statutory authority for major works. As to the second stage, if the interference is judged to amount to a nuisance the English courts have resolutely set their face against denying an injunction[12] on the ground of supposed public benefit, because of a belief that to do so would amount to granting without statutory authority a licence on payment of damages. The leading case is *Shelfer* v. *City of London Electric Lighting Co.*[13] Nor, where the interference with the plaintiff's rights is serious have the English courts shown any enthusiasm for refusing an injunction on the ground that compliance will involve a wholly disproportionate burden on the defendant. This has been the subject of considerable debate from an economic viewpoint and it has been argued that the practice of readily granting injunctions puts the plaintiff in an unusually strong bargaining position to claim to be "bought off" for a price higher than the loss he has actually suffered. American practice is rather different. For example, in *Boomer* v. *Atlantic Cement Co.*[14] the Court of Appeals of New York denied an injunction against a $45 million cement plant employing 300 people when the nuisance had reduced the value of the plaintiffs' properties by $185,000. Pointing out that the decision did not prevent public health agencies from seeking injunctive relief[15] the court commented that to award damages based on the plaintiff's loss "seems to do justice between the contending parties." Some American courts have experimented with the practice of granting an injunction on condition that the *plaintiff* compensates the *defendant* for the cost of closure or remedial works. There is no shadow of authority for this in England but it provides an interesting approach to the "coming to the nuisance" problem.

---

[12] There is power to award damages in lieu of an injunction.

[13] [1895] 1 Ch. 287. The refusal of an injunction in *Miller* v. *Jackson* (above) is dubious: see *Kennaway* v. *Thompson* [1981] Q.B. 88.

[14] 257 N.E. 2d 870 (1970).

[15] In England the majority of nuisances are probably dealt with by regulatory bodies under public health legislation. But a public body may take other factors than the complainant's interests into consideration and may be unwilling to act.

The defendant to a claim for nuisance is usually the occupier of the property from which it emanates, but this is not necessary, indeed the defendant need have no connection with the land at all: if A creates a nuisance on B's land which harms the land of C, A is liable to C. Can B the occupier also be liable in such a case? Yes, said the House of Lords in *Sedleigh-Denfield* v. *O'Callagahan*,[16] provided he knows or ought to know of the nuisance and fails to take reasonable steps to abate it. With some reluctance in some judicial quarters this principle has been extended to nuisances on the defendant's land which have been created by the operation of nature.[17] The price of the enjoyment of land is a duty to take affirmative action to protect neighbours against dangers arising on the land, but because the defendant has done nothing to create the danger he is to be judged by reference to what is reasonable to expect *him* to do, given *his* resources, not by the normal objective standard of the reasonable man. A landlord is not without more liable for a nuisance arising during a tenancy unless he has authorised it or it is a necessary consequence for the purpose for which the land has been let[18] but if the nuisance is a matter of non-repair this will very often be displaced because the landlord is responsible for damage to adjoining property or users of the highway wherever he is under an obligation to repair[19] or even if he has expressly or impliedly reserved a *right* to enter and repair. There is a very similar statutory liability under section 4 of the Defective Premises Act 1972.

The law gives a simpler answer to the question of who can sue. The plaintiff must have an interest in the affected land. He is usually the occupier, but a landlord out of possession can sue if there is permanent damage to the property. It is sometimes said to be anomalous that a member of the occupier's family cannot sue, but this is not really so. If the interference in question is truly with the enjoyment of the property there is no reason to extend the right of action beyond the occupier, since he can put a stop to it if he wishes. If the case arises from personal injury[20] or damage to property then anyone on the land affected has a claim for negligence and nuisance does not generally involve any strict liability.

Among the defences, statutory authority is probably the most important. As under the cognate rule in *Rylands* v. *Fletcher* the

---

[16] [1940] A.C. 880.

[17] See in particular *Leakey* v. *National Trust* [1980] Q.B. 485.

[18] See *Tetley* v. *Chitty* [1986] 1 All E.R. 663 (go-kart racing).

[19] There are various statutory obligations to repair, particularly under the Landlord and Tenant Act.

[20] Assuming nuisance to cover personal injuries even in a claim by the occupier, which is not wholly clear.

only wholly reliable rule is that the statute must be examined. Parliament may provide that the undertaker is to give full compensation for all interference with private rights or that his neighbours must put up with the effect of his activities upon the enjoyment of their property, or anything in between, but the Parliamentary intention often has to be guessed at rather than gathered by interpretation. It is common to find a clause to the effect that nothing in the Act "shall exonerate the undertakers from any action or other proceedings for nuisance" but even this is not treated as enough to preserve nuisance liability where this is the inevitable consequence of a statutory duty (as opposed to a power).[21] Where there is a statutory power and no "nuisance clause" the case will in effect turn on the degree of discretion given to the undertaker. In *Metropolitan Asylum District* v. *Hill*[22] the defendants established a smallpox hospital in Hampstead which was found by the jury to be a nuisance by reason of its situation. The defendants relied upon statutory authority to "purchase or hire, or to build . . . a building or buildings for [hospitals], of such nature and size, and according to such plan, and in such manner, as [they] think fit" but they failed in the House of Lords because their discretion as to the siting of the hospital rendered it impossible for them to show that the nuisance created by its siting *there* was an inevitable consequence of their statutory power to establish a smallpox hospital. By contrast, in *Hammersmith Ry.* v. *Brand*[23] the defendants had statutory authority to run trains along a track adjoining the plaintiffs' property, a process which inevitably, even where the railway was run with the greatest care, produced damaging vibration. As Lord Cairns put it, "if, therefore, it could not be used without vibration, and if vibration necessarily caused damage to the adjacent landowner, and if it was intended to preserve to the adjacent landowner his right of action, the consequence would be that action after action would be maintainable against the railway company for the damage which the landowner sustained; and after some actions had been brought, and had succeeded, the Court of Chancery would interfere by injunction, and would prevent the railway being worked—which, of course, is a *reductio ad absurdum*, and would defeat the intention of the Legislature. I have, therefore, no hesitation in arriving

---

[21] It has been suggested that such clauses may have been intended to have the effect that the undertaker could not be enjoined but would have to pay damages for the harm he caused, but that is not how they have been interpreted by the courts.

[22] (1881) 6 App.Cas. 193.

[23] (1869) L.R. 4 H.L. 171. See also *Allen* v. *Gulf Oil* [1981] A.C. 1004.

at the conclusion that no action could be maintained against the railway company."[24]

A defence virtually unique to nuisance is prescription. Provided the nuisance is of such a nature that it is capable of being an easement (that is, a right over someone else's land) it may be legalised by 20 years' user. Examples would be the discharge of water or effluent but a right to make a smell or smoke or a noise probably does not fall into this category because the degree of interference is too variable. In any event, time does not begin to run until the interference reaches a sufficient degree of severity to constitute a nuisance. Thus in *Miller* v. *Jackson*,[25] the cricket club case, the fact that cricket had been played on the field for 70 years did not (even assuming that a right to hit cricket balls into your neighbour's land is capable of subsisting as an easement) avail the defendants since the plaintiff's house had only been built four years before the action was brought.

Bearing in mind that coming to the nuisance is no defence, assumption of risk and contributory negligence are capable of application to a claim for damages for nuisance.

Some aspects of the law of nuisance are really part of land law and cannot be pursued here: examples are withdrawal of support from neighbouring land, obstruction of "ancient lights" (there is no natural right to light, still less to a view or privacy) or interference with water courses, and in many situations the common law has been substantially altered by statute. There is, however, one odd by-way of the law which causes recurrent difficulty. In *Bradford Corpn.* v. *Pickles*[26] the House of Lords confirmed the ancient rule of land law that there were no proprietary rights in percolating water (as opposed to water running in a defined channel), from which it followed that if the owner of higher land drained it off, even out of malice, a subjacent owner had no right to complain.[27] Where, as in *Bradford* v. *Pickles*, the damage to the plaintiff consists only in the loss of its water supply it may be possible to accept this result with equanimity but it has since been held that it is an inevitable logical consequence of that decision that the plaintiff has no claim even if the removal of underground water causes the foreseeable

---

[24] This case neatly demonstrates the frequent incoherence of compensation provisions. The legislation provided compensation to the owners of land "taken or injuriously affected by the construction" of the railway. This was held by the majority of the House of Lords not to extend to loss suffered by reason of the operation of the railway.

[25] [1977] Q.B. 966, p. 123, *ante.*

[26] [1895] A.C. 587.

[27] Hence this situation is to be contrasted with such matters as smoke and noise, where there must be a balance of respective rights.

collapse of buildings on his land and the result is the same even if the claim is framed in negligence.[28]

Public Nuisance

Public nuisance is a very different animal. Primarily it is a common law crime (though now rarely charged in view of the multiplicity of statutory offences governing public health and safety) which has been applied to a multitude of illegalities from selling rotten meat to obstructing the highway. Unlike private nuisance it has no connection with the enjoyment of land. The essence of a public nuisance is that it is something which affects the comfort and convenience of the public as a whole rather than of an individual complainant. Apart from the sanction of criminal prosecution the Attorney-General can bring a civil action for an injunction (a "relator" action) on the complaint of a member of the public. However, it has been recognised since the sixteenth century that a private individual has standing to sue for damages or an injunction in certain circumstances. Suppose that an oil refinery is discharging quantities of acid smuts which are causing damage to properties in the area. This may be a public nuisance for which the Attorney General can bring proceedings[29] but it is also a private nuisance *vis-à-vis* the individual householders, because their property rights have been interfered with. Individuals do not lose their rights in private nuisance because others suffer similar harm. Suppose, however, that another defendant in the area encroaches on the highway, causing serious obstruction.[30] The right to use the highway is a public right which is not dependent on ownership or occupation of land so the law of private nuisance is inapplicable. An individual may only bring an action in respect of this disturbance of the public right if he can show that he has suffered "special damage," a rule designed to prevent a multiplicity of suits by confining the remedy to those who can show they have suffered a loss which is clearly distinguishable from that of the public at large. Until that point is reached it is felt that the matter should be left to the proper representatives of the public, but once it has been passed the exceptional harm suffered by the plaintiff justifies giving him a private right of action. American courts have stuck fairly consistently to the requirement that special damage must be

---

[28] *Stephens* v. *Anglia Water Authority* [1987] 1 W.L.R. 1381.

[29] Other public bodies may have statutory rights to bring proceedings, *e.g.* a local authority under s.222 of the Local Government Act 1972.

[30] A highway authority is responsible for *failure to maintain* the highway under section 85 of the Highways Act 1980.

different in kind from that suffered by the public as a whole, but the weight of English authority is satisfied with a difference in degree. Mere inconvenience or delay is not actionable, but loss of livelihood or the need to incur greater expense is.

Though public nuisance is historically and conceptually distinct from the private variety it may involve a similar process of balancing competing rights by reference to a formula of reasonableness so that, for example, a partial obstruction of the highway may be justifiable for the purposes of repair or improvement of premises adjoining it, provided the defendant takes proper steps to minimise the interference. As Byles J. put it long ago, "as a general rule all the Queen's subjects have a right to the free and uninterrupted use of a public way: but, nevertheless, all persons have an equally undoubted right for a proper purpose to impede and obstruct the convenient access of the public through and along the same."[31]

Most public nuisances, like private ones, involve a patent and continuing state of affairs. Where they do not, there is no more reason in public than in private nuisance to believe that the tort involves any element of strict liability. If the defendant is doing that which is prima facie unlawful (for example, obstructing the highway) the burden may be on him to justify what he is doing, but that is not the same thing as saying his liability is strict.

---

[31] *Herring* v. *Metropolitan Board of Works* (1865) 19 C.B.(N.S.) 570. The common law is, of course, qualified by a multitude of statutory provisions.

CHAPTER EIGHT

Trespass to the Person and Related Wrongs

Trespass is the father of torts. Readers will be familiar with the plea in the Lord's Prayer to "forgive us our trespasses" and a moment's thought will lead to the conclusion that it is unlikely that the Deity is being asked for special absolution for the supplicant's comparatively venial sin in walking on someone else's land. The word is clearly being used in its old (and, in non-legal language, now archaic) sense of a "wrong."[1] Even in its legal context it may gradually be falling into disuse except with regard to land, but the meaning it has acquired in the developed common law is that of a direct, physical interference with the plaintiff's body, goods or land. It covers a blow, or theft or forcible entry, just the sort of straightforward wrongs one would expect an early legal system, concerned with keeping the peace and unconscious of any sophisticated distinction between "civil" and "criminal" law, to concern itself with. For harms which were done indirectly the writ of trespass provided no remedy but this gap was filled by the action "on the case," the origin of our modern law of negligence. The key element in all forms of trespass is that the wrong is actionable *per se*, that is to say, the plaintiff can sue even though he has suffered no damage,[2]

---

[1] But etymologically the word ultimately derives from the Latin *trans* (through) and *passus* (a pace) so that trespass to land is its "purest" meaning.
[2] Some doubt was raised in *Everitt* v. *Martin* [1953] N.Z.L.R. 298 whether trespass to goods is actionable *per se* but the doubt was expressed primarily in relation to unintentional trespass, and it is by no means clear that that form any longer exists in England: p. 146, *post*.

130

whereas the action on the case required (and its successor still requires) proof of damage as a necessary part of the plaintiff's claim. The reader may wonder how such wrongs can be of any practical importance, for who will risk litigation where he has suffered no harm from the defendant's conduct? There are several answers. First, some of the trespass torts are in practice concerned with matters which the man in the street would regard as "harm" even though they are not the sort of quantifiable physical loss which is the main concern of negligence, for example, loss of liberty, insult, outrage. In this respect their closest relative in torts is defamation. Secondly, trespass to land (and, to a lesser extent, trespass to goods) may be used as vehicles to determine questions of ownership so that there is a "real" issue going beyond the apparently pointless attempt to recover nominal damages. Finally, there are still circumstances in which a plaintiff who has suffered serious, tangible harm to person or property may gain an advantage by suing for trespass: the measure of damages is certainly one such advantage and in parts of the common law world the burden of proof may be affected.

For the purposes of exposition this area defies classification. Since both trespass to the person and trespass to goods are only part of a rather wider canvas which involves other forms of liability it would be confusing to devote a chapter to the "trespass torts" alone. Instead, this chapter deals with trespass to the person along with certain other matters which are intimately related in practice; the following chapter puts trespass to goods into the wider context of interference with goods; and a further chapter deals with defences which to some extent apply right across this area. Trespass to land is, as it were, "free-standing," though something will have to be said about the relationship of that tort to nuisance.

Trespass to the Person

Trespass to the person is the species of tort comprising the three sub-species of assault, battery and false imprisonment. Assault and battery nearly always occur together on the same facts and sometimes all three may be present, as in the case of wrongful arrest. All three torts are also crimes and many propositions of law about them tend to be supported by citation of authorities from criminal law. This is permissible and indeed necessary, provided we are on our guard against the assumption that civil and criminal law are always the same, particularly with regard to the mental element required.

The simplest form is battery, which is committed where the defendant intentionally and directly applies unlawful force to the plaintiff's body. The requirement of intention is a comparatively recent development in the civil law and would not be accepted in, say, Australia. To trace this point we must start with the decision of Diplock J. in *Fowler* v. *Lanning*[3] and attempt to explain the relationship between pleading and the substantive law. The plaintiff's statement of claim in that case simply stated, along with matters of time and place, that "the defendant shot the plaintiff." Under modern procedure the plaintiff's statement of claim must contain those factual elements which make up the tort in question and which he must prove by evidence (or admission) in order to succeed. If he fails to allege such elements the defendant may apply to have the claim "struck out as disclosing no cause of action," *i.e.* dismissed without trial on the facts. On such an application the judge must ask himself whether, if the plaintiff proves all he alleges and there is no other evidence in the case, judgment would be given for him. The statement of claim need not, however, deal with matters of "justification or excuse" for these are *defences* in the proper sense and it is up to the defendant to plead those in his turn and prove them at the trial. Thus is an action for false arrest against the police the plaintiff must prove that he was detained and it is for the police to raise in their pleading the point that they were entitled to detain the plaintiff because they reasonably believed him to be committing an offence. There is, therefore, an intimate connection between pleadings and the issues upon which the respective parties will be required to provide evidence at the trial. Now there was no doubt on facts like *Fowler* v. *Lanning* that the defendant would *not* have been liable if his gun had gone off wholly unpredictably while he was following all the safety rules applicable to a shooting party; if liability for trespass was ever "strict" it had certainly ceased to be so by 1600 at the latest. But the question starkly presented to Diplock J. by the plaintiff's pleading was "upon whom did the burden of proof lie?" Was it the law, as the plaintiff had asserted, that once he had pleaded a direct injury emanating from the defendant, he had done all that he was required to do and it was then up to the defendant to plead that the accident was not his fault ("inevitable accident" as the plea was known)? Or was the defendant right in saying that the statement of claim was fatally defective in omitting any allegation that the shooting of the plaintiff was negligent or intentional? At one time the plaintiff's argument would have commanded universal and unhesitating assent but Diplock J. concluded that the law had developed via a special rule in the 19th century for highway accidents to the position whereby, even in cases of trespass, the plaintiff had to

---

[3] [1959] 1 Q.B. 426.

plead and prove negligence on the defendant's part. If the plaintiff had no evidence as to how the incident occurred all would not necessarily be lost because the court might draw the necessary inference of negligence from the mere happening of the event[4] but the decision nonetheless went far towards depriving the plaintiff who could show a direct, trespassory injury of any advantage from that. Although only a first instance decision and assailed by some on historical grounds, *Fowler* v. *Lanning* is now firmly embedded in English practice.[5] The matter was taken further by a majority of the Court of Appeal in *Letang* v. *Cooper*[6] where the plaintiff had been run over by the defendant's car and the issue was whether the claim was time-barred by the normal three year period of limitation for personal injuries. In fact, it would have been enough to say that even if the plaintiff's claim could be framed as trespass it was, given the terms of the statute, governed by the three year period, but Lord Denning M.R. (with whom Danckwerts L.J. agreed) went further and in a robust judgment which really amounted to judicial legislation, declared that in the modern law trespass to the person lay only where the interference with the plaintiff's person was intentional. Diplock L.J. (as he had become) was more cautious but in saying that even if there could still be a claim for negligent trespass the plaintiff was required to prove damage he was effectively negating the cardinal element of trespass, that it is actionable *per se*. A "trespass" which requires proof of damage and puts the burden of proof on the plaintiff is negligence by another name. For England,[7] therefore, the law now appears to be as follows. If the defendant's interference with the plaintiff is direct and intentional[8] that is trespass (battery) and is actionable even though no harm has been suffered. Where, however, the defendant acts negligently then the plaintiff's claim is properly classified as negligence even if, as in *Letang* v. *Cooper*, the injury can properly be described as "direct." Whatever its historical validity this is, it is submitted, a reclassification of the law along rational lines, for it makes a great deal of sense to distinguish between defendants who act intentionally and negligently but little to distinguish between those who interfere directly and indirectly. In particular, there is a real need to give a remedy without proof of damage to the victim of an intentional wrong for

---

[4] *Res ipsa loquitur*, p. 70, *ante*.

[5] An American court had given a similar decision a century earlier: *Brown* v. *Kendall* 60 Mass. 292 (1850).

[6] [1965] 1 Q.B. 232.

[7] These developments have been rejected in Australia. See, *e.g. Venning* v. *Chin* (1974) 10 S.A.S.R. 299.

[8] For intentional, *indirect* harm, see p. 141, *post*.

the gist of the plaintiff's claim is then the outrage which stems from the fact that the act is intentional. We soon shrug off being knocked over by a clumsy person in a hurry provided we suffer no personal injury, but a slap in the face may be a different matter altogether.

The meaning of "intention" in the law of torts has already been touched upon.[9] In the context of trespass to the person it should certainly extend to the state of mind of one who actually foresees a risk even though he does not desire to bring about the result to which the risk relates. Unfortunately, the criminal law has fallen into some confusion over the mental element and it is possible (no more) that the crime of common assault may be committed by a person who simply fails to advert to a risk which would be obvious to any reasonable person. This is somewhere between the position of the conscious risk taker and ordinary negligence. Now it may seem strange if the mental element required for civil liability were narrower than for crime, so there is some temptation to apply this standard to tort, too. However, to do so would seriously undermine the rationalisation effected in *Letang* v. *Cooper*.

Even assuming that we are clear on the meaning of "intention" we have not answered the question "intentional as to what?" The point has great importance where a blow causes serious injury. If D strikes P and causes him harm he may intend to do any of the following: (a) to make the bodily movement but not to touch P; (b) to touch P unlawfully but not to harm him; (c) to cause P some moderate harm; (d) to cause P the serious harm he in fact suffers. It seems that for the purposes of battery the required intention is (b)[10] so that the defendant may be liable for *damage* he did not intend: the requirement of intention goes to the commission of the act of force, not its consequences. When combined when the proposition that the defendant takes his victim as he finds him,[11] that is to say, that he is liable even for consequences which are attributable to the plaintiff's unusual and unforeseeable susceptibility, this creates a powerful and far reaching liability. In the American case of *Vosburg* v. *Putney* one schoolboy "playfully" kicked another on the shin. He intended no harm and the blow was not hard, but it "revived" an earlier infection in the leg and caused such serious damage that the plaintiff lost the use of the limb. Though it granted a new trial on an

---

[9] See p. 14, *ante.*
[10] *Wilson* v. *Pringle* [1987] Q.B. 237. But there may be liability for assault in (a): p. 136, *post.*
[11] See p. 66, *ante.*

issue relating to the medical testimony the court had no doubt that such facts would give rise to liability.[12]

Not all intentional contact is, however, tortious, quite apart from cases of consent or matters of justification like arrest. The extra factor has, unfortunately, proved elusive. Lord Holt C.J. long ago said, "the least touching another in anger is a battery"[13] but that is not wide enough. If D presses an unwanted kiss upon the protesting P he is not "angry" but his act is unquestionably a battery. The American *Restatement* describes battery as a "harmful or offensive" contact but the Court of Appeal has described the necessary characteristic as "hostility."[14] Possibly this word in its ordinary meaning is too akin to anger, but the court specifically said that it should not be equated with ill-will or malevolence. Unwanted medical treatment may be forced on a plaintiff out of mistaken motives of kindness, but it is nevertheless a battery. But jostling in the supermarket queue or a touch to engage a person's attention is not tortious and even rough horseplay may fall on the non-tortious side of the line so that in *Wilson* v. *Pringle,* which arose out of schoolboy boisterousness, the trial judge was not justified in giving the plaintiff summary judgment under Order 14 of the Rules of the Supreme Court, which applies only if the defendant has no triable defence.[15]

Battery requires a direct, physical contact but flesh to flesh contact is unnecessary. For example, it would certainly be battery to spit in the plaintiff's face, to shoot him or to strike him where his body is covered in clothing and it would probably extend to snatching something from his hand or deliberately ramming the car in which he is riding. However, so long as the requirement of directness is retained (and it has been abandoned in the U.S.A. and Canada) there must be something at least *resembling* a blow, so that putting poison in food or digging a pit for the plaintiff to fall into probably do not qualify. Since such conduct is actionable under another head[16] this does not matter overmuch, but it would be desirable if the rationalisation began in *Fowler* v. *Lanning* could be carried further by dropping the requirement of directness and unifying all harmful or offensive intentional interference with the plaintiff's person under one head. This is not to deny that some pretty liberal interpretations have sometimes been put upon directness. In the famous case of *Scott*

[12] 50 N.W. 403 (Wis. 1891).
[13] *Cole* v. *Turner* (1704) 6 Mod. 149.
[14] *Wilson* v. *Pringle* [1987] Q.B. 237.
[15] Would the conduct in *Vosburg* v. *Putney* have fallen into the "non-hostile" category?
[16] See p. 141 *post.*

v. *Shepherd*[17] D threw a firework into a market. W picked it up and
threw it away. It landed near R, who did the same. It then landed
near P and exploded, injuring him. An action for trespass
succeeded. At the time a decision that the harm was indirect
would have been fatal to the plaintiff for he would have chosen
the wrong form of action (trespass, as opposed to case). Now that
the plaintiff does not have to choose a procedure to suit his claim
and, indeed, is not required to name his cause of action, the
matter would probably not trouble a modern court much.
Indeed, today we might approach *Scott* v. *Shepherd* as a case of
negligence with the principal issue being whether the chain of
events was sufficiently foreseeable for P to be owed a duty of care
by D and no doubt it would be.

Assault is an apprehended battery, the blow that misses or the
fist raised to strike. Unfortunately, it is used in popular speech
(and sometimes in a legal context) as a compendious word to
cover both assault proper *and* battery. Compared with battery it is
a rather "unphysical" tort for neither contact nor harm is
required, a point decided as early as 1348,[18] probably then more
for the purpose of discouraging breaches of the peace than for
compensating the mental disturbance likely to arise from a
threatened battery. Since there is no reason to believe that the
propositions stated in *Letang* v. *Cooper* are confined to battery it is
a tort of intention, but the intention goes to the impression
intended to be produced in the plaintiff, not to what the
defendant in fact ultimately intended to do. Thus, despite
various confusing and contradictory dicta, it is clearly an assault
to point an unloaded gun (or, indeed, a realistic imitation firearm)
at someone intending him to believe that he may be shot.[19] Much
ink has been spilled over the question whether words alone can
be an assault and those who assert that they may be certainly
have a strong argument in pointing to the absurdity of a
distinction between the highwayman who points his pistol and
says "Your money or your life"[20] and the one who sits still on his
horse while pronouncing the same threat. Since there will almost
always be some sort of movement which can be interpreted as a
threatening "act" (rolling up one's sleeves in one old case) it
would probably do no great harm to admit that words alone *can*
be an assault. This would not (and should not) lead to the result

---

[17] (1773) 2 Wm.Bl. 892.
[18] *I de S et Ux* v. *W de S* (1348) Y.L.Lib.Ass.f. 99, pl. 60. W attempted to break into
I's tavern "after hours" and swung his axe at I's wife, missing her.
[19] Hence it is not quite right to say that an assault is an attempted battery.
[20] The conditional nature of the threat does not render it lawful. But words may
make it plain that something which would otherwise be an assault is not
intended as such: *Turbervell* v. *Savadge* (1669) 1 Mod. 3.

that all threats of violence would be an assault for there must be some apprehension of an immediate or at least imminent battery. In criminal law this has been stretched to cover behaving in a threatening manner outside a window but could not extend, to, say, threats of future harm uttered over the telephone. Such conduct may, however, be tortious on another basis.[21]

Most batteries are immediately preceded by assaults, but not necessarily—for example a blow from behind would not arouse the "apprehension" necessary for assault. Apprehension must not, however, be equated with fear: it is still an assault even if the plaintiff can brush aside the defendant's puny attack on him.

False imprisonment is concerned with the protection of personal liberty but its name is rather misleading. "False" means "wrongful" or "unjustified" and "imprisonment" means restraint, even temporary restraint, and does not imply incarceration. Indeed, a person who is wrongly convicted and imprisoned can hardly ever sue for false imprisonment: the judge, witnesses and court officers are protected by an absolute privilege and the person who makes the accusation which leads to the charge cannot be sued because the link between his act and the imprisonment is regarded as broken by the independent decision of the prosecuting authority and the judgment of the court. In some cases the informant may be sued for malicious prosecution but that is a tort which is singularly hard to establish.[22] The typical case of false imprisonment in modern conditions is the unjustified arrest of the plaintiff by a police officer acting without warrant or the act of a store detective in

---

[21] See p. 141, *post*.

[22] Malicious prosecution hardly justifies its own chapter in an introductory book but from a historical and conceptual point of view it does not belong with any other tort. With the warning that it is certainly not a form of trespass (and hence not actionable *per se*) this seems a suitable point at which to summarise its requirements. The plaintiff must show: (1) That D prosecuted. Giving information to the police is not enough but he does not have to be the formal prosecutor: signing the charge or swearing out a warrant will do. (2) That the prosecution terminated in P's favour (which includes the quashing of a conviction on appeal). (3) That D had no probable cause for the prosecution (which, in a trial by jury, is a matter for the judge). This was defined in *Commonwealth Life Assurance Society* v. *Brain* (1935) 53 C.L.R. 343 as that which would lead a reasonable person to believe that "the probability of the accused's guilt is such that upon general grounds of justice a charge against him is warranted." But lack of honest belief in the charge is conclusive against D. (4) That D was actuated by malice, that is to say his predominant motive was not to vindicate the law. *All* the elements must be proved so that proof of malice (for example, a desire for revenge) gets P. nowhere if there is probable cause. Malicious civil proceedings (at least where they affect P's credit) are also actionable but the comparatively undeveloped state of the law on this is probably attributable to the power to award costs to the successful defendant and to stay proceedings as an abuse of the process of the court.

seeking to detain a person he mistakenly believes to be a shoplifter. As a variety of trespass the tort is actionable *per se* and since damages are "at large" even a short detention, if accompanied by circumstances of publicity, humiliation or distress may lead to a large award, still more so where a police officer is involved, for then there may be exemplary damages, too.[23]

False imprisonment will commonly be accompanied by a technical battery (a restraining hand, for example) or by an assault, but not necessarily so. It is by no means clear that a statement by a police officer, "you are under arrest" would be an assault but the submission of the plaintiff to the order would mean that there was an imprisonment. The law could hardly be otherwise, for while you are entitled to resist an unlawful arrest by using whatever force is reasonably necessary it would not normally be wise to do so, since the lawfulness of the arrest may turn on the arresting officer's reasonable perception of the facts, not the facts as they actually are. Hence, rather than oblige you to resist, the law allows you to submit and later test the reasonableness of the officer's belief by an action.

The restraint must be total to constitute false imprisonment, a point usually illustrated by *Bird* v. *Jones*[24] which arose from the attempts of the plaintiff (no doubt a stickler for the preservation of public rights) to proceed along an obstructed portion of the footpath on Hammersmith Bridge even though the carriage way was open to allow him to cross. As Coleridge J. graphically put it,

> "if, in the course of a night, both ends of a street were walled up, and there was no egress from the house but into the street, I should have no difficulty in saying that the inhabitants were thereby imprisoned, but, if only one end were walled up, and an armed force stationed outside to prevent any scaling of the wall or passage that way, I should feel equally clear that there was no imprisonment. If there were, the street would obviously be a prison; and yet, as obviously, none would be confined to it."

As always in connection with these torts it is important not to assume that the limits of this particular cause of action represent the whole of the law. If Bird had not been able to cross Hammersmith Bridge at all there would still have been no false imprisonment for not only could he roam through all the city on the north bank of the river but he could go to another bridge and use that; but if a person suffers damage as a result of obstruction

---

[23] See p. 206, *post.*
[24] (1845) 7 Q.B. 742.

of the highway (for example he has to go to much greater expense to deliver his goods) he may sue in public nuisance, an action on the case. No doubt in marginal cases there may be difficult in determining what amounts to total restraint. There would obviously be false imprisonment if the plaintiff were confined in an aircraft flying round the world and it is thought that the tort would also be committed by confining someone to a 100 acre park, but it is hard to believe that there could be false imprisonment if the plaintiff were free to move around the whole country provided he did not leave it. Similarly, a merely inconvenient but not dangerous means of escape which is known to the plaintiff or is obvious (for example, stepping out of a ground floor window) should negative the tort. An American decision which held that immobilising the plaintiff's car amounted to false imprisonment[25] may owe something to transatlantic notions of reasonable means of travel, but to immobilise the plaintiff's car in a remote place should amount to the tort.

A troublesome theoretical question, though rarely arising in practice, is whether the plaintiff must be conscious of the imprisonment. After conflicting authorities, the House of Lords has taken the view, *obiter*, that this consciousness is not necessary[25a] but there is a good deal to be said for the contrary view for in the absence of some actual damage (in which event there may be an action even if there is no trespassory tort) the wrong is essentially to the plaintiff's dignity and feelings and in this respect "what you don't know doesn't hurt." The necessity for knowledge has been accepted by the American *Restatement*. On the other hand, a person who was kidnapped while unconscious and then released before waking up might well have a powerful sense of outrage when he was later told of the facts[26] and this may be an area, like all the trespass torts, in which the civil law continues to have a quasi-criminal function.

Actions for false imprisonment have sometimes arisen when the defendant has refused to let the plaintiff out of an area which he entered voluntarily or in which his restraint was initially lawful. The law may be stated on the basis of the cases as follows—

1. Where there is a legal duty by contract or otherwise to let the plaintiff out a refusal to comply with this will be false

---

[25] *Cordell* v. *Standard Oil Co.* 289 P. 472 (Kan. 1930).
[25a] *Murray* v. *M.o.D.* [1988] 1 W.L.R. 692.
[26] Of course, the same might be true of the victim of an intended battery which was forestalled before he got to know of it. Consider *People* v. *Pape* 5 P. 621 (1885): D put gunpowder in P's stove to blow him up. Powder discovered and removed before P was told.

imprisonment, despite the general rule that failure to act cannot be trespass. If the law were otherwise it would not be false imprisonment to refuse to unlock the gaol door at the end of the term of imprisonment. The famous American case of *Whitaker* v. *Sandford*[27] is an example of this. The defendant, leader of a religious sect, got the plaintiff on to his yacht, assuring her that she could leave when she wished. On arrival in harbour he refused to furnish her with a boat so that she remained on board for a month.

2. Failure to release someone in the absence of such a duty is not false imprisonment, so that miners who downed tools and demanded to be brought up forthwith had no cause of action for false imprisonment. It should follow from proposition 1 that the result would have been different if the shift had come to an end or there had been an emergency.[28]

3. The conclusion can be drawn from the difficult case of *Robinson* v. *Balmain New Ferry Co.*[29] (like *Bird* v. *Jones* another warning against too zealous attempts to enforce what one conceives to be one's technical legal rights) that if the plaintiff has voluntarily entered the defendant's premises subject to a condition of which he is or ought to be aware (on the facts that he must either leave by ferryboat or pay a small sum of money for the privilege of leaving by the way he entered) then the defendant is entitled to take active steps, including the use of physical compulsion, to restrain him from breaking those conditions.

The cases which established propositions 2 and 3 have been criticised but they have never been overruled and they contain a good deal of common sense: a bus passenger cannot demand to be set down anywhere he chooses, but only where the company has scheduled stops. But they can also be criticised for failing to pay enough attention to the correct balance between the maintenance of contracts and personal liberty. A Canadian court has held that it can be false imprisonment for a hotelier to detain a guest who disputes a bill and leaves his name and address[30] but in many cases restraint might be justified on the alternative ground of arrest on reasonable suspicion of a criminal offence, to which we now turn.

A lawful power of arrest is the commonest justification for false imprisonment. It would be out of place here to try to give an account of this and it is likely to be covered in detail in a study of

---

[27] 85A 399 (1912).
[28] See *Herd* v. *Weardale Steel Co.* [1915] A.C. 67. But note that in the Court of Appeal the view was expressed that even failure to bring the men up at the end of the shift would be remediable only in contract, not in tort.
[29] [1910] A.C. 295.
[30] *Bahner* v. *Marwest Hotel* (1970) 12 D.L.R. (3d) 646.

Constitutional Law or Civil Liberties. There are likely to be very large variations from one jurisdiction to another, particularly where the law is overlaid with a written constitution or a bill of rights but the following salient characteristics of the English system are likely to be produced virtually everywhere. First, powers of arrest extend to circumstances where there is a reasonable suspicion that the accused person is committing an offence, though he is in fact not doing so. Secondly, the powers of police officers are rather wider under the general law than those of private citizens and they have numerous powers under particular statutes. Thirdly, the person who exercises the power bears the burden of showing that the arrest was lawful.

Non-trespassory Wrongs: the Action on the case

Though there are comparatively few cases, it is clear law that if the defendant intentionally and without justification causes personal injury (including "nervous shock") to the plaintiff he is liable even though his act cannot be classed as any form of trespass. In former times the action would have fallen within the category of actions on the case and the "action on the case for intentional harm" is, despite the archaism, probably the closest we can come to a name for the tort even now. One of the leading cases is *Janvier* v. *Sweeney*,[31] where the defendant, a private detective, misrepresented to the plaintiff that she was wanted for corresponding with a German spy (her fiancé, a German, was interned at the time), as a result of which she suffered a severe nervous illness, a consequence which, the jury found, the defendant contemplated as likely when he told the lies. The Court of Appeal upheld a verdict for the plaintiff and approved the earlier decision in *Wilkinson* v. *Downton*[32] a case of a practical joke, in which it is doubtful whether there could truly be said to be an intention to injure and which might now be more simply dealt with as a case of negligence. The conduct in *Janvier* v. *Sweeney* was certainly not an assault or battery and it would be straining language to describe it as negligent (though we might say that "negligence" is simply a convenient name for a wider tort of causing harm by legal "fault," of which it happens to be the most frequent example). Nor could we say that the lies amounted to deceit since the plaintiff had not acted in reliance upon them. Hence the recognition of the necessity of a residual category of intentional but indirectly caused harm. Though the English cases

---

[31] [1919] 2 K.B. 316.
[32] [1897] 2 Q.B. 57. *Cf.* the gruesome American case of *Blakeley* v. *Shortal's Estate* 20 N.W. 2d 28 (1945)—deceased cut his throat in the plaintiff's kitchen.

involve lies and nervous shock there is no reason to think that the principle is confined to such a situation and it would extend, for example, to frightening a person into falling (assuming this not to be an assault) and to surreptitious poisoning. It cannot, however, extend to financial loss such as loss of business (unless consequential upon physical injury) because the limits of the "economic torts" render it impossible to postulate any general principle of liability for intentional and unjustifiable infliction of harm of any description. Even in the area of bodily injury this tort can probably only arise if the conduct of the defendant can be described as in some way "unlawful," though not necessarily in the sense of a specific crime or tort. The lies in *Janvier* v. *Sweeney* no doubt fell within this. It has been suggested that if I obstruct the highway with the purpose of preventing a sick person getting to hospital I am liable in tort under this theory (whether or not it also amounts to a case of public nuisance); it does not follow that I would be liable if for the same purpose I refused the ambulance permission to cross my land.

The shock in *Janvier* v. *Sweeney* was an illness recognised by law and not mere distress or anger. The law has developed in the United States so that there is now a head of liability for what the *Restatement* calls "extreme and outrageous conduct intentionally or recklessly causing severe emotional distress." It appears that this distress need not amount to a recognisable psychiatric illness and what is extreme and outrageous is left at large. In *Nickerson* v. *Hodge*[33] damages were awarded when the defendants buried a pot containing stones in the back yard of a mentally infirm old lady, convinced her it was a pot of gold and persuaded her to take it to the local bank and open it in front of a laughing crowd. This topic provides a fascinating illustration of the development of "dignitary" law in a litigious society but even there it is recognised that it cannot be allowed to go too far lest it interfere with other protected rights:

> "there is still ... such a thing as a liberty to express an unflattering opinion of another, however wounding it may be to the other's feelings: and in the interest not only of freedom of speech but also of avoidance of other more dangerous conduct it is still very desirable that some safety valve be left through which irascible tempers may blow off relatively harmless steam."[34]

[33] 84 So 37 (1920).
[34] Prosser & Keeton, Torts, 5th ed., 59.

Other Remedies

Perhaps a few hundred civil actions are brought each year for trespass to the person[35] and most of them are probably brought against the police. Actions against private individuals are not unknown, even arising out of homicide (a mass-murderer in England was successfully sued in the early 1980's) but in most cases the chances of recovering substantial damages must be small for the defendant will not be insured, indeed *could not* be insured, against this sort of liability. In less serious cases it is much more likely that the criminal court which convicts an offender for, say, an assault, will exercise its power under the Powers of the Criminal Courts Act 1973 to order him to pay a limited sum of compensation directly to the victim. Indeed, there is a statutory rule that summary proceedings for assault are, in certain circumstances, a bar to a civil action.

Victims of violent crime would also of course be able to avail themselves of the normal social security benefits but a considerable number of common law jurisdictions have found it advisable to introduce systems of compensation funded by the state. A very early form of this, the liability of the local inhabitants for property damage caused by riot, may have rested upon the idea that the authorities were at fault in allowing the situation to arise, but the modern systems have cut loose altogether from this justification.[36] There is great variation in the scope and pattern of these schemes, but the English one is among the oldest and the most far-reaching. After a period of existence as an administrative scheme operating under the Royal Prerogative it is at the time of writing in process of conversion into a statutory scheme under the Criminal Justice Bill. The scheme covers personal injury directly attributable to a crime of violence or the apprehension of an offender or the attempted prevention of an offence. The awarding authority (the Criminal Injuries Compensation Board) has a wide discretion to withhold or reduce payments having regard to the conduct of the applicant before, during or after the events giving rise to the claim or even his character and way of life, matters which clearly go much further than any common law concept of contributory negligence. Compensation is assessed on the basis of common law damages, with a maximum for loss of earnings of twice average industrial earnings, but cases which

---

[35] The Judicial Statistics show about 500 High Court actions a year for a group of torts which includes trespass along with nuisance, fraud and conspiracy.

[36] In some circumstances an action for negligence may lie against a person who fails to control the criminal propensities of another, but the police are not liable in tort for failing to prevent crime: p. 43, *ante*.

would attract an award of less than £400 (or £500 in some circumstances) are excluded. Some awards are very substantial (there was one for £175,809 in 1986) though 95.3 per cent. are for less than £5000. In two respects the scheme is considerably less generous than that of litigation: there can be nothing in the award akin to exemplary damages and there is full deduction of all social security benefits,[37] though not of the proceeds of insurance effected and paid for by the victim. The procedures of the Board do not involve adversarial litigation and most applications are disposed of by single members on a paper adjudication. There is, however, provision for a hearing before three members. Between 1964 and 1986 the Board received 369,828 applications and paid out more than £261 million in compensation. The 1985–86 payment alone was over £41 million and it is not likely that tort damages in respect of criminal acts amounted to one tenth of this figure. The scheme has been attacked on the ground that, like the tort system, it singles out one particular group of unfortunates for preferential treatment, but given the scale of violent crime and the length of time it has been in operation its removal is politically out of the question without a truly dramatic increase in the level of state funded compensation for injury in general.

[37] *Cf.* p. 213, *post.*

CHAPTER NINE

Interference with Goods

This topic is important not so much in terms of the number of cases to which it gives rise but because it is the foundation of our whole law of personal (*i.e.* non-land) property. In its usual pragmatic, remedies-based way the common law does not pay very much attention to defining ownership of goods or what the rights of ownership consist of: rather, it concentrates on defining the remedies available for interference with goods and, subject to statutory modification, extends these well beyond the person who could be described as "owner" in any ordinary sense. The complexity of the law is to some extent based on the fact that its historical development involved the use of legal fictions designed to sidestep procedural inconveniences which have long since ceased to be relevant. In England, an attempt has been made at unifying and rationalising the law by legislation but that did not go so far as the recommendations of the law Reform Committee[1] and the law is arguably even more complicated than it was before. The subject is probably avoided in many torts courses and what is offered here is no more than an account of its salient features but its importance in gaining an understanding of the common law should not be minimised. Some knowledge of interference with goods is essential in order to grasp sections of the law of contract and of particular contractual transactions such as sale and hire purchase.

Trespass to goods

Trespass to goods is the unlawful, direct touching of or

[1] 18th Report, Cmnd. 4774 (1971).

application of force to goods in the possession of another. In the absence of any decisive modern authority it is to be hoped that an English court would follow the analogy of the cases on trespass to the person[2] and declare it to be a tort which can only be committed intentionally, leaving other cases to the law of negligence. We would then have a rational system in which intended interference was actionable *per se* (the hallmark of trespass), which is probably a necessary protection against officious intermeddlers, but other cases required proof of damage. "Intentional" of course would mean intentional as to contact with the goods: in the American case of *Ranson* v. *Kitner*[3] the defendant was liable when he shot the plaintiff's dog, mistakenly believing it to be a wolf (which he would have been entitled to shoot since it would have belonged to no one) and I am liable for trespass if I take your umbrella in mistake for mine.

Possession is vital for a true cause of action in trespass. Very broadly speaking possession means physical control. If I rent your car for a month then I (the bailee) have possession of it and you (the bailor) do not and I am the only person who can sue for trespass. This is much less significant than it looks because if someone seriously damages the car you have an action on the case, in other words, in modern terminology, an action for negligence.[4] Possession is not, however, confined to immediate physical control. I am in possession of my car when I fly away on holiday and leave it in the garage and the possession of a servant is treated as the possession of his employer. The common law took this emphasis on possession to its logical conclusion by allowing the possessor with a merely temporary interest (such as the bailee in the above example) to recover the full value of the goods where he was deprived of them or they were destroyed.[5] In England, this has been modified by statute, a point considered below.

Conversion

Trespass to goods is rather a simple tort. Conversion, because it looks to ownership as well as possession, is a very complicated one. Because of the many forms it can take it has been said that it "almost defies definition," but very broadly it is an intentional,

---

[2] See p. 133, *ante*.
[3] 31 Ill.App. 241 (1888).
[4] Or, if the damage is deliberate, under the principle applied in *Janvier* v. *Sweeney*: p. 141, *ante*.
[5] But if you have neither possession nor ownership at the time but merely a contractual right to become owner at a future time your loss is "economic" and you have no claim: see p. 53, *ante*.

wrongful interference of a substantial nature with the plaintiff's possession or right to possession of his goods—wrongfully seizing them with the intention of keeping them permanently or for an extended time; selling them or otherwise assisting in their disposition; destroying or misusing them; or, of course, refusing to return them on demand. Its old name was *trover* because it was based on a fictional allegation that the defendant had found (modern French "trouver") the goods; the present name comes from the second allegation, that he had converted them to his own use. There is a substantial overlap with trespass to goods and in cases of seizure or wilful destruction the two torts may well be committed at the same time. But there are two very important points of difference. First, trespass requires some physical act bringing about a direct contact with the goods, conversion does not: an auctioneer who sells goods without the authority of the true owner commits conversion but not trespass. Secondly, trespass is a wrong to possession only, whereas conversion in addition covers the case where at the time of the wrong the plaintiff had the "immediate right to possession." Thus in our example of the auctioneer it might be thought that he could be sued for trespass if he physically delivered the goods, but this would not be so for at the time of that act possession of the goods was in the wrongdoer (via his agent, the auctioneer) who put the goods up for sale. Nonetheless, the auctioneer's act is conversion because if the owner appeared he could demand the return of the goods without fulfilling any condition, that is, he had the immediate right to possession.

A person may be owner and yet not have an immediate right to possession (for example, someone who has hired out goods for an extended period or someone whose goods are subject to a lien). Such an owner has an action on the case (negligence) if the goods are damaged or destroyed by someone else's fault. It is not at all clear that he has any action if the goods are merely wrongfully taken and detained, though the question does not matter very much in practice since in many cases the person who had possession may be responsible for their loss or he may have to continue payments in respect of them (for example, the hirer under a hire purchase agreement) and in any case the immediate right to possession will sooner or later revert to the owner.

At common law conversion was an intentional tort, that is to say it could only be committed by a voluntary act in relation to the goods. Stealing someone's car was conversion, carelessly driving it over a cliff was not (though it was of course negligence). To this there is now one exception by statute, namely section 2(2) of the Torts (Interference with Goods) Act 1977, which provides that an action "lies in conversion for loss or destruction of goods which a

bailee has allowed to happen in breach of his duty to his bailor."
This subsection is a piece of intended simplification which makes
the understanding of the law more difficult. Its origin is
historical. Until the passing of the Act there was a further tort,
known as detinue, which substantially overlapped with
conversion. Indeed, conversion was mainly created in the 17th
century to remedy the procedural deficiencies of detinue. The
main form of detinue was refusal to return goods in the
defendant's possession (which was and is also of course
conversion) but it was also committed by someone who was
unable to return the goods because he had allowed them to
become lost or destroyed while they were in his custody. All
other forms of detinue were also conversion and when the Act of
1977 abolished detinue the course was taken of deeming this form
to be conversion. This in no way affects the general rule that
conversion requires an intentional act and it is not clear why
Parliament did not take the simpler course of leaving this
remaining form of detinue to the developed laws of negligence
and bailment. In the United States detinue disappeared long ago
without causing any apparent consequential difficulty.

An awkward area of conversion is the extent to which it may be
committed by a temporary interference with the plaintiff's goods.
If A lends his car to B to go from Leeds to Huddersfield and B uses
it to go to Brighton that is not trespass for B came lawfully into
possession of the vehicle. It is breach of B's duty as a bailee, which
may mean that he is liable for damage to the vehicle during the
deviation even without negligence on his part. But is it
conversion? Does a defendant commit conversion if, without
permission, he borrows his neighbour's lawnmower? In an old
English case, the wrongful wearing of the plaintiff's pearls was
held to be conversion.[6] In *Moorgate Mercantile* v. *Finch*[7] conversion
was established when the defendant used the plaintiff's car for
smuggling so that it was seized and forfeited by the authorities.
The plaintiff did, of course, *lose* his car but the basis of the
conversion claim was that the wrongful use exposed the car to the
risk of seizure, a risk which the defendant must have
contemplated, though he hoped it would not occur. But it can
hardly be the law that a person who hires a car for 24 hours is
guilty of conversion if he deliberately keeps it for an extra hour.
According to the American *Restatement* the question is one of
degree depending, *inter alia*, upon the extent and duration of the

---

[6] *Lord Petre* v. *Heneage* (1701) 12 Mod. 519.
[7] [1962] 1 Q.B. 701. There are a number of Australian cases involving wrongful use
of bottles, of which the best-known is *Penfolds Wines* v. *Elliott* (1946) 74 C.L.R.
204.

exercise of dominion over the goods, the harm done to them and the inconvenience and expense caused to the owner. While one cannot confidently say that this rather vague but sensible approach represents English law, one can at least say that there is no authority inconsistent with it. One case where a temporary interference was held not to be conversion is *Fouldes* v. *Willoughby*[8] where the defendant, in order to make the plaintiff leave his boat, put the plaintiff's wares ashore. This was trespass, but not conversion. On the other hand, in *Howard E. Perry* v. *British Railways*[9] a refusal to hand over the plaintiff's goods during industrial action of indefinite duration was conversion. The defendant's state of mind should certainly be a relevant factor: if D takes P's car by mistake and drives it a short distance but then discovers the truth and returns it, there should not be conversion, but a thief would commit conversion even though he had driven the car only a few yards and returned it because the police were in the vicinity. The paucity of cases on the point is probably explained by the fact that under English procedure it may not normally be a live issue. Although the primary remedy for conversion is a money judgment for the value of the goods the English practice seems to be to allow a defendant who offers to return the goods undamaged to apply for a stay of proceedings.[10] In other jurisdictions, however, conversion seems to have been looked on as a sort of forced sale, so it becomes very important to decide at what point misuse of the goods becomes the tort. It is not even obvious that the problem of conversion need arise when the goods are lost or destroyed since most cases could be taken care of by the principle that a bailee who goes outside the terms of his permission is treated as if he were an insurer of the goods.

Despite some doubt at common law, section 11(3) of the Torts (Interference with Goods) Act 1977 provides that a mere denial of the plaintiff's title to the goods, unaccompanied by any "dealing" with them, is not conversion, though it may be fraud or injurious falsehood.

To say that conversion is an intentional tort does not mean that it involves a knowledge of wrongdoing. In this sense, conversion is "strict." For example, it is clear that a person who in all innocence buys goods which have been stolen or otherwise wrongfully obtained from the true owner does not generally become owner himself and can therefore be sued for conversion. For reasons of commercial convenience it has been found necessary to create certain exceptions (most of which are found in

---

[8] (1841) 8 M. & W. 540.
[9] [1980] 1 W.L.R. 1375.
[10] In the *Howard Perry* case the remedy sought by the plaintiff was delivery up.

sections 21–26 of the Sale of Goods Act 1979) to the rule that innocent acquisition does not give a good title to property but that nevertheless remains the general rule. The severity of the law upon the innocent acquirer is demonstrated by the fact that he is liable for conversion even though, when he receives the demand for return from the true owner, he has disposed of them or consumed them. Thus if A steals P's goods and they subsequently pass through the hands of C, D, E and F, all of whom are innocent, any of them may be sued by P for the value of the goods. Everyone except A may have a right of indemnity under his contract of purchase, but the practical value of that may be dubious. Despite occasional suggestions that the law should be modified, there is no machinery for splitting the loss between P and the other victims of A's wrongdoing, even if P failed to take good care of his property.[11]

A different rule applies, however, to people like carriers or warehousemen who merely transport or store goods, for they are not liable if they act in the bona fide belief in the authority of the person who instructs them. The law could hardly be otherwise, for if it were it would be necessary to make the sort of enquiries that would seriously burden the operation of commerce. It is true that such liability might be covered by insurance (as it is, for example, in the case of the auctioneer, who is certainly liable for "innocent conversion") but the courts seem to have concluded that this answer is theoretical rather than practical: the loss of a person who has been defrauded out of his goods is not the sort of loss which calls out to be spread among British Rail, Pickfords and any other persons through whose hands they have passed. The rule has been explained on the ground that the carrier's act does not purport to affect the title to the goods (as the auctioneer's act of selling does) but merely their location—though he is certainly liable if he knows that the person giving him his orders has no authority to do so. Some difficulty has been experienced in defining what is a merely "ministerial" act not involving conversion. Blackburn J. in *Hollins* v. *Fowler*[12] said that the innocent handler was protected if the act were one which would be justified if done by the authority of a person who was a finder of the goods. This would clearly cover a warehouseman who takes goods into his safe keeping. On the other hand, in *National Mercantile Bank* v. *Rymill*[13] it was held that an auctioneer who, on the instructions of A, delivered the goods to B after a private sale

---

[11] See s.11(1) of the 1977 Act.
[12] (1875) L.R. 7 H.L. 757.
[13] (1881) 44 L.T. 307, criticised in *R.H. Willis & Son* v. *British Car Auctions* [1978] 1 W.L.R. 438.

by A to B was not liable. This would not be consistent with Blackburn J.'s view because a finder (*i.e.* what A is deemed to be for this purpose) has no authority to dispose of the goods. However, Blackburn J.'s view may be unduly narrow: if a railway is not normally liable in conversion when it innocently carries goods, the case should not be different because it knows that they have been sold by the consignor to the person to whom they are to be delivered.

Relativity of title and interference with goods: the "jus tertii"

This problem is exemplified by the case of the finder. A finds valuable goods on B's property. Assuming that A is not employed by B then if there is a dispute between A and B as to the right to keep the goods we resolve it primarily by asking whether B manifested a sufficient intention to exercise control over all things which may be on the premises. If he did not, then A has a better right than B.[14] But A's right is clearly inferior to that of the person who lost the goods, O, who is entitled to claim them (or their value) if he can trace them into A's hands. A's "title" is possessory only and liable to be defeated by someone with a prior and superior right to possess. If A's possession is disturbed by X, can X when sued raise the issue that O has a better right than A? The common law, concerned to protect security of possession answered "no," unless X was acting under the authority of O. In technical language, X was not allowed to plead the *jus tertii*, the title of the third party. The difficulty with this is that it leads to the possibility of X being liable twice over, for if he was successfully sued by A for the value of the converted goods he is exposed to the risk that at some later stage O may appear and raise the same claim, against which payment of damages to A would be no defence.[15] In England the law has been modified by the complicated provisions of sections 7 and 8 of the Torts (Interference with Goods) Act 1977 and associated rules of court. Briefly, the plaintiff is required to give particulars of other persons having a claim on the goods with the object of allowing such persons to be joined in the action so that the court may give judgment according to the value of the respective interests. Where the third party cannot be found (as in the famous case of the jewel found by the chimney sweep's boy, *Armory* v.

---

[14] As in *Parker* v. *British Airways* [1982] Q.B. 1004 where there is a full discussion of the law.

[15] In fact, the risk of double liability is not so great as it looks. By far the commonest situation in which a non-owner can sue for conversion is where he is a bailee and satisfaction of the bailee's judgment extinguishes the bailor's claim against the converter, leaving the bailor to his remedy against his bailee.

Delamirie)[16] or does not wish to participate in the proceedings, the original rule will continue to apply and the plaintiff may recover the full value of the goods even though his right in them is only possessory.

Since to some extent at least mere possession remains a good title against a wrongdoer the reader may well ask how far this is to be taken. Suppose that it is plain that A stole the goods from O but in proceedings by A against X for conversion O is untraceable. Would the court go so far as to allow A to recover damages notwithstanding the obvious criminality in his obtaining the goods? Professor Prosser commented with reference to American law that "no court ever has allowed an admitted or even clearly proved thief without claim of right to recover, and it seems improbable that one ever will."[17] In *Thackwell* v. *Barclays Bank*[18] it was suggested that when the court is aware of the illegal source of the plaintiff's "title" it may refuse him relief on the ground of public policy.

Remedies for Interference with Goods

There is little to be said on trespass: the plaintiff may recover damages (nominal damages even if there is no loss) and in a suitable case no doubt an injunction could be granted to restrain trespass to goods. Conversion is rather more complicated and once again the common law has been modified by the 1977 Act. The relief now available to the plaintiff may be in one of the following forms.

1. An order for the delivery of the goods, together with consequential damages (for example, for loss of use). The reader may be surprised to find that there is no *right* to such an order and the matter is in the court's discretion. The discretion to order such specific restitution has traditionally been said to be exercisable on somewhat similar lines to the granting of specific performance of a contract, that is to say, it will not be granted in respect of an ordinary article of commerce because damages would be an adequate remedy. It would therefore be granted for unique chattels such as works of art but refused where the plaintiff would be just as well off by using his damages to buy a substitute in the open market. The fact that the market was not functioning properly because of industrial action should clearly be a circumstance justifying specific restitution.

---

[16] (1721) 1 Stra. 505.

[17] *Torts*, 5th ed., 103.

[18] [1986] 1 All E.R. 676. The case concerned conversion of a cheque and was not one where the plaintiff was in possession at the time of the alleged wrong but the reasoning could be applicable even to such a case.

2. If the case is not a suitable one for an order for specific delivery the plaintiff has a free choice between two remedies. He may either claim damages[19] (the value of the goods plus consequential loss) or an order which gives the defendant the option of returning the goods or paying damages. When the defendant has paid damages representing the full value of the plaintiff's interest in the goods (including the case where the damages have been reduced on account of contributory negligence) the plaintiff's title is extinguished.

---

[19] At common law this was the only remedy for conversion. The other remedies now existing could only be sought in an action for detinue.

CHAPTER TEN

Trespass to Land

Trespass to land is even more part of the law of property than is trespass to goods: in the great majority of cases the object of proceedings is either to stop further intrusion by injunction or, by getting a judgment which may well be for nominal damages, to settle some dispute as to title or rights over the land.[1] For the latter reason it is particularly important that the tort is actionable *per se*. Trespass also acts as a peg upon which the landowner may base his right to use reasonable force to expel unwanted intruders, though more and more systems find the need to supplement the civil law of trespass by criminal provisions which allow the landowner to call on the assistance of the police, so that we may be moving gradually towards the position, as in trespass to the person, where the criminal law is more practically significant than the tort. A farmer whose fields are taken over for a "bikers' festival" has a perfect right to throw them off and sue for damages and/or an injunction in the county court but he is likely to reply that he lacks the private army necessary to do the first and the financial resources necessary for the other course. Nevertheless, despite various statutory modifications[2] it remains generally true that trespass is not a crime.

Like trespass to goods, a claim for trespass to land may be brought only by the person in possession when the wrong was done, which means that it does not lie, for example, at the suit of a

---

[1] However, there is a separate action for recovery of land of which the claimant has been dispossessed. Land is specifically recoverable as a matter of course, whereas personal property is not.
[2] See in particular Part V of the Public Order Act 1986.

landlord but at that of his tenant.[3] This is no great hardship, because if any damage is done which is great enough to affect the value of the land when it comes back to him at the end of the lease (for example, demolishing buildings) the landlord has an immediate action which in former times would have been classified as an action on the case. Possession need not be lawful: if A, the lawful owner, is dispossessed by B, a squatter, and then C enters the land without B's permission, B may sue C for trespass. C cannot set up A's superior title (the *jus tertii*) and the law is as it was in relation to goods before the Torts (Interference with Goods) Act 1977. A cannot sue C because he was not in possession at the time, though his superior title will, of course, allow him to recover the land from B[4] and an owner out of possession may, by re-entry, be able to sue for earlier trespasses under the doctrine of "trespass by relation."

Given the characteristics ascribed to all actions of trespass there must be some voluntary "direct" action by the defendant, usually in the form of an entry on the land, but remaining there after the expiry of the landowner's permission is clearly trespass. Despite the apparent analogy with the authorities on trespass to the person it may be that even a negligent entry will suffice but the point is not likely to trouble the court since almost all entries are intentional even though they may not be intentionally *wrongful*, as where they are made under a mistaken claim of right. It is as much trespass for me to throw rocks on to your land from across the boundary as it is to walk on it but there is no trespass when I allow tree branches to grow across the fence or fail to keep my drains in order so that your land is befouled, for it is then not my *act* which leads to the offending material being there. Such things are, however, actionable as nuisance,[5] which requires proof of damage. There is not much authority on the meaning of "direct" in this context but in an American case where the defendants dumped asphalt which in due course slid into a stream which carried it into the plaintiff's fish pond that was held to be direct and hence a trespass.[6] The plaintiff's land must be invaded by something tangible, so that noise and vibrations do not amount to trespass, but smoke and gases are more problematical since they are made up of microscopic particles. It is thought unlikely that an English court would be so ready to bring them within

---

[3] But a lodger does not have possession.

[4] But B's title will become good against A after 12 years' "adverse possession."

[5] If a cricket club is liable at all for balls hit over the boundary it is in nuisance, not trespass; but the *batsman* may be liable for trespass.

[6] *Rushing* v. *Hooper McDonald Inc.* 300 So. 2d 94 (1974). But in *Southport Corpn.* v. *Esso Petroleum* [1954] 2 Q.B. 182, [1956] A.C. 218 (discharge of oil from a ship) differing opinions were expressed.

trespass as have some courts in America, where the point has been quite widely litigated. The question whether this is trespass is not without importance, for interference with the plaintiff's land is only actionable as nuisance if it is of such a degree that it is unreasonable (usually by reference to the character of the locality) whereas any trespass is actionable even if its effects are trivial.[7]

Unless land has been divided laterally (which is quite common) a landowner will be in possession not only of the surface but also of the area above and below it. Neither sector, however, extends infinitely for the purposes of the law of tresspass. Issues of subterranean trespass might arise over, for example, mining or the injection of water into strata to bring up oil or gas but in England statutory authority is always sought for such activity and this limits the likelihood of any action coming before the courts.[8] Trespass to airspace by aircraft flights was fully considered in *Bernstein* v. *Skyviews*,[9] where the court concluded that the landowner's rights extended only to the height reasonably necessary for the enjoyment of the land so that an overflight at some hundreds of feet was not trespass even though it was made for the purpose of photographing the land. There is also statutory authority for flights at a reasonable height. Conflicts between landowners and aircraft operators may also arise in the reverse way, as when the defendant erects high structures in the vicinity of an area where aircraft take off or land. In principle, obstruction of aircraft might be a public nuisance but there are no rights of way in the air and protection of the aircraft operators' interests is more likely to come via planning controls on building and legislation governing the operation of airports. Airspace trespass is a not infrequent problem in connection with construction work which requires cranes to swing over adjoining property. This is trespass no matter how high the crane and no matter how safely operated it may be and, coupled with the proposition that a landowner is entitled to an injunction against trespass even if it is causing him no damage,[10] may put him in a strong position to demand a large "rental payment" from the other party for the privilege of the use of his airspace.

There are many justifications for entry on the land of another and most of them really belong to the study of other branches of the law, such as real property. Examples are a licence from the landowner, the exercise of a private right of way for the benefit of

---

[7] But as to whether an injunction may be obtained, see p. 220, *post*.
[8] For an interesting American case about a cave system see *Edwards* v. *Sims* 24 S.W. 2d 619 (1930).
[9] [1978] Q.B. 479.
[10] On this, see further, p. 220.

those who live on adjoining land or of a public right of way. Technically, every public right of way is a "highway" though motor roads will usually be vested in a highway authority rather than in the person whose land they cross. The highway is for passage, so that "on a highway I may stand still for a reasonably short time, but I must not put my bed upon the highway and permanently occupy a portion of it. I may stoop to tie up my shoelace, but I may not occupy a pitch and invite people to come upon it and have their hair cut. I may let my van stand still long enough to deliver and load goods, but I must not turn my van into a permanent stall."[11] Usually, misuse of the highway will be controlled by the police with reference to various offences of obstruction but occasionally the civil law of trespass may be relevant, as it was in *Hickman* v. *Maisey*[12] where a racing tout used the highway traversing the plaintiff's land to spy upon his racehorse trials. The student may be surprised to find that even the beach has an owner (below high water mark it is the Crown) and that the public have no right of access to it except for fishing and "navigation"—a good example of legal theory being divorced from practice.

[11] *Iveagh* v. *Martin* [1961] 1 Q.B. 232.
[12] [1900] 1 Q.B. 752.

CHAPTER ELEVEN

Defences to Intentional Torts to Person and Property

As we have noted in the discussion of trespass to the person, a "defence" in the proper sense is something which must be raised and proved by the defendant if the plaintiff makes out the basic elements of the tort. "I didn't hit him" is not a defence in this sense but simply a denial of the plaintiff's case and it is up to the plaintiff to prove that the defendant *did* strike him. If, however, the defendant says, "Yes, I did strike him, but I did it in a reasonable effort to stop him assaulting me," then he is raising a defence and he must (a) plead it and (b) establish it by evidence. A point may move in time from one side to the other. In the 17th century an assertion that the defendant in trespass acted without intention or negligence when he struck the plaintiff was a defence; since *Fowler* v. *Lanning* the courts in England say that the plaintiff must establish the requisite "mental element."

We have already mentioned one of the most important defences to trespass to the person, lawful authority in the form of powers of arrest. What follows is an account of other defences which are particularly prominent in the context of intentional torts to person and property, though it is by no means a complete list of defences.

Consent

There is no doubt that consent renders many things lawful which would be unlawful if done without it—a kiss, borrowing someone's lawnmower, walking on another's land, all would be tortious without the element of consent. Though the matter is not beyond doubt, we are probably in strict law incorrect in including it in this chapter for the balance of English authority is that it is not a defence but something the absence of which must be established as part of the plaintiff's case. Lord Denman in *Christopherson* v. *Bare*[1] said that consent should be shown under the "general denial" in the defendant's pleading for "to say that the defendant assaulted the plaintiff by his permission" is a manifest contradiction in terms. Now that we are less concerned with the niceties of pleading we might respond that the basic element of the tort is that the defendant made an intentional bodily contact with the plaintiff and to say that this was done with consent is not self-contradictory. The courts in Canada seem to have come round to the view that consent is a defence and even if this is not the law in England it is certainly true that whatever the formal burden of pleading and proof the *defendant* is likely in most cases to have to adduce evidence to raise the issue. On balance, it is thought that this is the best place for an account of consent.

A defendant is entitled to rely on the outward appearance of consent even though the plaintiff harbours secret reservations, for life would be impossible on any other basis. The justification for medical treatment of unconscious persons has been explained on the basis that consent is "implied" but it has also been said that it is not tortious simply because it lacks the element of "hostility" necessary for a trespass, even though the same act against a conscious but non-consenting person would clearly be wrongful. Where an adult is mentally incapable of giving a consent there is no power in anyone else to give it on his behalf but necessary medical treatment of such a person, though tortious, has been declared lawful, a paradoxical situation.[2] Parental consent to treatment is effective in the case of young children, but by section 8 of the Family Law Reform Act 1969 the consent of a minor who has reached 16 is fully effective and after that age the parent certainly could not override the minor's wishes by purporting to consent on his behalf. The statute is not, however, the end of the story for it provides only a clear line of an age above which the minor's consent will *always* be effective and a consent given by a person below the age of 16 may still be effective at common law if he has sufficient intelligence and understanding to have a full grasp of what is proposed and of its implications.[3] Such matters are much more likely to arise in criminal prosecutions or wardship proceedings than in tort actions. What has spawned a

---

[1] (1848) 11 Q.B. 473.
[2] *T.* v. *T.* [1988] 2 W.L.R. 189.
[3] *Gillick* v. *West Norfolk A.H.A.* [1986] A.C. 112.

plethora of tort cases is the situation where the plaintiff gives his consent to a particular medical procedure and the doctor, acting in good faith for what he conceives to be the patient's benefit, performs some further procedure. The law is simple, though the doctor may say that in some respects it does not give him an easy guide to apply. The fundamental proposition is that the patient of full age and understanding is master of his own body and it is he and he alone who decides what is to be done with it, so that his refusal of consent is binding even if there is a grave emergency in which most people would believe that his conduct was eccentric or foolish.[4] It is true that in *Leigh* v. *Gladstone*[5] an action by an imprisoned suffragette based on forcible feeding was dismissed but at that time suicide was a crime and it is thought that the decision became wholly obsolete when the crime was abolished or (less satisfactorily) that it turned upon the view that a prisoner was to be equated with a child of tender years.[6] If we were to seek to build on it some doctrine of medical necessity which could override the plaintiff's clear wishes we would have to accept that, for example, a gravely ill person could lawfully be restrained from leaving hospital and no one has suggested that that is the law. It will, however, be a fairly unusual case in which the patient has forbidden a particular course of treatment. More likely he will have given his consent to operation A and during the performance of that the surgeon discovers condition B, which also requires treatment. There are a number of Canadian cases on this and the upshot of them seems to be a sensible rule that the further treatment is justifiable if (a) the patient is not known positively to object to it, (b) the treatment is urgently necessary and (c) it would be unreasonable to bring the patient round to seek further consent—it is not enough that it is merely convenient to carry out the procedure without further ado. The effect of the general consent forms which purport to give consent to any such procedures as the surgeon may deem necessary has not been considered in England. It is unlikely that they are wholly ineffective but the courts might approach them with caution.

Another variation on the theme of consent to medical procedures is the problem of "informed" consent. The English courts have steadfastly maintained that a consent is valid if it is based on an understanding of the nature of what is being done and it is *not* ineffective because of a failure to explain the risks inherent in the procedure: doctors who are paternalistic or even

---

[4] See *Mulloy* v. *Hop Sang* [1935] 1 W.W.R. 714.
[5] (1909) 26 T.L.R. 139.
[6] Some American jurisdictions have legislated for the compulsory medication of pregnant women.

high-handed about what their patients should know are not to be put into the same legal category as muggers. However, as part of his duty of care to the patient the doctor owes him a duty to explain any major risks attached to the procedure and if he fails in this duty and the patient can establish that he would not have consented with full knowledge then there may be liability for resulting harm even if the procedure has been carried out with all due care and skill. This principle is universal to common law jurisdictions but its application varies widely according to how the content of the duty is prescribed by the courts. The English courts have rejected a test oriented towards the expectations of the patient and use one which measures the adequacy of disclosure by reference to the normal custom of the profession. Although the judges reserve the ultimate right, in all cases of negligence, to brand the whole profession as wrong it will be a very unusual case in which they do so. If the patient asks specific questions he is entitled to truthful answers (though here, too, there remains some scope for the doctor's judgment of what the patient will understand) but even breach of this duty, it seems, is actionable as negligence or fraud rather than trespass. What English authority there is is to the effect that a consent obtained by fraudulent misrepresentation is still consent if the plaintiff understands the *nature* of what is being done and this must be equally so in a case of non-disclosure. Hence, if D has sexual intercourse with P knowing that he (D) is HIV-positive that is not battery. This may be rather startling, but its importance is reduced by the fact that if an infection is transmitted or other damage caused there is liability for negligence or for the intentional infliction of harm.

Mistake

Mistake in the civil law is not so significant as in the equivalent areas of crime, where it often negatives the necessary mental element. Because we conclude that the defendant should be spared the stigma of criminality it does not follow that we should also throw the risk of his mistake upon the plaintiff in a civil suit. For example, an honest belief by the defendant that he was lawfully entitled to seize the plaintiff's property for non-payment of a debt would protect him from a charge of theft but not from a claim of conversion. Nor even does a mistaken belief in ownership suffice: if A walks on B's land believing it to be A's, that is trespass. Mistake may, however, enable the defendant to shelter under a privilege which he believes, erroneously, to exist on the facts. Thus a reasonable but mistaken belief that the plaintiff has committed an arrestable offence will justify a police arrest[7] and a person may be able to rely on self-defence on a similar basis.

Necessity

Where necessity arises from another's wrongdoing that is the law of self-defence, which is clear enough, though sometimes hard to apply: anyone is privileged to use such force as is reasonable in the circumstances to defend himself, his property or others. But where P suffers from action taken by D in response to a situation for which P is not to blame the law, far from accepting the maxim "necessity knows no bounds," draws the bounds very tightly indeed. Since it is clear law that to kill another under pressure of hunger or because one's own life is threatened by a third party (duress) is the crime of murder, we may safely say that it is also the tort of battery; and in *Southwark London Borough* v. *Williams*[8] the Court of Appeal rejected an argument that necessity could be a defence to trespass by homeless persons in empty public housing, for "if homelessness were once admitted as a defence... no one's house would be safe." This may be criticised on the basis that many other defences are allowed in law even though they may be open to abuse but it is probably true that the boundaries of necessity would be peculiarly difficult to draw. Nonetheless, the defence of private necessity has been recognised in some cases. A lower landowner is not required to receive water draining unchannelled through his neighbour's land and may erect barriers to keep it out even though it causes the higher land to flood; and in *Greyvenstein* v. *Hattingh*[9] (a South African appeal) the defendant was allowed to divert locusts from his own land to that of the plaintiff. It is hard to believe that in the latter case the defendant would have been liable if the locusts had already settled for a few moments and he had driven them *out* of his land rather than diverted them, but in *Whalley* v. *Lancs. & Yorks. Ry.*[10] the defendants were liable when they pierced their embankment so as to release flood water which had accumulated on their land. No English case of private necessity appears to have recognised that the defendant who acts under its compulsion may have to compensate the plaintiff even though he

---

[7] The law in this area is complex. A private citizen can justify an arrest of the wrong person but not an arrest where no offence has been committed by anyone: a reasonable mistake is relevant to the first issue but not to the second.

[8] [1971] Ch. 734.

[9] [1911] A.C. 355.

[10] (1884) 13 Q.B.D. 131.

has committed no legal wrong[11] but in the famous American case of *Vincent* v. *Lake Erie Transportation Co.*[12] the court held that where the defendants lashed their vessel to the plaintiff's wharf so as to prevent her being driven out into a storm they were obliged to pay for the damage to the wharf even though they had not committed trespass and the plaintiff could not lawfully have cast them adrift. Such a rule will presumably lead to the sacrifice of the less valuable of the two items of property. It could be argued that this approach should also be taken where D takes P's property to save X's life for why should P bear the financial burden of saving one he was under no legal duty to rescue? However, this would create a risk that rescuers might hesitate to take property[13] even in order to save life and if an English court were to accept the *Lake Erie* solution it is unlikely it would be extended to this situation.

Action taken to save life may be regarded as an example of "public necessity," the paradigm example of which is destruction of property by the authorities to prevent the spread of fire.[14] In *Burmah Oil Co.* v. *Lord Advocate*[15] the House of Lords held that the Crown, acting lawfully under the Royal Prerogative in destroying the plaintiffs' oilfields during the retreat from Burma in 1942, was nonetheless obliged to pay compensation. However, it does not follow that a doctrine which applies to the Crown applies to a private individual and in any event action taken to deny the enemy resources ("economic warfare") is pretty far removed from emergency action taken to avert imminent peril, which is much more likely to be the action of an individual. In fact such emergency action might be regarded as akin to what was described in *Burmah Oil* as "battle damage," in respect of which it was accepted that no compensation was payable.

What if the defendant is mistaken as to the necessity for action? It seems from *Cope* v. *Sharpe*,[16] which concerned trespass to land to protect game, that the danger must actually exist; but the defendant is justified in doing what appears reasonably

---

[11] But the maritime law of general average contribution, which is designed to spread loss among cargo owners where the property of one is sacrificed to save the ship, may be regarded as an example of such a principle.

[12] 124 N.W. 221 (1910).

[13] If X were at fault, no doubt he could be made to indemnify D: p. 77, *ante*.

[14] As in *Scirocco* v. *Geary* 3 Cal. 69 (1853) arising from the San Francisco fire of 1849. Since the plaintiffs' house would have been consumed by the blaze its value for the purpose of damages would have been small, but the substance of their complaint seems to have been that they were prevented from recovering the contents.

[15] [1965] A.C. 75.

[16] [1912] 1 K.B. 496.

necessary and he is not liable because the danger is in fact averted by other means.

Contributory Negligence and Illegality

We have seen that contributory negligence was at common law a complete defence to the tort of negligence and now, under the Law Reform (Contributory Negligence) Act 1945 goes to reduce damages. Neither the common law defence nor the Act has any application to conversion, a policy reflected in the parallel rule that the owner of converted goods is not estopped from asserting his title against an innocent party merely because his carelessness has facilitated a rogue's making off with them. It also seems most unlikely that contributory negligence would have been regarded at common law as a defence to an intentional trespass to the person and it is widely thought that legislation like the 1945 Act applies only in those situations where the full defence would have applied at common law. This is the predominant view in Australia, but in England the Court of Appeal has contemplated the application of the 1945 Act as a possibility.[17] If the concept of contributory negligence is at all applicable to intentional trespass to the person it is likely to be in the form of provocation and it is universally agreed that such conduct can go to reduce the exemplary or aggravated damages element in the award. Since the purpose of the former is to punish the defendant and of the latter to salve the injury to the plaintiff's feelings arising from the outrageousness of the defendant's behaviour it would be difficult to take any other course.

Illegality is an obscure area of torts. It is certainly not the law that the plaintiff is barred from suing because he was engaged in criminal conduct when the tort was committed against him: no one suggests that the plaintiff's exceeding the speed limit necessarily provides a complete defence in a road accident case. But to exclude illegality altogether would bring the law into disrepute. For example, it was surely right to reject the claim under the Fatal Accidents Act of the dependants of a deceased burglar for loss of support caused by his wrongful death, not because they were implicated in his illegal conduct but because they were in effect asking for compensation for having been deprived of the support of the proceeds of crime[18]; and it was similarly right to deny the existence of any duty of care between two robbers escaping in a get-away car from the scene of the

---

[17] *Barnes* v. *Nayer, The Times*, December 19, 1986.
[18] *Burns* v. *Edman* [1970] 2 Q.B. 541.

crime.[19] In both cases the plaintiff was required to reveal circumstances of criminality serious enough to offend the court's conscience. Beyond this point, however, the cases become hard to reconcile. In *Singh* v. *Ali*[20] the plaintiff was allowed to sue for what is now conversion in respect of a lorry which had previously been transferred to him by the defendant under an illegal contract, on the basis that the plaintiff's property rights would be protected even though they had an illegal source.[21] Yet in *Thackwell* v. *Barclay's Bank*[22] the plaintiff's action for conversion of his cheque by dealing with it on the basis of a forged endorsement was dismissed when the evidence showed that the cheque was the proceeds of a fraudulent refinancing agreement of which he was aware. Indeed, the Court of Appeal in *Saunders* v. *Edwards*[23] (a case where the plaintiff successfully claimed damages for fraud in respect of a contract tainted by illegality) spoke of a "pragmatic approach . . . seeking where possible to see that genuine wrongs are righted so long as the court does not thereby promote or countenance a nefarious object or bargain which it is bound to condemn." This may not be very satisfying, but it may be the best that a practical system of law can do. There is no doubt that any rigid classification of illegality by reference solely to the seriousness of the offence involved is doomed to failure.

---

[19] *Ashton* v. *Turner* [1981] Q.B. 137.
[20] [1960] A.C. 160.
[21] Compare the common law principle that a defendant in conversion cannot raise the *jus tertii*: p. 151, *ante*.
[22] [1986] 1 All E.R. 676.
[23] [1987] 1 W.L.R. 1116.

CHAPTER TWELVE

Defamation

The law of defamation is very entertaining (though not for those whose litigation goes to make it, since they risk utter financial ruin) and very complex. It is also a troublesome area for those who maintain that the law of torts is all about compensation. Certainly the law is in form concerned with loss of reputation rather than insult (as witness the strict requirement that the defamatory statement must be made to third parties) and reputation may be regarded as a sort of asset. Further, there are certainly instances where plaintiffs have pleaded and proved financial loss as a result of a false accusation but in the majority of cases it is not necessary for the plaintiff to prove any loss at all, for it is presumed. In *Youssoupoff* v. *M.G.M.*[1] the plaintiff, an emigre Russian princess, recovered £25,000 damages for a film which implied that she had been raped by Rasputin. No doubt her social life was considerably affected but it is a strange system of "compensation" which gives her a sum at least a hundred times the average annual wage. In *Cassell & Co.* v. *Broome*[2] a retired naval officer recovered some £200,000 (in the money of 1987) for an accusation of cowardice which none of his acquaintances believed; and a millionaire novelist recovered £500,000 in 1987 for a newspaper's claim that he had consorted with a prostitute.[3] It is not simply that we are dealing with losses which are even less easily quantifiable in money than the lives and arms and legs of personal injury litigation (though that certainly plays a part) for it

---

[1] (1934) 50 T.L.R. 581.
[2] [1972] A.C. 1027.
[3] The case is that of Jeffrey Archer against "The Star" newspaper.

must be recognised that the English law of defamation has strong elements of what Roman law knew as "delict," that is, the notion of a penalty imposed upon the wrongdoer. In its form the common law differs very markedly from some other modern legal systems which make defamation primarily a criminal matter with small or even token monetary compensation, but it is possible to argue that what the common law has in fact done is to dress up in civil clothing what is in truth a penal process, with the very large "fine" going to the complainant rather than to the state. In so far as the law allows exemplary or punitive damages (and defamation is one of the few areas where those still flourish in England) this is frankly recognised but even where the damages are technically compensatory the fact that they are "at large" as the technical phrase puts it means that an appellate court cannot effectively moderate even a substantial (but not extravagant) award, which may in fact be penal upon the defendant. Further, compensatory damages may be "aggravated" on account of the defendant's malice and bad behaviour. In theory this does no violence to the principle of compensation because the plaintiff's loss is increased by the defendant's conduct, but in truth this is "satisfaction" rather than compensation, it is the law's substitute for the duel. The form of defamation known as libel is also a crime but prosecutions are these days very rare and in former times it was largely used to muzzle criticism of public figures. The Law Commission proposed in 1985 that there should be a new, statutory crime to punish serious and deliberate "character assassination" but nothing has yet been done to implement this. However, behind this generous protection of reputation there is another side to the story, for defamation litigation is a risky business not lightly to be undertaken. There is no legal aid for plaintiff or defendant and costs are said to be substantially increased by the fact that a jury trial (which is the norm for defamation, though it has disappeared in England for most tort litigation) proceeds at a slower pace than trial by judge alone. Nor is trial by jury a guarantee of a large award, for though it is probably true that juries generally award much larger sums than would be awarded by judges sitting alone they are also perhaps more likely to take a "broad" view of the overall justice of the case (they are not required to give reasons) and occasionally produce a low or derisory award.

While one can still speak of a "common law" of defamation, this branch of torts has undergone more detailed modification than most in the various jurisdictions. American law has been revolutionised by the impact of the Constitution and this is briefly outlined at the appropriate point in this chapter. Some Australian states have had a codified law of defamation for very many years and there is the prospect of a uniform defamation law for that country though this had not been implemented at the time of writing.

What is defamatory?

Not every untrue statement is defamatory. If I said that you had gone shopping yesterday that might be untrue but it would not, in the absence of some other facts, reflect on your reputation, the protection of which is the basis of the tort. The final arbiter of whether an imputation is defamatory is the jury but the judge has power to withdraw it from the jury if it is incapable in law of being defamatory. At the first stage, therefore, the question of whether a statement is defamatory is a matter of law. There is no statutory definition and the courts have (perhaps wisely) declined to tie themselves down with too much precision. The most influential judicial statement is probably that of Lord Atkin in *Sim* v. *Stretch*[4] where he asked, "would the words tend to lower the plaintiff in the estimation of right-thinking members of society generally?" A statement is most commonly defamatory because it imputes something disgraceful but reputation may suffer in other ways. For example, professional incompetence is the basis of a good many defamation claims (an amusing example is the charge that an Australian rugby player was too fat to play first grade rugby)[5] and while such accusations may well make people avoid the plaintiff, to his financial loss, they hardly import disgrace. Poverty is a Christian virtue, but an American court left to the jury as potentially defamatory an accusation that the plaintiffs were so poor that their child would have to go to a pauper's grave.[6] It is doubtful if even the *Sim* v. *Stretch* formula will reach this case (or the allegation of rape in *Youssoupoff* v. *M.G.M.*) and some residual category is necessary which will cover the situation where the natural effect of the words will make people avoid the plaintiff, even from embarrassment, though nothing dishonourable is imputed.

The appeal to "right thinking" persons in the *Sim* v. *Stretch* formula may mean that an accusation cannot be defamatory if what is alleged would be regarded by ordinary people with indifference even though it may cause the plaintiff to suffer serious loss of reputation with the particular group with which he is associated. In setting this standard, English law may assume a

---

[4] [1936] 2 All E.R. 1237, 1240.
[5] *Boyd* v. *Mirror Newspapers* [1980] 2 N.S.W.L.R. 449.
[6] *Katapodis* v. *Brooklyn Spectator* 38 N.E. 2d 112 (1941).

homogeneity of opinion greater than actually exists but the problem has not been too troublesome in practice because an accusation that the plaintiff has done something of which "his" group disapproves may carry an implied imputation of disloyalty or hypocrisy of which all, even non-members, would disapprove. So, it would no doubt be defamatory of a Kosher butcher to put him on a list of bacon retailers or of a temperance campaigner to picture him as endorsing a brand of whisky. The plaintiff will face more difficulty when the allegation is that he has informed the authorities about a crime, even though one suspects that most people would think ill of him if the offence were trivial.[7] This is understandable because, whatever the realities of the situation, the law can hardly be seen to condone the view that it is wrong to put it in motion. Of course, if the plaintiff can show that from the circumstances in which the accusation was made there is in fact an implied comment that he thereby behaved dishonourably he may succeed on that.

Practitioners' works on defamation sometimes include long lists of particular statements which have or have not been held to be capable of a defamatory meaning, together with the salutary warning that meanings and attitudes may vary from one society to another and from time to time. For example, a case from the United States in the 1950's concerning a charge of communism would be of limited persuasive value in England today and popular literature will demonstrate that a certain degree of anti-semitism or colour prejudice was perfectly respectable in "polite" society half a century ago. One of the best known defamation cases is *Tolley* v. *Fry & Sons*[8] where the defendants' advertisement was held to be defamatory in that it implied that the plaintiff, a well-known amateur golfer, had agreed to lend his name and likeness for reward to the advertising campaign, something which at the time would have led to his being drummed out of any respectable club. The *principle* of the case is as valid now as it ever was, but it would be unsafe to assume that it could be applied without qualification in modern conditions to other sports, where financial reward and amateurism are not necessarily wholly incompatible. *Tolley* v. *Fry* also demonstrates that a defamatory meaning need not be direct but may be implied or allusive, what the layman rather inaccurately calls an innuendo. Technically speaking, an innuendo is that part of his statement of claim in which the plaintiff sets out facts which are not in the words published and are not part of their ordinary

---

[7] See *Byrne* v. *Deane* [1937] 1 K.B. 818 (plaintiff falsely alleged to have reported illegal gambling at golf club).

[8] [1931] A.C. 333.

meaning[9] but which were known to the reader and which give the allegation its defamatory sting—for example, to say that "X is regularly seen coming out of No.—Lyddon Terrace" is wholly unexceptionable unless the reader knows that that address is a brothel. But to say of a businessman that he will win no prizes for business ethics is not an innuendo in this sense at all: while it is *capable* of being construed as harmless, for prizes fall to few, its obvious and irresistible real meaning is that the plaintiff is a crook. In modern practice the plaintiff is required to give particulars of what he alleges the words mean wherever the defamatory meaning is not explicit, so this technical distinction between an innuendo and an allusive statement is no longer of such importance.

Libel and Slander

So far we have spoken of defamation, but English law continues to attach importance to the form which the defamation takes and we have two torts, libel and slander. Broadly speaking, libel is that which is in written or other "permanent" form (for example, a statue), slander is spoken or otherwise transient (for example, a gesture). This is something of a rationalisation from dicta and generations of law students have been regaled with hypotheticals about talking parrots, flag signals at sea and so on.[10] In England much potential difficulty has been avoided by statutory provisions which classify radio and television broadcasting and the theatre as libel but the fundamentally unsatisfactory state of the law is demonstrated by the fact that it is not easy to give a wholly confident answer to the simple question whether reading aloud a defamatory letter is libel or slander. Though there is authority that it is the first, there is much to be said for the second. When the legislature acted to classify broadcasting as libel it did not do so on the basis of whether on the traditional test it was "closer" to spoken or written words. Fundamentally, the decision was one of policy as to whether we applied the more rigorous libel liability to the activity or gave it some degree of protection by imposing on the plaintiff the extra requirements of a slander suit. The English legislature was no doubt influenced by the wide dissemination of broadcasting and its great potential for harming reputation; in some American jurisdictions the media have constituted a more powerful pressure group and have had

---

[9] Strictly, the technical concept of innuendo extends to foreign words or technical and slang terms which are not known to people generally.

[10] Among the more bizarre examples in the decided cases are erecting a gallows before the plaintiff's door and putting up a lantern so as to indicate a brothel.

broadcasting legislatively classified as slander. Of the various options the simplest is to abolish the separate category of slander and to apply the present libel law to all defamations, and the risk of an increase in petty actions arising out of spoken words seems more theoretical than real.

Libel is more favourable to the plaintiff because it is actionable *per se* or, in plain English, the plaintiff is entitled to put a libel before a jury and seek an award, perhaps a very large award, of general damages without any proof of material loss whatever. If his claim is for slander he will normally fail altogether, no matter how wounding the allegation, unless he can show "special damage," which means some loss of a material or financial nature. To show that you have lost your job, even temporarily, will do but not to show that your former friends will no longer speak to you, even if the effect of this is far worse. To this rule there are four exceptions, where slander is actionable *per se*, namely, imputation of unchastity to a female (this is statutory in origin), imputation of a "loathsome" disease (an exception which may gain new importance with the advent of AIDS), imputation of a crime punishable by imprisonment and an imputation reflecting on the plaintiff in his trade or calling. The last two exceptions cover much ground and go far to minimising the problems of the libel/slander distinction in practice but it may be noted that of the three famous cases referred to at the beginning of this chapter in which very large damages were awarded one might well have failed altogether had the wrong been slander and another would have raised at least some difficulty on the point.

Publication

We have already seen that a defamatory statement is only actionable if it is conveyed to the attention of a third party. Face to face insult without witnesses is not defamation in English law, though such conduct might be some other tort if done with intent to cause harm (for example a heart attack).[11] This element of the tort has been saddled with the unfortunate name of "publication," but nothing like a newspaper or a book is necessary: if the defamer speaks or writes to just one person that is all that is required, provided that person understands the words to refer to the plaintiff.[12] Of course the majority of actions are brought in respect of widespread media publications and in that situation everyone is a "publisher" and therefore liable who takes an active part in the production and dissemination of the

---

[11] See p. 141, *ante*.
[12] It is *not* necessary that he should believe them to be true.

material—author, newspaper proprietor, journalist, compositor, wholesale distributor and even news vendor.[13] Nor is this wide-ranging liability wholly theoretical for printers and distributors have sometimes been sued when the originator of the material was not worth powder and shot and the threat of action against a distributor (who may not consider it worthwhile strenuously to fight a case involving only one among his many wares) can be an effective means of denying the originator the means for wide dissemination of his allegations. However, an unqualified liability in a distributor for everything he sold would be intolerable and the law allows him a defence ("innocent dissemination") if he can show that he neither knew nor ought to have known that the article contained defamatory material. This does not extend to the printer, who is regarded, like the author, as an originator and whose position is unenviable, as was recognised by a committee which examined the English law of defamation in 1975.[14] That a radio or T.V. station is an originator for this purpose and hence responsible for an unscripted defamatory remark by a participant in a live programme does not seem to have been doubted here, though a few American cases have treated them as mere distributors. The Post Office is by statute exempt from any liability for defamation in respect of the mail it delivers, so there is not much point in pursuing the question of whether it is a mere distributor, but the statute governing telecommunications only exempts the undertaker from liability for deficiencies in the service. A New York court categorically stated that the telephone service had no more published a defamatory call which it carried than, say, the owner of a leased typewriter published when the machine was used by the lessee to type a libel[15]; but a different attitude would no doubt be taken if defamatory matter were incorporated in one of the many pre-recorded services available on the telephone.

Publication is normally a deliberate act but there may be liability for an accidental publication where there is a failure to take reasonable care, as where a defamatory document is left lying around for anyone to see or where a letter is sent to the victim of the defamation in circumstances where the sender knows that it is likely to be opened by others, for example, by a clerk acting in the ordinary course of business. Similarly, an initial publisher may be liable for a republication by another

---

[13] Technically, each successive step involves a separate publication, and each copy of the offending piece is a separate publication.
[14] The Faulks Committee (Cmnd. 5909).
[15] *Anderson* v. *New York Telephone Co.* 320 N.E. 2d 647 (1974).

where he authorises it or foresees it as a likely consequence of his actions, for example when answering press questions.

Reference to the Plaintiff

Words are only defamatory of the plaintiff if they are understood by a reasonable person to refer to him. This is the key to the problem of "group defamation." It is often said that you cannot defame a group or class of persons. This is literally true in the sense that the group cannot sue because it has no legal personality and practically true because it is usually the case that no member of the group can sue. The latter point, however, is to be explained not by reference to any special rule but by the fact that claims like "all lawyers are thieves" are vulgar generalisations from which no reasonable person would draw the inference that any individual member of the profession was being aimed at. If, on the other hand, the defendant makes it plain that he *does* level the charge against every member of the group then any member can sue. In practice, the smaller the group the more likely the plaintiff is to make out such a case. Racial or religious slurs get little or no redress from the law of defamation though they may be dealt with by other branches of the law.[16]

A recurring situation is that where D publishes material which is in fact defamatory of P but D had no intention of referring to P, for example, because he intended the subject of the material to be a fictitious character or because he intended to refer to X and did not know of circumstances from which the reader might deduce that P was intended.[17] Prima facie the writer is liable, for as it was put in an American case, "the question is not who is aimed at, but who was hit," and liability is strict. This is a quite remarkable level of protection for reputation but it does not mean that if I write a novel in which the villain is called John Smith (or even Wimperis) all the John Smiths (or Wimperises) in the world can sue me, for mere coincidence of name is not enough for the reader reasonably to draw the conclusion that the statement refers to the plaintiff.[18] However, the law reports contain enough instances of greater concatenations of coincidences to show that the rule operates hardly and is not a reasonable balance between protection of reputation and freedom to communicate. In

---

[16] Usually the criminal law. But in Manitoba a race or religious "libel" entitles an individual member of the group to seek an injunction against repetition.

[17] The two situations are exemplified by *Hulton* v. *Jones* [1910] A.C. 20 and *Newstead* v. *London Express* [1940] 1 K.B. 377.

[18] It must be debatable whether this issue should ever have been left to the jury in the great case of *Hulton* v. *Jones*, though there *was* rather more than coincidence of name.

England the law has been substantially altered by section 4 of the Defamation Act 1952, though the strict liability remains where the conditions of that section are not complied with. The section applies where the publisher did not intend to refer to the plaintiff *or* where, though he did intend to refer to the plaintiff, the words were not defamatory on the face of them and the publisher did not know of circumstances which made them defamatory (the example often given is the newspaper story that Mrs. X has given birth to twins, the newspaper being unaware that Mrs. X has only been married a month). The section is complicated and probably excessively cumbersome in practice but essentially it requires that the publisher make an offer of amends (for example, costs and an apology) as soon as practicable. If this is not accepted it provides a defence to the action if the publisher shows that he has exercised all reasonable care in relation to the publication, though the lack of reported cases on the defence does not make it easy to predict what will amount to reasonable care in a given situation.

The Defamation Act 1952 has no application to another type of "innocent" defendant, he who makes a statement which is defamatory on its face but which he sincerely—even reasonably—believes to be true. His protection, if any, is to be found in the law of privilege, which is outlined in the next section. However, it is always open to any defendant to publish an apology (indeed, it is common and perhaps even advisable for the plaintiff to demand one before commencing action as a means of showing he is concerned with his reputation and is not just "in it for the money") which, although it will not provide a defence, may mitigate the damages awarded. Further, if the defendant pays money into court he may exert tactical pressure on the plaintiff to settle because of the rule that if the damages eventually awarded do not exceed the amount of the payment in, the plaintiff loses on costs incurred from the time of the payment.

Defences

The primary defence to defamation is truth. The English common law has committed itself firmly to the stance that what is to be protected is not the reputation the plaintiff enjoys but that to which he is entitled. Unfortunately, the technical name for the defence is "justification," which may give the wholly incorrect impression that publication of the truth is only legally defensible if it serves some moral or social purpose. Curiously, this *is* the law with regard to the crime of libel (though the crime is not of much practical importance) but in tort the defendant is generally free to

publish the truth even for purely malicious motives,[19] provided
he takes care to avoid the implication that past misdeeds affect
the plaintiff's present character, in which case he would have to
prove the truth of the imputation. This state of affairs is widely
thought to be undesirable and produces calls for the grant of a
right of action for invasion of privacy but the practical task of
balancing a right of privacy with the demands of a free press
raises formidable problems of defining the limits of legitimate
public interest in what the subjects of that interest may regard as
their private affairs. Few would doubt that the press should be
able to publish the fact that a general is having an affair with a
Soviet spy, but what of the politician whose peccadilloes carry no
security risk, nor interfere with his work in government; or the
politician who was thrown out of law school 30 years ago for
cheating in his examinations? Nor could one sensibly confine
invasion of privacy to revelations of embarrassing past events,
which would be the effect of simply injecting a "public benefit"
requirement into the defence of justification (though this is the
law in some Australian jurisdictions). We cannot deny the press
the right to report the details of the Hungerford massacre even
though it may cause distress to the relatives of the victims, but
how far do we allow disclosure of the details of the lives of the
relatives themselves or intensive visits and telephone calls by
journalists? Phrases like "public figure" only conceal the
unpleasant fact that some matters are of strong public interest
even though they do not involve iniquity and the subject of the
interest has not sought public attention. Of course it would be a
gross exaggeration to say that the legal system could not cope
with the introduction of a right of privacy (it is widely recognized
in civil law systems) but there is some reason for the suspicion
that a cure based upon an action for damages might be worse
than the disease and that the undoubted, regular and flagrant
lapses of parts of the media from "decent" standards are best
dealt with by the less draconian methods of complaint to the
Press Council and Broadcasting Complaints Commission, both of
which have unwarranted invasions of privacy within their terms
of reference.[20] There is certainly a highly developed law of
privacy in the United States but it has to some extent been
curtailed in the light of the First Amendment to the Constitution,
which is discussed below in relation to defamation. A case

---

[19] "Generally," because the Rehabilitation of Offenders Act 1974 derogates from
this principle with regard to "spent" convictions. Further, a combination by
two or more persons maliciously to publish the truth may fall within the tort of
conspiracy: (see p. 198, *post*).
[20] For the role of these bodies in relation to defamatory statements see p. 183, *post*.

constantly cited by those who support the introduction of an actionable right of privacy is *Melvin* v. *Reid*,[21] which involved revelations of the very respectable plaintiff's lurid past, including her trial for murder, but it is ironic that the case is probably inconsistent with a later Supreme Court decision denying any claim to privacy in respect of matters of public record.

To return to the law as it is, a defamatory statement is presumed to be untrue so that although it is for the plaintiff to show that the words have a defamatory meaning it is for the defendant to establish that they are true, not on the criminal standard of "beyond reasonable doubt" but on the civil standard of balance of probabilities, qualified by the principle that as the charge increases in gravity so must the cogency of the evidence to prove it. Some of the old cases are comical in their insistence on justification being established in every detail, but the modern principle is that the defendant has only to justify the "sting" of the imputation. If I write that X took £100 from me on Monday and spent it on heroin obtained in Bradford, I would succeed in my defence by showing that £99 was taken and the heroin obtained in Halifax. I might well, however, fail as to the second charge if I could show only that the drug was cannabis because people probably consider that a less serious matter. There is also a rather obscure provision in section 5 of the Defamation Act 1952 to the effect that where there are two or more distinct charges "a defence of justification shall not fail by reason only that the truth of any charge is not proved if the words not proved to be true do not materially injure the plaintiff's reputation having regard to the truth of the remaining charges." This is wider than the common law in that it would allow the jury to dismiss the plaintiff's claim altogether even though the defendant had wholly failed to justify some minor accusations (for example if in our example above there was added an allegation of exceeding the speed limit on the way to Bradford)[22] but it is not clear how far and by reference to what principles the judge can direct the jury that the unproven charge does not as a matter of law injure the plaintiff's reputation and so take the matter out of their hands.

What may loosely be called "partial justification" raises complex issues in what has been described as the "artificial minuet" of libel pleading, which may appear aridly technical but have considerable practical implications. It will be a very simple case in which the defendant is unable to support *anything* in what he has written about the plaintiff. It is much more likely that the

---

[21] 297 P. 91 (1931).
[22] The jury might in the event award contemptuous damages in such a case, which would mean that the "successful" plaintiff would lose on costs.

plaintiff's advisers will recognise that they must concede the accuracy of A, B and C, are confident that they D and E are wholly unfounded and regard F and G as doubtful. Can they bring the action solely in respect of D and E and exclude the other elements in the case altogether? As well as affecting the eventual outcome this is important because the wider the defendant can range over the issues the greater will be the costs—and in the typical case of an individual plaintiff against a major newspaper corporation the ability to "raise the stakes" by increasing costs can be a powerful deterrent to the plaintiff's persevering with his claim. The first point is that the plaintiff cannot, by taking a "blue pencil" alter the meaning of what the defendant has said. To take an example from an old case, if the defendant says, "T is a damned thief; and I can prove it. T received the earnings from the ship and ought to pay the wages," the second sentence makes it plain what the first means, *viz.* not that T has really committed theft but is guilty of a breach of contract or trust. The defendant cannot, by selecting the first sentence alone, prevent the plaintiff justifying the whole allegation by proving the truth of the second. If, on the other hand, the defendant makes *distinct* charges against the plaintiff the latter is at liberty to select certain of them and thereby prevent the defendant giving evidence in justification of the others. If he does this, section 5 of the Defamation Act 1952 has no relevance for that refers to "an action . . . *in respect of* words containing two or more distinct charges" which means that it applies only to those charges in respect of which the plaintiff chooses to sue. Nor can the defendant side-step the problem by putting the other matters in evidence in reduction of damages for while it is well established that evidence which is given pursuant to an unsuccessful plea of justification may go to reduce the damages it is equally the case that you cannot for this purpose give evidence of specific acts of misconduct outside the words complained of. For this purpose one might say that the law *does* look at the reputation a plaintiff enjoys, not that which he deserves, and while the rule has been subject to strong criticism for the inequitable results to which it leads, even the critics admit that to abolish it creates some risk of allowing defendants to prolong trials by raising collateral issues.

The above discussion assumes that each imputation made by the defendant has a single, clear meaning. Unfortunately, the imperfections of language and the ingenuity of lawyers ensure that this is rarely so, which adds a further layer of complexity to libel proceedings. It has, however, been held that in pleading justification the defendant is not tied to the meaning which the plaintiff says the words bear: he is entitled to seek to justify any meaning which a jury might reasonably find to be the meaning of the words so long as he does so with sufficient particularity to enable the plaintiff to know what case he has to meet.[23] The line between justifying a "lesser" defamatory meaning in this way and giving evidence of specific acts of misconduct to reduce damages may sometimes be very fine.

The defendant may base what he says upon the reports of others—for example, a newspaper relying on its "sources"—but he cannot justify by showing that he is accurately repeating what he was told, nor can he hide behind "it is rumoured that...," even if rumours are in fact circulating widely. Indeed, he cannot put the rumours in evidence in reduction of damages. This does not mean that it is impossible to report that a person's affairs are under investigation by the police if that is in fact the case for that statement would not, in the law's view, be interpreted by the reasonable man as a statement of guilt. Any other rule would render the publication of news impossible but it possibly represents a rather generous view of the fairness and high mindedness of the typical reader.

There is a curious historical byway to the law of justification. If the charge was that the plaintiff was guilty of crime the law struggled on for years with an amazing rule that the fact of a criminal conviction was no evidence at all that he was guilty and in one case a plaintiff serving a sentence for an offence won an action for damages in respect of a statement in a policeman's memoirs that he had committed the offence. Fortunately, this rule was abolished by statute in 1968 and the conviction is now *conclusive* proof of guilt in a defamation action.

Privilege

Again an unfortunate name, since in popular usage it often carries connotations of inequality or unfairness, but it is not easy to find a better one. Privilege is at the heart of defamation law, for it is the concept which excuses untrue defamatory statements because of the purpose for which they were made. It recognises that there are situations in which the need for free communication is so great that it requires the defendant to be protected from liability even though this is at the price of serious harm to the reputation of another. The subject is large and complex and some aspects of it are regrettably, though probably inevitably, vague, and no more than an outline is attempted here.

First come matters covered by "absolute" privilege where no action may be brought in any circumstances whatever—even, for example, if it is crystal clear that the defendant knew the untruth

[23] *Prager* v. *Times Newspapers* [1988] 1 W.L.R. 77.

of what he said, was actuated by spite and had the purpose of causing harm to the plaintiff. In these situations free discussion altogether eclipses protection of reputation. The privilege is not granted for the purpose of conferring immunity on those who abuse it from malicious motives but to ensure that those who engage in honest debate have freedom from even the fear of litigation; it is simply an unfortunate fact of life that this can only effectively be achieved by a rule which sometimes does protect the malicious. Few would dispute the necessity of such absolute privilege in respect of statements made in Parliament (indeed, so fundamental is this rule that it is part of our constitutional law in the Bill of Rights) or in judicial proceedings,[24] though it is strange that *reports* of the former enjoy only the qualified privilege described below while most reports of the latter are granted the higher protection. More difficult is the absolute privilege granted in respect of communications between officers of state, for it is not clear how far down the scale of public service it descends, nor whether there is any distinction to be drawn between the civil and military services. The matter is further clouded by the fact that the courts have power to refuse to order disclosure or even to allow the putting in evidence of documents if to do so would be against the "public interest" (for example, it is highly unlikely that Cabinet minutes would be the subject of disclosure). The basis of this form of "privilege" is the need for candour in communications between those concerned with government and policy. It is not coterminous with absolute privilege protecting the maker of a defamatory statement (in particular the privilege relating to documents is essentially discretionary, the court having to balance the requirements of justice with the needs of the public service) but it cannot be ignored in the defamation context: if the plaintiff cannot obtain disclosure of material which is vital to his case he may lose even if the court would not be prepared to extend the protection of the defamation privilege to the document in question.

Beyond the categories of absolute privilege lie the much more numerous situations where there is still a need to protect free speech but it is not so strong as to exclude defamation law altogether. The law attempts to effect a balance by making the statement the subject of qualified privilege: the defendant who can show that the statement was made on a privileged occasion escapes liability unless the plaintiff can show that it was made with "malice." Malice means *either* that the defendant speaks without belief in the truth of what he says or, where, although he believes it to be true, he acts from improper motives and not for

---

[24] A similar privilege protects communications between solicitor and client.

the purpose for which the law grants the privilege. An illustration of the latter variant is *Royal Aquarium* v. *Parkinson*[25] where the defendant disapproved of music halls and, in his determination to ensure that the London County Council did not grant the plaintiffs a licence, had managed to convince himself that a perfectly innocent performance was indecent. If, however, his motives are proper, then he is not malicious in law even if he is careless in arriving at his belief or even if it is produced by "irrational prejudice"—good faith is all that is required. The unreasonableness of a belief may of course be evidence that it is not actually held by the defendant, but the ultimate issue is still "what did the defendant believe?"

Many instances of qualified privilege are based upon statute. The Defamation Act 1952 protects a wide range of reports of proceedings (for example, of foreign legislatures, public inquiries, trade associations and public meetings) though in some cases the defence is only available if the defendant has complied with a request to publish a reasonable statement by way of explanation or contradiction. It is more difficult to state when qualified privilege arises at common law because it is granted for the "common convenience and welfare of society" and the law must be adaptable to both novel situations and changing circumstances. Very broadly, the common law examples can be grouped under two heads: (a) statements made in connection with a public or private duty and (b) statements in which maker and recipient have a common interest. Examples of the first (which is by no means confined to a legally enforceable duty) are an employer giving a reference in respect of a former employee; a witness of a crime giving information to the police; or a complaint to the authorities about the misconduct of a public officer. In the last case one might say that there was a "public duty" to report wrongdoing in the public service or that the privilege was based upon the duty of the recipient to investigate charges against its servants. The point is of no real importance and anyone who expects anything more than flexibility bordering on vagueness in the categories of qualified privilege will be disappointed. Examples of the second category are communications by an employer to his workers about the conduct of a fellow-worker, statements by a creditor to a person holding his debtor's assets, or replies by a person whose character or conduct has been the subject of attack. What is essential in all cases is that there should be reciprocity (of interest or of duty and interest) between the maker of the statement and the person to whom it is addressed, and it seems that it is not enough that the defendant honestly

[25] [1892] 1 Q.B. 431.

believed that it existed. However, it may be that courts nowadays will take a rather more generous view than that displayed in some of the older authorities and find that a person has a sufficient interest even when he lacks formal powers of correction and discipline. The privilege covers what is reasonably done under it and this may mean that it is not lost even if others who are not in reciprocity come to know of the statement. It may well be unreasonable to convey a potentially defamatory imputation by telegram or postcard rather than in a sealed letter, but the privilege is not lost where the letter is dictated to a secretary; again, where a person is being detained on suspicion of theft one may (indeed must) inform him of the reason for his detention even though others are within earshot. There may even be occasions on which a defendant may properly use the press for the dissemination of a defamatory statement without losing the protection of privilege, as where he replies in the press to an attack made on him in the press. In that event the newspaper, like any other intermediary used for a privileged publication, has an "ancillary" privilege, for otherwise the privilege of the author could be effectively negated by the risk that the intermediary might be sued. However, the press occupies no "privileged" (if one may for once use the word in its popular sense) position in the law of defamation except in so far as it is conferred by statute. There is no common law privilege to publish material (believed by the newspaper to be true) on the ground that it concerns matters of public interest.

It is useful at this point to give some account of the way the common law has been transformed in the United States by the application, one might almost say the discovery, of the guarantee of free speech and freedom of the press found in the First Amendment to the Constitution, which has considerably extended the liberty of the press at the expense of the defamed. Of course the First Amendment does not apply here or elsewhere in the common law world, nor is it likely to do so in the foreseeable future, but some equivalent protection is from time to time advocated in this country by representatives of the press. The two leading American decisions are *N.Y. Times* v. *Sullivan*,[26] in which the Supreme Court held that statements about public figures or public officials only attracted the law of defamation if they were made with knowledge of their falsity or "recklessly," that is with actual consciousness that they might be false; and *Gertz* v. *Robert Welch*,[27] which prescribes that media statements about private persons are actionable only if the publisher was

---

[26] 376 U.S. 254 (1964).
[27] 418 U.S. 323 (1974).

negligent as to the truth of what he said. It seems that it is still possible for the laws of the individual states to apply the common law strict liability standard to non-media statements about private persons but the trend is likely to be that the *Gertz* rule will be adopted for these cases, too. The *N.Y. Times* rule renders the common law of qualified privilege redundant because by adopting a standard of knowledge or falsity the law has in effect made *all* statements about public figures subject to qualified privilege. Under *Gertz* the common law remains relevant, for where the statement is made on a privileged occasion even a negligent falsehood may be protected if the publisher has an honest belief in its truth, but its importance is clearly much reduced.

The American developments are a reaction to the consequences of the common law's insistence that the virtually exclusive remedy for defamation is an award of damages[28] which leads to irreconcilable tensions between the protection of free speech and the protection of reputation. Where damages are not very tightly controlled (and the trial jury in *N.Y. Times* awarded about $2.5 million in today's money) there is a serious risk that press reporting and discussion, which are generally thought to be necessary elements in a free society, will be silenced by the threat of crippling awards. On the other hand, the grant to the press of immunity from defamation in the absence of knowledge of falsity means that the victim of accusations which are in fact untrue (though believed to be true by the newspaper, perhaps on flimsy evidence) has no means of redress: if he sues he will simply lose the case because the law looks to the mental state of the defendant, not to the truth of statement and the verdict of the jury may well give no indication of *why* they concluded as they did, thereby depriving the plaintiff even of the comfort of knowing that they regard him as defamed.[29] The solutions that spring to mind are (a) a speedily enforceable right to require the defendant to publish a correction and (b) some procedure for a declaratory judgment but it is not easy to see how either of them could be made to work if a newspaper "stuck to its story." How are large legal costs to be avoided in relation to (a) if, as seems inevitable, the newspaper were given the right to contest the accuracy of the correction? And in relation to (b), even a system

---

[28] It is not possible to obtain an injunction in respect of defamation in the U.S.A. In England it is very difficult to obtain an interlocutory injunction (for that would amount to pre-censorship) and an injunction is rarely necessary after trial.

[29] It has to be admitted that the same problem can arise at common law where the statement is made on a privileged occasion, but the *N.Y. Times* rules greatly increases it.

which allowed normal legal costs to the successful claimant would be likely to leave him heavily out of pocket. A person who merely wishes to clear his name can at present go to the Press Council or the Broadcasting Complaints Commission. These bodies have power to require publication of their adjudication and recourse to them generally precludes any action for damages in the courts. On present evidence it seems unlikely that, short of very extensive increases in these powers (which would in itself have implications for press freedom), they will wholly supplant the law of defamation. More likely is some "moderation" of the common law by restricting or abolishing trial by jury and exemplary damages.

Fair Comment

As is implicit in the very existence of this defence, comment or opinion may be defamatory, but words cannot be fair comment in law unless they rest upon some substratum of fact which is stated or indicated with the comment. The matter is very clearly put in *Kemsley* v. *Foot*[30]:

> "If the defendant accurately states what some public man has really done, and asserts that 'such conduct is disgraceful' this is merely an expression of his opinion, his comment on the plaintiff's conduct. So, if without setting it out, he identifies the conduct on which he comments by a clear reference. In either case the defendant enables his readers to judge for themselves how far his opinion is well founded; and, therefore, what would otherwise be an allegation of fact becomes merely a comment. But if he asserts that the plaintiff has been guilty of disgraceful conduct, and does not state what that conduct was, this is an allegation of fact for which there is no defence but privilege or truth."

In an ideal world, therefore, the writer will first set out the facts upon which he relies (which, generally, he must be able to show are true, since you cannot comment upon untrue facts)[31] and be careful to separate his comments thereon in such a way as to

---

[30] [1952] A.C. 345, 356.

[31] A fuller statement of the law is: (1) By section 6 of the Defamation Act 1952 a defence of fair comment "shall not fail by reason only that the truth of every allegation of fact is not proved if the expression of opinion is fair comment having regard to such of the facts alleged or referred to . . . as are proved." (2) In so far as the facts alleged are defamatory they can be protected *only* by a plea of justification. (3) But if the facts upon which the comment is based were published on a privileged occasion (*e.g.* in judicial proceedings) the commentator is entitled to assume them to be true.

make the distinction plain to the reader. Unfortunately, few writers are constantly thinking in terms of the law of libel and the line between the two categories can be extraordinarily difficult to draw. For example, the defendant in *London Artists Ltd.* v. *Littler*[32] spoke of "what appears to be a plan to close the run" of a play. Was this a statement of fact that there was such a plot or a statement by the defendant that from other facts he inferred the existence of such a plan? If the latter the statement would be comment. The Court of Appeal concluded on the totality of the communication that it was a statement of fact, though this may have been assisted by the fact that until a late stage of the proceedings the defendant had strenuously been advancing the defence of justification.

A comment only falls within the defence if it is on a matter of public interest but this is an extremely wide concept, much wider than that of "interest" in qualified privilege. Lord Denning M.R. in *London Artists* v. *Littler* said that it should not be confined "within narrow limits. Whenever a matter is such as to affect people at large, so that they may be legitimately interested in, or concerned at, what is going on, or what may happen to them or to others; then it is a matter of public interest on which everyone is entitled to make fair comment." It is certainly not confined to matter which the plaintiff has put before the public, such as a play or a novel, but extends to matters which the plaintiff may wish to conceal, so long as they are of a nature in which the public has a legitimate concern. Even the "private life" of a public figure is fair game so far as it reflects on his fitness for public office.

The adjective "fair" in the title of the defence must be the favourite in a strong field of defamation contenders for the title of most misleading expression in the law. One thing is clear, the defence is not a form of justification so that the commentator escapes liability even if the jury strongly disagrees with it and considers it "unfair" in the sense that it is exaggerated or unbalanced.[33] Indeed, we can almost say that the law is precisely the opposite and that the only issue is whether the comment is the honest expression of the defendant's views: if it is, it is protected even though he is obstinate, unreasonable and cantankerous. To this, however, there is certainly one and possibly there are two qualifications. First, the judicial formulations draw a distinction, albeit imprecisely, between criticism and mere invective or abuse, which is not protected even if it accurately reflects the defendant's state of mind. The

---

[32] [1969] 2 Q.B. 375.
[33] At least this is the theory of it, though it assumes that the jury understands the judge's explanation that "fair" does not really mean "fair" at all.

test put to the jury by Diplock J. in *Silkin* v. *Beaverbrook Newspapers*,[34] was "would a fair-minded man, holding strong views, obstinate views, prejudiced views, have been capable of making this comment?" The other qualification is that where a comment imputes dishonesty or dishonourable motives some cases impose the requirement that the imputation must be reasonable or even warranted upon the facts, creating, in effect, a form of justification. Since the meaning of "dishonourable" is so vague this could encroach severely upon the fundamentally "subjective" nature of the defence of fair comment, though it is probably true to say that the modern cases seem to have ignored the possibility of any special rule in such situations.

Like qualified privilege, fair comment is displaced by the existence of "malice," the burden of proof of which again lies upon the plaintiff. There are some dark corners here. If the defendant expressed an opinion he did not in fact hold that is conclusive evidence of malice, that is clear enough.[35] It has, however, been said that even a comment which is objectively fair may fall outside the defence if the defendant was writing not as a genuine critic but with the intention of injuring the plaintiff. The trouble with this is that it does not allow for mixed motives: would it really extend to a case where the defendant publishes his genuine opinion and at the same time takes pleasure in the hurt it will cause because of personal animosity between him and the plaintiff? In practice it is likely that the personal animosity will colour the opinion and we have the express decision of the Court of Appeal that "comment distorted by malice cannot be fair on the part of the person who made it"[36] but this is not easy to square with the proposition that comment which does not descend to invective is allowable even if unreasonable and prejudiced.

---

[34] [1958] 2 W.L.R. 743.
[35] It is assumed that the defendant is the originator of the comment. A newspaper publishing a letter is not (at least in England) required to share the opinion of the writer.
[36] *Thomas* v. *Bradbury, Agnew* [1906] 2 K.B. 627.

CHAPTER THIRTEEN

Business and Economic Torts

All the torts in this chapter are primarily concerned with the intentional causing of economic loss, though beyond that their characteristics are so diverse that they do not fit neatly into any scheme of classification. For example, if we remove the central mental element from deceit (fraud) it appears to have much more in common with liability for negligent misstatement than with, say, interference with contract and there may be a practical link in that a claim which failed as deceit could conceivably succeed on the basis of *Hedley Byrne* v. *Heller*. Nonetheless, it is thought that there is a marginal advantage in an introductory book in keeping deceit separate from the uncertainties of modern negligence law. More important than niceties of classification is that it is the torts in this chapter which above all have tended to be squeezed out of the law school syllabus before the seemingly inexorable increase in complexity of negligence law. Up to a point this is justifiable because their focus is in other areas of the curriculum: for example, interference with contract would, in England, receive a good deal of attention in employment law since industrial disputes have been the source of most of the case law for a century or more. What is more, there are areas in which the common law of torts has a part to play but in which it is supplemented and even overshadowed by statutory provisions: no one could advise on what was lawful competition who knew the law of injurious falsehood and passing off but not the law of trademarks, copyrights, patents and designs, not to speak of the restrictive practices legislation or the competition provisions of the European Community Treaty. When all this is said, however, it is a pity that these torts are so often ignored, because some of them raise very fundamental questions of the limits of civil responsibility which are likely to continue to trouble the law after much of negligence law has been replaced by more cost-effective methods of compensating losses.

A. TORTS INVOLVING MISREPRESENTATION

Deceit

The early law of deceit was primarily concerned with false "warranties" about goods sold. Gradually, the law of warranty ceased to be regarded as concerned with false statements of fact (tort) and shifted its focus to the notion of promise (contract) so that in the modern law a warranty is a contractual term, breach of which involves no element of dishonesty nor even of fault. However, at about the time when this process was complete the Court of King's Bench in *Pasley* v. *Freeman*[1] allowed an action of deceit to lie where D had falsely represented to P that P might safely extend credit to X.[2] The crucial point was that deceit was henceforth available even when there was no contractual relationship between the plaintiff and the defendant. Of course, the existence of a contract between the parties does not render the law of deceit inapplicable. If a contract is induced by fraudulent misrepresentation the plaintiff may have both (a) a claim to rescind the contract and (b) a claim for deceit, but the latter is firmly grounded in tort, a point which is significant for the law of damages.[3]

The tort is committed when D makes to P a statement of fact which he knows is or may be false with the consequence (intended by D) that P acts upon it to his loss. It is vital to note that the tort applies only to statements of fact, for it is only a statement of fact that can be true or untrue. If I sell you my car, saying it has done 50,000 miles that is a statement of fact; but if I say that I will deliver it on the first of next month that is a promise, which is neither "true" nor "untrue" but which is remedied by the law of contract if it is broken—a broken promise is not a lie. However, if the overall structure of law is to be understood two qualifications must be made to these propositions. First, if it can be shown that when I made the promise I had no intention of fulfilling it, that is a false statement of fact, that is to say, the fact of my present state of mind. Secondly, a factual statement such as the mileage of my car may also be regarded by the law of contract as a promise ("I

---

[1] (1789) 3 T.R. 51.
[2] *Cf. Hedley Byrne* v. *Heller*, p. 84, *ante*.
[3] See p. 189, *post*.

warrant that the car has done 50,000 miles") if an intention to give a contractual undertaking can be deduced from the demeanour of the speaker, in which event the recipient gains the benefit of the (generally superior) remedies for breach of contract if the promise is unfulfilled. In the language of contract, "the car has done 50,000 miles" may be either a representation or a warranty but "I will deliver on the first of the month" is, in the absence of fraud, a warranty only.

Mere negligence as to the falsity of the statement will not found a claim for deceit, though it may lead to liability under *Hedley Byrne* v. *Heller*. The required mental element was clearly stated by Lord Herschell L.C. in *Derry* v. *Peek*[4]:

> "First, in order to sustain an action of deceit, there must be proof of fraud, and nothing short of that will suffice. Secondly, fraud is proved when it is shewn that a false representation has been made (1) knowingly, or (2) without belief in its truth, or (3) recklessly, careless whether it be true or false. . . . To prevent a false statement being fraudulent there must, I think, always be an honest belief in its truth, and this probably covers the whole ground, for one who knowingly alleges that which is false has obviously no such honest belief."

Hence in that case the honest but mistaken belief of the promoters of a tramway company that they had power to use steam traction protected them from liability in an action for damages by a purchaser of shares.

Circumstances and beliefs may change and in deceit the operative time for determining whether a statement is false is when it is acted upon. It is possible that a statement may be true when made but become false (to the maker's knowledge) when it is relied upon; alternatively, the defendant may make a false statement believing it to be true and then discover its falsity. In either event it seems that he commits deceit if he fails to correct the statement, though it must be admitted that the case law concentrates upon the avoidance of a contract on the ground of misrepresentation, where knowledge of falsity is unnecessary. In so far as the law in these cases casts upon the representor a duty to speak out it is an exception to the general rule that silence is not misrepresentation: one is allowed to acquiesce in the self deception of another provided one neither acts to confirm his false belief nor takes active steps to conceal defects in what one is selling. In a very limited class of cases the law of contract imposes a duty from the commencement of negotiations to disclose

---

[4] (1889) 14 App.Cas. 337, 374.

matters which would affect the other party in his decision to enter the contract (insurance is the best known example). If such non-disclosure is made knowingly it does not give rise to a claim for damages, though in the vast majority of cases the representee will be adequately protected by his right to avoid the contract.[5]

The requirement that the plaintiff must have acted on the representation means that there is no liability if he discovers the truth or if it is clear that he would have gone ahead anyway, though as to the latter point the law accepts that a representation may be operative even though it is only one among a number of factors that influenced the plaintiff. It seems that we must take literally the proposition that the defendant should intend the *plaintiff* to rely on the statement for in the leading case false statements in a prospectus were held not to be actionable by persons who, no doubt foreseeably, relied on the prospectus when, after issue, they bought shares on the market from those who had applied for and been allotted them on the basis of the prospectus.[6] It is not of course necessary that the defendant communicate directly with the plaintiff: in modern conditions a request for credit information, for example, would often come through the plaintiff's bank, but it would be clear that it is the plaintiff, not the bank, who is intended to act upon the answer.

The damage suffered by the plaintiff through his reliance is nearly always financial loss, for example, money wasted on the purchase of worthless shares, though the tort has occasionally been applied to other, less usual losses: in one case to personal injuries suffered in a military expedition into which the plaintiff had been tricked and in another (in Canada) to the distress suffered by the plaintiff when induced to enter into a marriage which turned out to be bigamous. However, the fact that a claim for deceit is one in tort excludes the loss of profit or "expectation" element which is available in an action for breach of contract. Suppose D sells P a chair for £1000 warranting it to be the work of H. A chair by H would have a market value of £1100. The chair is not by H and has a market value of £900. P is entitled, in his claim for breach of contract, to be put in the position he would have been in if the contractual warranty had been fulfilled, so the damages are £1100 less the £900 value received, £200. If, however, the statement is not a term of the contract but a fraudulent misrepresentation inducing it, the plaintiff is entitled to be put in the position he would have been in if the fraud had

---

[5] *Banque Keyser Ullmann* v. *Skandia Insurance* [1988] N.L.J. 287 (a case of negligence, but the reasoning seems equally applicable to other forms of misrepresentation).

[6] *Peek* v. *Gurney* (1873) L.R. 6 H.L. 377. As to negligence, see p. 88, *ante*.

not been committed. This is the £1000 expenditure, less the £900 value received, £100. This is undoubtedly the law in England, but so odd is the proposition that a fraudster should pay less than a contract breaker[7] that some American jurisdictions have applied the contract measure to deceit. As to remoteness of damage, deceit is more generous to the plaintiff than negligence so that the defendant will be liable for direct consequences even if they were unforeseeable. This provides a partial answer to the question why the plaintiff should choose to allege deceit (a serious charge of which the tribunal of fact will require convincing proof),[8] given the development of liability for negligent misstatement. Another reason is that aggravated damages are certainly available for deceit and exemplary damages may be.[9] It is also said that the plaintiff in deceit does not have to show that there was a "special relationship" between him and the defendant but there does not seem much in this in view of the requirement that the defendant must have intended the plaintiff to rely on his statement. The law of deceit is narrower rather than wider than the law of negligence.

Injurious Falsehood

Deceit is committed where A lies to B and B acts upon the lie to his (B's) detriment. This tort covers the situation where A lies to B and B acts upon the lie to C's detriment. It is often called "slander of title" or "slander of goods" because it can be committed by a trader (A) falsely disparaging to potential customers (B) the wares of a rival (C).[10] If the statement reflects upon B's reputation ("B's beer is of poor quality because he drinks too much of it himself") it is also defamatory and bearing in mind that (a) a charge of business inefficiency is capable of being defamatory and (b) a company can be defamed in its trading capacity there is a good deal of potential overlap between the two torts. However, defamation would have been no use in *Joyce* v. *Motor Surveys*[11] where the defendant in an effort to get rid of his tenant, the plaintiff, falsely informed customers and the trade association that the plaintiff had ceased to trade.

---

[7] It will be observed that if P had made a bad bargain, *i.e.* the goods would have been worth less than the price even if as warranted, the tort measure will be more favourable.

[8] Deceit will very often be a crime as well.

[9] *Post*, p. 206.

[10] If the customers suffered loss in relying on A's statements *they* can sue for deceit.

[11] [1948] Ch. 252.

Injurious falsehood requires "malice"—knowledge of falsity (or at least lack of belief in the truth of the statement) or pursuit of an improper motive, that is to say, injuring the plaintiff's business rather than advancing the defendant's own. Hence it does not require the paraphernalia of privilege which we find in the law of defamation; in the United States, where some authorities make liability stricter, the tort has attracted the "constitutional privilege" of free speech.[12] Nor is fair comment relevant as such, though something akin to this defence is found in the principle that mere claims to the superiority of the plaintiff's wares over those of his rivals are not actionable. Despite the strict requirement of malice in injurious falsehood there are some indications that the law of negligence may intrude into some examples of our paradigm three party situation. In *Lawton* v. *BOC Transhield*[13] it was held that where an employer (A) gives a reference on a former employee (C) to a new employer (B) he owes a duty of care to C as well as to B. Given the very close "proximity" between A and C this decision seems justifiable. Indeed, it is not that far distant from the *Hedley Byrne* situation, for C may be said to rely upon A's taking due care. It is not, however, directly applicable because C does not ask for the information nor rely upon it in framing his own conduct.

Passing off

A trader's business reputation and "good will" is a valuable asset. The tort of passing off is aimed not at those who disparage his wares but at those who attempt to "cash in" on his good reputation by representing their goods as his. It resembles injurious falsehood in that it is not the plaintiff but third parties who are deceived by the falsity, but it is usually regarded as a separate tort based upon interference with the plaintiff's proprietary rights. In practice there is a good deal of overlap between passing off and the statutory law protecting trade marks, proceedings under which may be cheaper for the plaintiff. However, a trade mark is only protected if registered as such and the legislation does not cover distinctive presentation or packaging which cannot be described as a "mark." Thus a distinctive soft drink bottle is outside the trade mark legislation but copying of it might constitute passing off. The elements of passing off are (1) a misrepresentation (2) made by a trader in the course of trade (3) to prospective customers of his or ultimate consumers of goods or services supplied by him, (4) which is

[12] See p. 181 *ante*.
[13] [1987] 2 All E.R. 608.

calculated to and does injure the business or goodwill of another. The key issue is whether the way in which the defendant's product is marketed is likely to cause confusion in the minds of the public. If not, it is no tort to launch a similar product and exploit a market which has been built up entirely by the plaintiff's own efforts for the common law has no general concept of "unfair competition."[14]

B. CAUSING LOSS BY UNLAWFUL MEANS AND RELATED MATTERS

One eminent Commonwealth court has contemplated the existence of a tort whereby liability exists for "harm or loss as the inevitable consequence of the unlawful, intentional and positive acts of another."[15] This is certainly not the law in England for at the very least we should have to add the requirement that the defendant intended to cause the harm or contemplated that it would occur. It may be that in the last analysis English law does come close to the proposition that loss intentionally caused by unlawful means is actionable but the law has developed by means of separate, nominate torts and it is only by reference to these that it can be understood. The law is straightforward enough with regard to personal injury or property damage intentionally caused: most cases will fall within one of the varieties of trespass and those which do not are covered by the "action on the case for intentional harm."[16] Loss of an economic nature is a much more complicated matter.

Most of the case law in England has arisen from industrial strife but since 1906 Parliament has given a modicum of protection from these torts to those involved in industrial disputes. Unfortunately this matter is something of a political football, subject to constant revision, so no attempt will be made to give an account of it here. Let it suffice to say that things done "in contemplation or furtherance of a trade dispute" are not actionable in tort on the ground that they interfere with, or threaten interference with a contract, so that a trade union leader cannot be sued for calling his members out on strike. However, this is limited in two ways: first, action which is taken without the ballot required by the Employment Act 1984 may not be protected; secondly, there may be no protection for "secondary action," that is to say, calling out employees of a supplier of the employer who is involved in the dispute.

---

[14] *Moorgate Tobacco* v. *Phillip Morris* (1984) 186 C.L.R. 414 (High Ct. of Australia).
[15] *Beaudesert Shire Council* v. *Smith* (1966) 120 C.L.R. 145 (High Ct. of Australia).
[16] See p. 141, *ante*.

Interference with Contract

There was an ancient tort of enticing or harbouring the servant of another. Long obsolete, it was abolished in England in 1982. It seems to have had its origins in the view that the master's interest in his servant's labour was of a proprietary nature thus according with the old view that such relations were more a matter of status than of contract. However, in 1853 in *Lumley* v. *Gye*[17] an impresario recovered damages against a rival who had procured the plaintiff's star, Johanna Wagner, to repudiate her contract with him. Miss Wagner was clearly not a servant in the technical sense of that term and though the case did involve a contract for personal services the principle of it was wider and was soon accepted as extending to all contracts.

Those judges who opposed this development in the law argued that the doctrine amounted to the creation of an exception to the requirement of privity of contract and laid stress upon the fact that the plaintiff had his remedy on the contract itself against the party who succumbed to the persuasion (indeed, Lumley did obtain an injunction against Miss Wagner's breach). The first criticism is misdirected, for the plaintiff sues not on the contract but for the interference with the legitimate expectation that others will not interfere with his contractual rights. As Erle J. put it, "He who procures the non-delivery of goods according to contract may inflict an injury the same as he who procures the abstraction of goods after delivery; and both ought on the same ground to be made responsible." As to the second point, in many cases the contractual action would probably not be worth pursuing; this is what has made the tort so important in the industrial context, for the right of action for breach of contract against individual strikers is more theoretical than real.

The form of the tort in *Lumley* v. *Gye* was direct persuasion. A's entering into a contract with B which A knows to be inconsistent with the performance of B's prior contract with C may also constitute the tort, though probably not where B is the sole instigator. If A refuses to deal with B because of a contract between B and C of which A disapproves he is not liable even if he knows this may cause B to break the contract, for A is free to decide with whom he will deal; but if his purpose is to persuade B to break the contract the tort is committed. Though persuasion is the simplest form of the tort it may be committed in other ways, by some form of intervention which causes B to break his contract against his will. Such intervention may be direct (as where A steals B's equipment or kidnaps him) or indirect (as where A calls

[17] (1853) 2 El. & Bl. 216.

B's employees out on strike).[18] When the intervention is indirect it is clearly established that some independently unlawful means must be employed[19] but the matter is more doubtful when A intervenes directly. On balance, however, unlawful means are probably required here, too: If A buys up all the goods of a particular description on the market to strike at his rival C by depriving C of his expected supplies under his contract with B he commits no tort against C.[20]

What are "unlawful means" for the purposes of wrongful interference with contract? Acts which amount to torts or breaches of contract between A and B certainly are, but the position is less clear where A's act is a crime but not also a tort against B. The House of Lords has held in *Lonrho* v. *Shell Petroleum (No. 2)*[21] that a statutory offence which does not give rise to liability for the tort of breach of statutory duty is not unlawful means for the purposes of the tort of interference with trade or business by unlawful means.[22] It cannot be assumed that "unlawful means" necessarily bears the same meaning wherever it occurs but it has been said that the tort considered in *Lonrho* is the genus of which interference with contract is one species so it is hard to see how the concept can sensibly differ between the torts.

So far we have assumed that the result of A's conduct is a *breach* of contract by B and this is certainly necessary when persuasion is used: it is legitimate for A to persuade B lawfully to terminate his contractual relations with C and to deal with A, and *a fortiori* it is not a tort for A to persuade B not to enter into a contract with C. Such a requirement would not, however, be very satisfactory where there is intervention by unlawful means. Had Gye kidnapped Johanna Wagner it is more than likely that she would have been excused from her contractual duty to appear at Lumley's theatre while she was under restraint, but that is hardly a satisfactory reason to deny Gye's tort liability to Lumley and it is tolerably clear that the law accepts this.[23]

Interference with contract is a tort of "intention" and therefore in no way contradicts the proposition that A is not liable in

---

[18] It is assumed that the conduct is not protected by the trade disputes legislation.
[19] In the example given the unlawful means used to strike at C is the tort (against B) of directly persuading B's employees to break their contracts of employment.
[20] This seems more satisfactory than saying that A is presumptively liable to C but his purpose of diverting C's trade to himself provides him with a defence of justification.
[21] [1982] A.C. 173, p. 199, *post*
[22] See p. 200, *post*.
[23] *Torquay Hotel Co.* v. *Cousins* [1969] 2 Ch. 106, though some of the dicta in the case go too far.

negligence where his conduct brings about a breach of a contract between B and C.[24] But it is not wholly clear what intention means. One view is that the defendant's *purpose* must be to strike at C so that C cannot sue if his loss is an inevitable "spin-off" from an act aimed at B. On the other hand, it is possible that it is sufficient that A knows his conduct will inevitably disrupt a contract between B and C. On this view a transport union acting outside the protection of trade disputes legislation could be liable to a passenger whose existing travel arrangements were disrupted. All are agreed, however, that no malice need be shown towards C — it is no defence that A is motivated by the desire to advance his own interests. A need not have detailed knowledge of the terms of the contract between B and C. Thus in *Merkur Island Shipping Corpn.* v. *Laughton*[25] a seamen's union could not deny that in "blacking" a ship they were aware that they would be interfering with performance of contracts between the owner and charterers or cargo owners, for in modern conditions a ship carrying the owner's own goods would be wholly exceptional.

When (apart from cases of statutory authority) can interference with contractual relations be justified? If A has a prior contract with B and B makes another contract with C which is inconsistent with this, A may certainly seek to persuade B not to perform the latter (though C is probably entitled to use like persuasion if he did not know about the prior contract when he made his). It is, however, difficult to say how far the law goes in allowing interference on the ground of the public interest. In *Brimelow* v. *Casson*[26] a plea of justification was successful where the defendant induced breaches of contracts between the plaintiff and theatres where his troupe was to play, on the ground that the plaintiff paid so badly that his employees were driven to prostitution. However, beyond remarking that if justification did not exist on the facts he could hardly conceive of a case in which it would, Russell J. disclaimed any attempt to state a general test. A potential area for the application of this defence is that concerning confidential information. An employee clearly owes a duty to preserve his employer's secrets but there is no right to confidentiality in respect of matters involving illegality. It would seem to follow that if A persuades B to reveal information relating to illegal conduct by C then A has the defence of justification in an action by C.

---

[24] See p. 50, *ante*.
[25] [1983] 2 A.C. 570.
[26] [1924] 1 Ch. 302.

Intimidation

The leading authority on this tort is *Rookes* v. *Barnard*,[27] where the
defendants in order to preserve a "closed shop" threatened strike
action unless the plaintiff's employment was terminated. The
employers yielded to this pressure and lawfully terminated the
plaintiff's employment. The ordinary form of interference with
contract did not avail the plaintiff for, while the defendants had
certainly threatened breaches of the employment contracts of
those they represented, they had not yet brought them about;
but, in any event, the Trade Disputes Act 1906 protected persons
engaged in a trade dispute from liability on the ground only that
they induced breaches of contracts of employment. Neither
point, however, was an objection to a claim for intimidation,
which is committed where A, to strike at C, threatens B with an
unlawful act unless B acts to C's detriment. Though B will often
have a contract with C (as in *Rookes* v. *Barnard*) this is not
necessary—the tort extends to protecting benefits to which C had
merely an expectation, but no right. This form of liability was not
new (for example, in 1793 a defendant was held liable for firing
cannons at the plaintiff's African customers to deter them from
coming to trade with the plaintiff)[28] but before *Rookes* v. *Barnard* it
had been confined to threats of violence and the significance of
that case was to extend the scope of unlawful means in this tort to
threats to breach a contract.[29] This development has been subjected to strong criticism on the ground that it amounts to an
unwarranted exception to the doctrine that generally speaking
only a party to a contract can sue or be sued on it (a similar
complaint was made in relation to *Lumley* v. *Gye*) but the defen-
ders of the decision argue that this is to miss the point: the rule is
based on A threatening unlawful means against B as a vehicle for
inflicting damage upon C. Having adverted to the fact that a
threat to commit a *tort* against B was already established as intimidation actionable by C, Lord Reid in *Rookes* v. *Barnard* went on:

> "A person is no more entitled to sue in respect of loss which
> he suffers by reason of a tort committed against someone else
> than he is entitled to sue in respect of loss which he suffers by
> reason of breach of a contract to which he is not a party. What
> he sues for in each case is loss caused to him by the use of an
> unlawful weapon against him—intimidation of another per-
> son by unlawful means."

---

[27] [1964] A.C. 1129.
[28] *Tarleton* v. *McGawley* (1793) Peake NP 270.
[29] In so far as it concerned threats to breach *employment* contracts the decision has
been abrogated by statute, but the general principle is unaffected.

In this respect, therefore, *Rookes* v. *Barnard* merely recognised that in some circumstances a threat of a breach of contract may be just as coercive as a threat of violence—a point also reflected a few years later in the extension of duress in the law of contract to cover "economic duress." However, at unlawful acts the law stops and a threat of action which the defendant is at liberty to take (for example a threat to cease, without breach of contract, to trade with B[30]) gives rise to no liability. This distinction between lawful and unlawful threats may appear arbitrary but it is a thread which runs right through this area of English law; we have already encountered it in connection with interference with contract and it recurs in the remaining torts in this chapter.

If A commits a tort against C by threatening unlawful acts against B which coerce B into acting to C's loss is it also tortious for A to coerce C directly by threatening unlawful action against him? The general view is in the affirmative and it would be difficult to justify on logical grounds a rule of non-liability in the simple, two-party case if it exists in the complex, three-party situation. However, the paucity of authority on the point suggests that intimidation is less necessary in the two-party case: C will often have a right to obtain a *quia timet* injunction to restrain the threatened unlawful act and if it is committed he has his action for tort (for example, assault) or breach of contract as the case may be. Further, if the purpose of the intimidation was to get C to pay money or transfer property to A ("your money or your life") the transfer will be voidable at C's option if it amounts to duress. It would be fair to say that the problems of two party intimidation have not been fully worked out,[31] in particular where the threat is of a breach of a contract between the two parties.

Conspiracy

Here is one of the stranger and more obscure areas of tort. Two torts under one name, one of great potential but virtually strangled at birth, the other now an almost redundant fossil. The first variety is commonly known as "conspiracy to injure" and reaches its modern form in the decision of House of Lords in

---

[30] This may be a little too sweeping: it is possible that acts contravening restrictive practices legislation or "abuse of a dominant position" under the provisions of the EEC Treaty might be unlawful means.

[31] Does a blackmailer commit intimidation? The problem is that although the threat to expose his victim is not of itself unlawful the law makes it criminal to make the threat for the purposes of extortion.

Crofter Hand Woven Harris Tweed Co. v. *Veitch*.[32] It is committed
where damage is caused to the plaintiff by a combination of two
or more persons with the purpose of causing such damage. The
crucial point is that the tort is committed even though the conduct
of the defendants is such that if done by an individual it would be
subject to no legal sanction. Hence a concerted refusal to deal
without any breach of contract, price cutting so as to divert away
the plaintiff's trade or even, it seems, an agreement to tell the
world the unpleasant truth about the plaintiff[33] can be actionable
as torts by virtue of the element of combination. If, therefore, A
and B, to settle a grudge against C, the local barber, set up in
business at cut rates with the sole purpose of ruining C that is a
tort, whereas if A did the same thing alone it is not. Attempts
have been made to justify this on the ground that increased
numbers bring greater power but, while this is often the case, it is
not necessarily so: a massive supermarket chain will have
infinitely greater economic power than two corner grocers.[34]
However, the point hardly matters, for the tort is of scant
practical importance, since it requires that the defendant's
purpose be to cause harm to the plaintiff and it is not enough that
he contemplates a high likelihood or even a certainty of this as a
result of his actions. In the *Crofter* case the defendant union
officials took industrial action against the supply of yarn to small
wool producers in the Isle of Lewis with the object of reducing
competition against the large mill owners, who employed their
members. There was no liability because their purpose was to
advance the interests of their members by increasing the ability of
the mill owners to pay higher wages.[35] The tort catches the
disinterestedly malevolent, the vengeful, but it does not touch
those who ruthlessly pursue self-interest to the exclusion of all
consideration of others and persons in this latter category greatly
outnumber those in the former. Another way of looking at this
part of the law is to say that there is liability for combining so as
knowingly to inflict harm without justification—always bearing
in mind that naked self-interest is a justification. This would
allow the imposition of liability upon interfering busybodies, of
whom it might be difficult to say that their purpose was to injure.
However, it should not be thought that once the plaintiff shows
harm as a necessary or foreseeable consequence of a combination

---

[32] [1942] A.C. 435.

[33] When done by an individual this is covered by the absolute defamation defence
of justification.

[34] The chain is in law one person and there is no conspiracy between an employer
and employees acting in the course of business.

[35] Hence the statutory protection given by English trade disputes legislation
against this form of conspiracy liability is hardly necessary.

the burden of proof shifts to the defendants to justify their actions. Though the dicta are not all consistent, the law probably is that the burden throughout is on the plaintiff. In practice, the evidence produced by the plaintiff may put the defendants at risk of an adverse decision unless they produce evidence of a "proper" motive but that is no more than a reflection of the general principle that inferences which may properly be drawn from evidence may need to be rebutted by the party in whose favour the formal burden of proof inclines.

The other form of conspiracy is known as "unlawful means conspiracy." It is a tort for A and B to combine to use unlawful means to cause damage to C. The question of what amounts to unlawful means is as obscure here as elsewhere in the economic torts, but it probably includes breaches of contract, torts (and threats to commit such acts) and crimes—though, paradoxically, the last point is by no means clear. However, the difficulty of defining unlawful means need not trouble us too much since the tort is now of very limited ambit. First, the tort (unlike the equivalent criminal offence at common law) requires some overt act causing damage to the plaintiff and if this is a tort or breach of contract against him a claim for conspiracy adds little except perhaps to "aggravate" the damages[36] and, perhaps, to make it easier to show that a defendant is a joint tortfeasor even though he has not himself done any act to carry the combination into execution. More important, however, is the restriction put upon this form of the tort in *Lonrho* v. *Shell Petroleum (No. 2)*[37] in which the House of Lords seems to have held that even where unlawful means are used it must be the defendant's purpose to inflict harm upon the plaintiff. On the assumed facts the defendants, oil companies, were taken to have conspired to "bust" the sanctions order against the illegal Rhodesian regime by covert imports of oil, a serious offence under the sanctions legislation. The effect of this was to prolong the rebellion and cause loss to the plaintiffs, whose business was to supply oil to Rhodesia by pipeline and who were prevented from carrying on that activity while the rebellion continued. However, while the defendants might well contemplate that this would be the effect of their conduct it was certainly not their purpose to bring it about and the claim failed on this ground. At its narrowest the decision could be taken as applying only to those cases where the unlawfulness alleged is breach of a criminal statute which does not of itself give rise to a civil claim, but it probably applies to other unlawful means cases as well and on this basis this form of conspiracy adds little or

---

[36] *Post*, p. 205.
[37] [1982] A.C. 173.

nothing to the *Crofter* form. The Supreme Court of Canada, on the other hand, has retained some scope for unlawful means conspiracy by holding that it applies where the conduct is directed towards the plaintiff and the defendant should know that injury to the plaintiff is likely to and does result.[38] There are now conflicting first instance decisions on the meaning of *Lonrho* and the matter needs to be settled by an appellate court.[38a].

Interference with Trade or Business by Unlawful Means

The case of *Merkur Island Shipping Corpn.* v. *Laughton*[39] was primarily about the interpretation of legislation concerned with trade union immunity and the plaintiffs' claim was based upon the well-established wrong, outlined earlier in this chapter, of interference by unlawful means with a subsisting contract. However, Lord Diplock also said that "the evidence also establishes a prima facie case of the common law tort... of interfering with the trade or business of another person by doing unlawful acts. To fall within this genus of torts the unlawful act need not involve procuring another person to break a subsisting contract or to interfere with the performance of an existing contract." He went on to say that procuring the breach of a subsisting contract "is but one species of the wider genus of tort." But if this "genus" exists the *Crofter* form of conspiracy is clearly outside it for the essence of that tort is that the combination renders unlawful what would otherwise be lawful action. Possibly, we should also exclude the simple form of interference with contract, that is to say the case where the defendant procures a breach of that contract,[40] for the persuasion itself is wrongful and no unlawful means are required. We are then left with (1) indirect interference with a subsisting contract (2) intimidation and (3) unlawful means conspiracy (if that still has any life after *Lonrho*) as the three species within the genus. The genus, however, is wider than the species. Suppose, for example, that various people wish to enter into business contracts with the plaintiff but the defendant uses unlawful means (other than threats against those others) with the purpose and effect of preventing them doing so. This is not interference with contract, since there is no subsisting contract; nor is it conspiracy, since the defendant acts alone; and intimidation is

---

[38] *Canada Cement* v. *B.C. Lightweight Aggregate* (1983) 145 D.L.R. (3d) 385.

[38a] *Allied Arab Bank Ltd.* v. *Hajjar (No. 2)* [1988] 3 W.L.R. 533; *Metall und Rohstoff A.G.* v. *Donaldson Lufkin & Jenrette Inc.* [1988] 3 W.L.R. 548.

[39] [1983] 2 A.C. 570.

[40] There was persuasion in *Merkur Island* but it was directed at a contract several times removed from that to which the plaintiff was a party.

inapplicable because there is no threat. Yet the case presumably falls within the genus tort stated by Lord Diplock and it may be observed that the law would be absurd were it otherwise, for if a threat of an unlawful act renders conduct actionable in tort, so also should the actual doing of the act.

There are, however, at least three difficulties to be surmounted before we can fully accept this rationalisation of the law. First, if there is in fact a genus, has not the time come to abandon the species? Logically, the present law is that wherever the species tort is committed, so also is the genus one. Secondly, what state of mind is required for the genus? In interference with contract and (probably) intimidation, it is enough that the defendant intends (not necessarily desires) to cause loss to the plaintiff, but from *Lonrho* it seems that the mental element of unlawful means conspiracy is single-minded vindictiveness and it is hard to see how the genus can embrace different meanings of "intention." By far the most serious difficulty is the third, a point upon which we have already touched, namely, the grave uncertainty surrounding the concept of unlawful means, which lies at the heart of the supposed tort.[41]

There is no doubt that an act which is itself a tort is unlawful means[42] so that a tort committed or threatened by A against B may be the foundation of an action against A by C. Less obvious but just as certain, is that a breach of contract is unlawful means: that was the very point decided in *Rookes* v. *Barnard*.[43] The most important (and most controversial) decision is once again the *Lonrho* case, the facts of which have already been given. As an alternative to conspiracy, the plaintiffs' claim was presented as one of causing loss by unlawful means, the unlawful means in question being the criminal contravention of the Rhodesian Sanctions Order. This was decisively rejected by the House of Lords. There was a well recognised category of cases in which a civil action lay for a breach of statutory duty[44]; civil liability might also arise where a statute created a public right and the plaintiff suffered special damage peculiar to himself from the interference with that right. But the Sanctions Order was in neither category, it was a mere criminal prohibition upon members of the public from doing what it would otherwise be lawful for them to do. The plaintiffs' argument amounted to the assertion of a general liability for the foreseen harmful consequences of a crime and that

---

[41] The difficulty of course remains even if there is no genus tort since "unlawful means" forms a main component of all the species.
[42] It must be stressed that this outline ignores the English trade disputes legislation.
[43] See p. 196, *ante*.
[44] See Chap. 5.

is not the law. The same presumably goes for common law crimes which are not also matched by equivalent nominate torts, which explains why in *Chapman* v. *Honig*[45] contempt of court by victimising the plaintiff gave rise to no civil claim. Other matters which are neither crimes nor torts have been suggested as unlawful means but are not clearly established as such, in particular breaches of confidence and agreements contravening the restrictive practices legislation.[46] The latter would be particularly significant, for it would introduce the action for damages into an area, the regulation of competition, in which Parliament has opted for other methods of control.[47]

We have seen in the context of intimidation that it may be that that tort is committed against C not only when A threatens B in order to strike at C but also if he directly threatens C. We have also seen that to some extent the very existence of this background tort of interference with trade or business by unlawful means is a necessary consequence of the existence of intimidation. Can this "symmetry" be followed into the two party situation? If A breaks his contract to B in order to harm C he commits the tort. If A breaks his contract with C is he liable in tort as well as for breach of contract? The point is not entirely academic for the measure and remoteness of damage differ between the two heads of liability. Logical though the contrary view may be, however, it can safely be said that it is not the law that every deliberate breach of contract is also a tort. Similarly, if I steal your stock-in-trade that is the tort of conversion, but it is not *also* the tort of interference with trade by unlawful means.

The reader who has to struggle with the modern case law on unlawful means may come away with two impressions. The first is that the courts have generally found it difficult to resist the seductive logic of extending the notion of unlawfulness (though the *Lonrho* case may signal a general brake on expansion). The second is that liability can turn on the almost random chance that the defendant has in some way infringed the law. If A wishes to ruin C he is liable if he wrongfully repudiates a long term supply contract with B, on whose business, as A knows, C depends, or even if he engineers the breach of some remoter contract which is vital to B's trade with C; but if he simply refuses to have any further dealings with B with precisely the same motive, he is not. Some say that the law should abandon the requirement of

---

[45] [1963] 2 Q.B. 502.

[46] But agreements in restraint of trade at common law are not unlawful means: *Mogul SS Co.* v. *McGregor Gow* [1892] A.C. 25.

[47] But as to EEC Competition law see *Garden Cottage Foods* v. *Milk Marketing Board* [1984] A.C. 130.

unlawfulness and embrace a broader doctrine whereby wilful harm requires justification in all cases. In the United States a doctrine known as "prima facie tort" has developed from a statement by Bowen L.J. in the *Mogul* case[48] that "intentionally to do that which is calculated in the ordinary course of events to damage, and which does, in fact, damage another in that person's property or trade, is actionable if done without just cause of excuse." But a few years later in *Allen* v. *Flood*[49] Lord Herschell commented that "for the purpose then in hand the statement of the law may be accurate enough, but if it means that a man is bound in law to justify or excuse every wilful act which may damage another in his property or trade, then, I say, with all respect, the proposition is far too wide; everything depends on the nature of the act and whether it is wrongful or not."

[48] (1889) 23 Q.B.D. 598, 613.
[49] [1898] A.C. 1, 139.

CHAPTER FOURTEEN

Remedies and Limitation

A. REMEDIES

The action for damages is the remedy sought in the overwhelming majority of tort cases and in many it is the only practicable remedy because the act has been done, the harm has been suffered and it is not likely to be repeated. Indeed, it may be that the availability of the action for unliquidated[1] damages is the hallmark of a true tort.

Most damages awards are, or are intended to be, compensatory in their purpose and what Lord Blackburn said about the matter in 1880 is as true now as it was then, namely, that "where any injury is to be compensated by damages, in settling the sum of money to be given for reparation of damages, you should as nearly as possible get at the sum of money which will put the party who has been injured, or who has suffered, in the same position as he would have been in if he had not sustained the wrong for which he is now getting his compensation."[2] These words were of course spoken at a time when most damages were assessed by jury. The disappearance of the civil jury (except in actions for defamation) has certainly led to greater appellate control of awards and to the development of a large and complex "law of damages." The principal focus of this

---

[1] A sum of money is liquidated when it has been fixed in advance (*e.g.* the agreed damages payable for delay under a building contract) or where its ascertainment is a mere matter of arithmetic (*e.g.* the price of a quantity of goods sold and delivered at so much per unit). Damages in some tort cases may be closely predictable, but they are never liquidated in this sense.

[2] *Livingstone* v. *Rawyards Coal Co.* (1880) 5 App.Cas. 25, 39.

Chapter will be on damages for personal injuries and death but we need first to look at those categories of damages which do not fit, or at least do not fit neatly, into the general principle of "compensation" as that idea might generally be understood.

In torts actionable *per se* (for example, trespass to land) the plaintiff is entitled to nominal damages for the mere infringement of his right. Such an award (which seems to vary from about 10 pence to £10) may well indicate that the plaintiff's conduct in bringing the action was a proper vindication of his rights and is to be distinguished from the "contemptuous' damages (one penny) sometimes awarded in defamation suits, the usual consequence of which will be that the plaintiff is saddled with costs. Sometimes damages are said to be "at large," which means that a substantial sum may be awarded for the loss the plaintiff has suffered even though he is wholly unable to quantify it in terms of lost property or wages. The best example is damages for loss of reputation in libel. An analogy is sometimes drawn between these cases and the non-pecuniary elements in personal injury cases and this is valid in so far as in both situations an arbitrary financial *quantum* is being placed upon that which is inherently incapable of expression in money, but the analogy is not exact: the consequences of personal injury are at least sufficiently similar to allow the creation of a broad "tariff"—£X to £Y for loss of an eye, £Y to £Z for loss of a foot—but no similar grading is possible in libel. Had trial by jury been abolished in libel the courts might have gravitated towards a fixed or "conventional" sum under this head, if only because a judge, unprotected by the collegiate anonymity of the jury room, would have found it impossible to give reasons why his award was £1,000 or £10,000. As it is, large awards are tolerated in the name of jury autonomy, until they become "wholly unreasonable."[3]

Two categories of damages are affected by the defendant's conduct. "Aggravated" damages may be awarded in circumstances where wilful or high handed conduct increases the loss suffered by the plaintiff,[4] as by exposing him to humiliation or ridicule. This in no way conflicts with the principle of compensation and in a sense these cases do not form a separate category at all for they are merely concerned with the quantification of the loss, but it is a rather different sort of compensation from that in respect of a broken leg or a wrecked car. Furthermore, they can in practice be difficult to disentangle

---

[3] A good example is *Blackshaw* v. *Lord* [1984] Q.B. 1. "My own opinion is that it was too much, but I do not think it was beyond the bounds of reason." (Fox L.J.).

[4] An award of aggravated damages for negligence, no matter how crass, is not possible in England.

from the other category, that of exemplary (or punitive) damages. These are clearly not reconcilable with the principle of compensation, for their avowed purpose is to punish the defendant for his acts. They had been regularly awarded, though on no very clear principle, until the House of Lords restated the law in 1964 in *Rookes* v. *Barnard*,[5] the result of which is that they may now be awarded in only two[6] types of case. The first is where there is oppressive or unconstitutional conduct by servants of the State (who, for this purpose, include the police). The protection of civil liberties is obviously the key to this. The second covers those cases where the defendant calculates that the "profit" to be made by committing the tort is greater than the loss for which he is likely to have to compensate the plaintiff, in which calculation is of course included the chance that the plaintiff may not sue. The idea is that the defendant must be shown that "tort does not pay." The archetypal case is that of a newspaper publishing a story it knows or suspects not to be true with the purpose of boosting its circulation, but the principle is not confined to these cases: it would, for instance, cover the Canadian case of *Nantel* v. *Parisien*,[7] where a property developer, wishing to get the plaintiff out, moved in with bulldozers and simply demolished the building. Logically, exemplary damages are refused where a criminal court has already dealt with the defendant, for the punitive function has already been fulfilled. Less logically, English courts (but not Australian and Canadian ones) have held that the sum awarded in exemplary damages against joint tortfeasors must be that which is merited by the *least* blameworthy of them. It will be observed that if a defendant who is not part of a State agency engages in outrageous conduct not for profit but out of pure malice he falls outside the *Rookes* v. *Barnard* categories. Thus aggravated damages may be awarded against a rapist (for battery) but not exemplary damages, a state of affairs that can be explained, though it cannot be defended, by reference to the fact that the House of Lords in *Rookes* v. *Barnard* would probably have preferred to erase exemplary damages altogether but instead rationalised the existing authorities in the narrowest possible manner. The subsequent decision of the same court in *Cassell & Co.* v. *Broome* revealed some considerable differences of opinion on the fundamental question of the desirability of exemplary damages but at the end of the day the

---

[5] [1964] A.C. 1129, which must be read with *Cassell & Co.* v.*Broome* [1972] A.C. 1027.
[6] *Rookes* v. *Barnard* allowed for a third category, where such damages were permitted by statute, but it is unlikely that any examples exist.
[7] (1981) 18 C.C.L.T. 79.

Rookes compromise was left untouched. It is indicative of the present unsatisfactory state of the law that it should still be uncertain whether exemplary damages can be awarded, even where the case falls squarely within the second category, if the tort in question is one where such an award had not been made before 1964 (for example, nuisance). Those who oppose exemplary damages say that they confuse the roles of the civil and criminal law and deprive the defendant of those extra safeguards which the common law has traditionally built into the criminal process. Certainly, there already exist or could easily be created alternative legal mechanisms for achieving the goals of confiscation and punishment aimed at by exemplary damages. For example, it would not be difficult to shape a direct restitutionary remedy to deprive a newspaper of the profits of libel and there is already the possibility of a criminal prosecution of an erring police officer, not to mention disciplinary procedures. But others argue that it is an over-simplification to allocate wholly separate functions to rigid and exclusive categories and that while, say, the tort of negligence may be overwhelmingly about compensation, libel and false imprisonment are at least as such about deterrence, admonition and vindication. Suffice it to say that other Commonwealth jurisdictions have given *Rookes* v. *Barnard* a hostile reception and have maintained a wider field of operation for these damages. The law is very different in the United States, exemplary damages being given a wider field of operation than they ever had here, in part perhaps because of the absence of any general provision for the recovery of legal costs from the defendant. Thus they have been awarded in product liability cases where the evidence has shown that the manufacturer has "cut corners" with safety in order to maximise profits. Despite the resemblance of these cases to the second category under *Rookes* v. *Barnard* such awards could certainly not be made here, for the cause of action put at its highest is negligence. Exemplary damages in the United States have not only played a role in contributing to the crisis over liability insurance[8] but have actually worked against the compensatory role of tort: one massive exemplary award can so reduce the assets of a corporation or its insurer as to render it unable to meet awards to other victims.

---

[8] It must, however, be admitted that some of the most notorious instances did not survive an appeal: *Grimshaw* v. *Ford Motor Co.* 174 Cal.Rptr. 345 ($125m. award in respect of car design); *Duke* v. *Housen* 589 P. 2d 334 (1979) ($1.3m for venereal infection).

Damages for Personal Injury and Death

First, so-called non-pecuniary losses. A plaintiff who has suffered personal injury (which includes disease and mental impairment) is entitled to damages for "pain and suffering." This head of damages is clearly subjective, that is to say, it is based on that of which the plaintiff is aware and no award is to be made under this head for periods of unconsciousness. It is not, however, confined to physical pain and the plaintiff is entitled to recover in respect of worry attributable to his condition and treatment and, where his life expectation has been reduced by the accident, to mental suffering consequent upon that.[9] In practice the exercise of making a reasoned assessment of this sort of loss would be impossible and the award is usually included with that for loss of amenities (below); where there is more than normal pain and suffering the "tariff" figure for that injury is simply increased.

The principal head of non-pecuniary damages in English law is "loss of amenities." These damages are awarded for loss of the general enjoyment of life consequent upon the injury. At least three theoretical approaches can be made to the purpose of these damages. First, they may be looked on as compensation for loss of an asset, each limb or function having a value, rather on the lines of the "bot" of Anglo-Saxon law. Secondly, the law may seek to compensate for the loss of happiness of the individual victim. Thirdly, we may abandon any attempt to value the *injury* and instead seek to provide the plaintiff with a sum which will give him reasonable solace (perhaps in the form of alternative activities) for the loss he has suffered. These conflicting ideas have come prominently to the fore in cases where the plaintiff has suffered such grievous injuries that he is not aware of his condition. The law of England was settled by the House of Lords in *H. West & Son* v. *Shephard*,[10] to the effect that a substantial award was to be made for the "objective" loss of amenity even in cases of total unconsciousness, the award being increased where there is consciousness of the loss. In the money of 1987 English courts seem to regard about £40–45,000 as a suitable figure "for cases of total loss of amenity in which the plaintiff is no more than a vegetable, with no appreciation of the catastrophe that has overcome him,"[11] with about £80–85,000 being the sum for a

---

[9] Until 1983 a conventional sum was recoverable for "loss of expectation of life" whether or not the plaintiff was conscious of the fact.

[10] [1964] A.C. 326.

[11] *Young* v. *Redmond* 1982 C.A. No. 147. All non-pecuniary awards must, for comparative purposes, be scaled up to allow for inflation.

typical case of conscious quadripilegia. Around £100,000 would mark the upper limit of awards for total disability. The period since *West* v. *Shephard* has undoubtedly seen a decline in this head of damages, since in real terms the level of even the "worst case" award is below that upheld in that decision, but the sums are still substantial, even in cases of unconsciousness. In other parts of the Commonwealth different attitudes have been taken to the unconscious plaintiff. In Australia the High Court in *Skelton* v. *Collins*[12] rejected *West* v. *Shephard* on the basis that if it was improper to award substantial compensation to the estate of a *deceased* person for the loss of the enjoyment of life, so also was it improper to attempt the exercise in a case of "living death." The Supreme Court of Canada in *Andrews* v. *Grand & Toy Alberta Ltd.*[13] firmly committed itself to the third approach mentioned above and added an upper limit for non-pecuniary damages of $100,000 in the money of that time. Though the logic of this approach would seem to require detailed evidence of how the plaintiff proposes to use his damages, this does not seem to have happened and it may be that where the plaintiff is capable of managing his own affairs the difference between the Canadian approach and that adopted in England is more a matter of form than of substance.

None of the judicial solutions to the problem of loss of amenities can be said to accord completely with the compensation principle. It has been fairly said that all figures in any jurisdiction could be halved or doubled overnight without being in any way less defensible (or indefensible) and that the tariffs[14] adopted by the judges are no more than their perception of what is "fair" given the overall standard of living and the resources likely to be available to meet awards as a whole. Those critics of the tort system who would prefer to establish a more broadly based system independent of fault recognise that any replacement could not, without greatly increased funding, compensate all accident victims at the current rate of damages and most of them would give compensation for non-pecuniary loss a lower priority than replacement of lost income and reimbursement of expenses—indeed, some would not cover it at all unless and until "full" compensation is achievable under other heads. However, even the New Zealand system, which is the most radical of

---

[12] (1966) 115 C.L.R. 94.
[13] [1978] 1 W.W.R. 577.
[14] It is not suggested that there is a precise figure for each injury. Rather, there is a "bracket" within which the Court of Appeal will not interfere.

the alternatives to tort currently in existence,[15] makes a limited degree of provision for non-pecuniary losses.

The largest item in many personal injury awards is damages for loss of earnings (though in serious cases of long term disability expenses can loom even larger). The plaintiff is entitled to be compensated for this at the rate of his actual lost earnings even if they are far in excess of the average and foreseeability has nothing to do with this, for the defendant takes his victim as he finds him in this respect. The major problem is that damages can generally be awarded as a once-for-all lump sum[16] so the court must attempt to assess the value of a loss which may extend thirty or forty years into the future. The court is required to guess not only at what will happen to the plaintiff during the ensuing years (for example, his condition may worsen or improve, or he may die prematurely from some cause unconnected with the accident) but also what *would* have happened to him if the accident had not occurred, for that is a necessary part of determining what he has lost. As Lord Scarman bleakly commented in *Lim v. Camden and Islington A.H.A.*[17] "knowledge of the future being denied to mankind, so much of the award as is to be attributable to future loss and suffering—in many cases the major part of the award— will almost certainly be wrong. There is really only one certainty: the future will prove the award to be either too high or too low." In this respect the tort system contrasts with social security, which generally utilises periodical (usually variable) payments for all but the most minor awards of benefit, which makes it more likely that "true" compensation will be achieved (within the financial limits of the benefit) in an individual case. Among other alleged defects in the lump sum system are the danger of the plaintiff's dissipating his award through fecklessness or incompetence in handling large sums and the lack of incentive for rehabilitation before judgment or settlement. On the other hand, it must be said that there are serious practical difficulties about introducing periodical payments into the tort system. Any worthwhile scheme would presumably allow for some process of review, with the prospect of increased costs and court

---

[15] See Chap. 15. *Cf.* the Australian Northern Territories motor accident compensation scheme (1979). This gives a modest level of compensation for non-pecuniary items but preserves the common law action for pain and suffering and loss of amenities.

[16] There is one major qualification in England to the lump sum rule. Under the Administration of Justice Act 1982 the court may make a provisional award of damages if there is a chance that the plaintiff's condition will deteriorate and revise it if that contingency occurs. This, however, is meant only for cases where there is real doubt about the medical prognosis.

[17] [1980] A.C. 183.

congestion. Further, one must always bear in mind that the system's money is coming from the funds of commercial insurers, whose overhead costs would rise and who do not have the same capacity to undertake open ended commitments as the State, with its taxing power.[18] Nor is it irrelevant that the evidence suggests a plaintiff preference (whether wise or not) for lump sums and it would be difficult to impose a periodic payments system on the overwhelming majority of claims which are settled out of court. Nevertheless, the very high level of awards now being made in some cases (into seven figures) may gradually bring about changes in the attitude of insurers. In Canada and the United States there have been some experiments with "structured settlements" whereby the parties agree on an overall amount of compensation and then arrange for it to be paid in instalments. There is no reason why this should not be done in England if the parties so wish.

For the foreseeable future most cases are likely to end with a lump sum judgment or settlement. The practice of the courts is to determine the plaintiff's annual loss of earnings (after deduction of income tax,[19] social security contributions and other outgoings which would have been necessary to earn the income) and apply a "multiplier" to this figure. Thus a man in his thirties who has suffered permanent incapacitating injury and whose annual earnings loss is £10,000 might receive 15 × £10,000 (£150,000) under this head. It will be observed that the multiplier is considerably less (by about 50 per cent. in this example) than the average working life expectancy of a person of that age, but the theory of the matter is that the income from the capital sum, supplemented by drawings on the capital (low in the initial years, higher as time goes on) will provide the plaintiff with the equivalent of his total net earnings throughout the period. Clearly, to award 30 × £10,000 would be substantially to overcompensate him, because, assuming a rate of return (gross) of 5 per cent., that would give him an income of £15,000 per year (a little more, after deductions, than his assumed net loss) *and leave his capital untouched.* Furthermore, such an award would make no allowance for the "vicissitudes of life" (for example, premature death) which may affect the plaintiff after the accident or which *might* have affected him but for the accident. In other words, the multi-

---

[18] Social security benefits are mostly paid from current tax revenue, not from any actuarially based fund.

[19] The lump sum of damages is not taxable in his hands, though the income its investment produces is. The latter factor should, arguably, attract some increase in the award since the initial annual loss has been calculated net of tax, but this is not done unless the award is large enough to push the plaintiff into higher tax brackets.

plier is set at a figure which takes into account both the fact that a capital sum capable of investment is more valuable than an equivalent aggregate of income over a period of time *and* the chance that the plaintiff might anyway not have earned all that income. The correct multiplier is a matter of law in the sense that it depends upon the figures chosen by other courts in cases of plaintiffs of the same age, subject to a degree of flexibility to take account of circumstances peculiar to the individual case, but it has been said that the English practice assumes a return on capital of between 4 and 5 per cent.[20] The significant feature is that the multipliers remain constant even though the actual rates of return on invested capital may fluctuate widely around this 4–5 per cent. line. Hence, it is argued, the system automatically takes care of inflation, for inflation is accompanied by high interest rates which will increase the plaintiff's return on capital well beyond the assumed 4–5 per cent.[21] and the plaintiff will be earning a significantly higher income from his damages than it was assumed they would produce when they were awarded. Even if it is true that there is a consistent relationship between sharp falls in the value of money and high rates of interest there are a number of objections to this thesis. First, it is inapplicable to the later period of the loss when the plaintiff is assumed to be making large drawings on capital.[22] Secondly, it does not allow for the "ratchet" effect on prices when a period of high inflation is followed by a period of stability—prices do not return to their pre-inflation levels but returns on capital do. Most important is the fact that a decision of the House of Lords on another aspect of damages[23] proceeds on the assumption that the "real" rate of return on investments (that is to say, when interest rates are shorn of their inflation element) remains at a fairly constant 2 per cent. If so, all plaintiffs are being undercompensated by the difference between that figure and the return assumed by the multipliers. So far, however, the courts have rejected the

---

[20] In some jurisdictions (*e.g.* Australia) the practice is not to use a multiplier but to take the plaintiff's full working life expectancy, apply a small reduction for "vicissitudes" and then apply to the final figure a mathematical discount table. This is only another way of performing the same process—*i.e.* converting a stream of income into a capital sum of equivalent value.

[21] Interest is the sum a borrower pays a lender for the latter's being kept out of his money. But only part of the rate represents the payment for the use of the money; the balance represents the lender's estimate of the additional sum he will require to restore his lent capital, on repayment, to its original, pre-inflation purchasing power.

[22] But since there is little evidence that any plaintiffs actually manage their funds in the way assumed by the legal model perhaps this does not matter too much!

[23] *Wright* v. *B.R.B.* [1983] 2 A.C. 773 (interest on damages for non-pecuniary loss before trial).

suggestion that the multipliers should be modified, probably because of fears of the effect of the sudden and massive increases which would occur in awards in the more serious cases. The relationship between inflation and interest rates has also troubled Commonwealth courts. Some earlier Australian decisions made the disastrous assumption that high interest rates should be reflected in high discount rates (up to 9 per cent.) but in *Todorovic v. Waller*[24] the High Court set a standard rate of 3 per cent. An even lower rate now seems to prevail in Canada, so that given an equal annual loss, damages for future loss of earnings should be higher in both jurisdictions than in England.

In some cases the plaintiff will suffer no immediate loss of earnings but his injuries may put him at some future time in a disadvantageous position on the labour market. Damages are commonly awarded for this (an exceedingly speculative exercise) under the head of "loss of earning capacity." Confusingly, this expression is also sometimes used to mean what has been described above as loss of earnings.

It would be a most unusual case in which, even though the plaintiff is totally disabled, he will be wholly without income as a result of the accident. In practice, sums will come to him from various sources (social security, charity, occupational pension, private insurance) and the question then arises of how far these benefits are to be taken into account in calculating his loss. The issue is one of the most important in the law of damages, for it is by no means unusual, particularly at the lower end of the income scale, for the aggregate of these benefits to exceed the earnings lost as a result of the accident. Full details of this topic would be beyond the scope of an introduction and the issue is one on which there are extremely wide divergences from one jurisdiction to another, but the English position is essentially a compromise dictated more by expediency than by underlying principle.

The proceeds of private insurance and of charitable benevolence (for example, payments from a disaster fund) are left wholly out of account and it is unlikely that any other rule would be acceptable to public opinion. In the case of insurance most people would feel that the plaintiff should be rewarded for his foresight and thrift by "double recovery"[25] and there is an obvious risk that the springs of charity would dry up if gifts went

---

[24] (1982) 37 A.L.R. 381.

[25] But where the policy is one of *indemnity*, a plaintiff who has claimed on the policy would hold any damages recovered from the tortfeasor on trust for the insurer. A policy is one of indemnity where it pays the objective, market value of the plaintiff's loss (for example, the comprehensive cover against damage to a motor car). Policies covering death and personal accident are not policies of indemnity.

ultimately to relieve the tortfeasor of his burden of damages. In other areas, the tendency is to ask whether the payment received by the victim is properly to be regarded as an equivalent or replacement for what he has lost. Thus sick pay, even of a very long term nature, is brought into account in calculating the plaintiff's loss of earnings but a disability pension payable on termination of the employment is not[26]—the two payments are of a different nature. Social security benefits are partly governed by statute, the Law Reform (Personal Injuries) Act 1948, which provides that the specified benefits are to be brought into account only as to 50 per cent. of what is receivable in the five years after the accident. This completely arbitrary formula represents the original compromise struck at the birth of the present welfare state system. Some important benefits are not, however, mentioned in the statute and the courts have had to struggle to discern a legislative intention as to their relationship with tort damages. The general tendency is towards bringing these sums into account. The argument that no offset should be made because the effect is to relieve the tortfeasor of his liability has been mentioned above in connection with charitable payments. It is sometimes also heard in relation to sick pay and social security payments but there are at least two serious objections to it. First, tort damages in accident cases are concerned with compensating the plaintiff, not punishing the defendant, so if one concludes that the plaintiff's losses have been fully met there is no basis for the involvement of the law of torts.[27] Litigation being necessarily a slow process it is almost inevitable that the plaintiff will have had to call on these alternative sources of funds and the defendant may be regarded as having caused a loss to their providers by creating the occasion for their disbursement. As a matter of theory there is something to be said for giving these providers a right of recourse against the defendant, but in practice shifting funds around in this way is too expensive to be workable. The doctrine of subrogation in insurance law (whereby an insurer who has paid out on an indemnity policy may take over the rights of the insured against the defendant who has caused the loss) may be thought to provide a favourable analogy but subrogation is little exercised except where large sums are at issue. It is significant that in motor insurance, which produces a

---

[26] Though it would be brought into account against an item in the plaintiff's claim alleging a reduction in his annual employment pension as a result of his employment being terminated prematurely.

[27] The non-deduction of insurance and charitable payments could still be justified: the first because the plaintiff has bought an "extra," the second because the intention of the donors prevents them being regarded as full compensation.

very large number of comparatively small claims in respect of property damage, the right of subrogation has been abandoned by most insurers.[28] The second point is that the law of tort damages should be looked at as part of the wider system aimed at covering the financial consequences of misfortune and since the funding of all sectors of this system is inherently limited all possible effort should be made to avoid wasteful "double compensation." If D has to pay less damages to P because P's receipt of benefit "X" is regarded as reducing P's loss then D's funds (in reality those of his liability insurer) will be augmented and thereby more capable of meeting other claims—though only, of course, those in respect of which a tort can be established.

The present system of offsets is a patchwork and there is unlikely to be enough to be gained by "fine-tuning" it to repay the effort of reform. The Pearson Commission in 1978[29] proposed a much greater degree of deduction of social security benefits, a step which would have fundamentally altered the balance of the system between tort compensation and state payments (as well as greatly reducing the tort recovery of low to middle income earners) but it now seems unlikely that this will be implemented.

One state benefit comes in kind, not in cash—care and treatment under the National Health Service. The hospitalised plaintiff will receive board and lodging for the equivalent of which he would have had to pay if he had not been injured and the consequent saving to him is brought into account against his loss of earnings.

So far we have spoken in terms of giving the plaintiff redress for what he would have received but for the accident and will no longer receive. But he is also entitled to recover damages for expenses incurred as a result of the tort, provided that they are reasonable. Private treatment is reasonable even though public facilities are available but the uncertainty of recovering damages against the tortfeasor probably means that it is unlikely that the plaintiff will avail himself of private treatment solely or mainly because the law allows the cost to be recovered from the defendant. In cases of long term disability the cost of nursing care may run into hundreds of thousands of pounds, but the question of what is recoverable is not to be determined solely by the cheapest method of providing the minimum care. For example, the court may conclude that it is reasonable for the plaintiff to live at home with his family even though equivalent facilities could be provided in a nursing home at less cost. It is in the recovery of this sort of expense that the tort plaintiff really scores in comparison

---

[28] This is the so-called "knock-for-knock" agreement.
[29] See p. 229, *post.*

with the victims of other misfortune. An area which once caused difficulty is compensation for services rendered gratuitously by relatives, for example the mother who gives up work to look after an injured child. It would be conceptually difficult under the present law of negligence to give a direct right of action to the relative (indeed, it might well be undesirable to do, since a multiplicity of claims arising out of one injury is not to be encouraged) but the courts have dealt with the problem by allowing the *victim* to recover the value of the services rendered to him: he is expected (though perhaps he cannot be compelled) to use that portion of his damages to recompense the relative. The same principle probably allows recovery of the amount of expenditure by a third party which can fairly be said to be incurred in promoting the victim's well-being and recovery (for example, visits by a spouse or parents to the victim in hospital). Where a non-earner has provided gratuitous household services he may recover the sum reasonably necessary to replace these. This rather obvious point was only clearly recognised late in the development of damages law, perhaps because the ancient, anachronistic and now abolished action of the husband for loss of his wife's services allowed another method of recovery in the majority of cases.

As to death, the common law concluded nearly two hundred years ago that "the death of a human being could not be complained of as an injury in a civil court." This astonishing rule has long gone but the structure of the law is different from and rather more complex than that governing personal injuries.

The first point to grasp is that the "estate" of a deceased person lives on after him for the purposes of winding up his affairs, distributing his property and so on. This legal entity can sue and be sued for torts (except defamation) so that even in a case of instantaneous death the estate of the victim has a cause of action against the tortfeasor in respect of the death[30]—and if the tortfeasor, too, is dead, the claim is against *his* estate. In some American jurisdictions there is little more to say, the estate being able to recover the earnings the deceased would have acquired during his life had he not been prematurely killed and these being distributable in accordance with his will or the law of succession, usually to close relatives dependent on him. English law recently and briefly flirted with such an approach (known as the doctrine of the "lost years") but Parliament restored the law to what it was formerly thought to be so that the estate cannot sue for loss of

[30] The law is in the Law Reform (Miscellaneous Provisions) Act 1934, as amended.

earnings in the period after death.[31] Where death is instantaneous the estate's recovery will be minimal, no more than funeral expenses; but if the victim lingers on there may be a substantial claim involving all the personal injury elements outlined above, except, of course, that there will be no problem of assessing *future* loss.

Alongside the claim of the estate and usually far eclipsing it in amount, is the claim of the dependants of the deceased person under the Fatal Accidents Act 1976,[32] the purpose of which is to compensate them for the loss they have suffered as a result of the death. The death is not a wrong to them at common law but the statute gives them a right to recover in respect of it. Analytically, the claim is an odd hybrid, for although it is undoubtedly personal to the dependants, that is to say, they are not pursuing the deceased's own claim, it depends upon there being a wrong in respect of which the deceased could have sued at the time of his death (so that, for example, a judgment or settlement in his favour extinguishes any potential claim by the dependants) and their damages are affected by this contributory negligence. The original Act of 1846 ("Lord Campbell's Act") was extremely influential and it can be recognised today in many forms throughout the common law world.

As a result of an amendment in 1982 spouses and parents of minor children can claim a conventional sum of £3,500 as damages for bereavement but the Act is otherwise concerned only with financial loss arising from the death, the support from the deceased of which the dependants have been deprived. The list of eligible dependants is very wide and includes a person who had been living with the deceased as a spouse even though they were not in fact married. Though each dependant has a separate claim, in the common case of a surviving spouse and minor children it is usual to assess the loss as a whole and give most of the damages to the spouse, who will continue to be responsible for the children's upbringing. The process of assessment is not dissimilar from that in a personal injury case, with a multiplier and multiplicand, although the multiplicand in fatal cases will be lower because one must deduct the sums which the deceased would have spent exclusively on himself. This, coupled with the fact that apart from the very limited exception mentioned above there are no damages for non-pecuniary items, means that

---

[31] A living plaintiff whose life expectancy has been reduced can still recover the earnings of the "lost years."

[32] Both the estate's claim and the Fatal Accidents Act claim will be brought by the executor or administrator of the deceased's estate, but this is a matter of machinery and should not obscure the different legal nature of the claims.

damages in a fatal accident case will be lower than those for a seriously disabling personal injury: it is cheaper to kill than to maim. However, this difference is reduced by the much more generous treatment under the Fatal Accidents Act with regard to offsetting of benefits. Under section 4 of the Act "benefits which have accrued or will accrue to any person from [the estate of the deceased] or otherwise shall be disregarded," so that dependants may be considerably financially better off as a result of the death. It is not self-evident that there should be so sharp a contrast between fatal cases and others and the contrast is even greater between the Act and the Criminal Injuries Compensation Scheme, under which all benefits other than life insurance paid for by the deceased are deductible. A further remarkable feature of the Act at present is the provision whereby both the remarriage and the prospects of remarriage of a widow (but not a widower!) are to be ignored in assessing the loss suffered by her. Once it is borne in mind that the Act is concerned with financial dependency this is, of course, wholly illogical, for the widow may be supported by a new husband at a standard of living equal to or higher than that which she previously enjoyed. Accordingly, these matters were originally taken into account, but some judges found the task of assessing remarriage prospects distasteful (as it undoubtedly was) and said so in forthright terms. This fuelled one of those well-intentioned but not very carefully reasoned "campaigns" which afflict accident compensation law from time to time and this led to legislation in 1971. It is truly astonishing (though understandable for practical reasons) that even the *fact* of remarriage before trial is to be ignored. Certainly the supposed vice of double compensation has not been pursued with the same vigour in death cases as in others.

Property damage

This is a complex subject which generates a good deal of case law but only the barest of outlines can be attempted here. Again the basic theme is compensation but the courts have been reluctant to commit themselves to a rigid formula by which that compensation is to be measured. In many cases the measure of damages will be the diminution in value of the property at the time when the wrong was done (together with interest up to judgment) but other formulae may be adopted if the justice of the case demands. Thus the cost of repair may be awarded, even though it exceeds the diminution in value where it is reasonable for the plaintiff to retain that particular property[33]; and it may be

---

[33] *Ward* v. *Cannock Chase D.C.* [1986] Ch. 456 is a good and entertaining example.

justifiable to postpone the effecting of repairs until the outcome of litigation is known even though inflation in repair costs may then lead to a higher award than the cost of repair immediately after the wrong plus interest.[34] As well as an award for the damage itself, the plaintiff can also recover for loss of use (for example, the profits he would have made with the property) subject, as is the case with all damages, to the duty to act reasonably to mitigate his loss, as for example by hiring a substitute.

Remedies other than Damages

The main tort remedy other than an award of damages is the injunction, an order of the court requiring the defendant to refrain or desist from some wrongful course of conduct. The injunction is the dominant remedy in some areas, particularly nuisance and the "economic torts." Since it may be some time before the case can be tried and it may be necessary to preserve the *status quo* the plaintiff may obtain an interlocutory injunction if he can show that there is a "serious question" to be tried, that damages would not adequately compensate for any harm he may suffer before trial and that the balance of justice favours a temporary order. The plaintiff will be required to give an undertaking to compensate the defendant for losses he has suffered if the plaintiff should subsequently fail at the trial, but in some cases the grant of an interlocutory injunction will effectively settle the matter once and for all. For example, the defendant in a passing off action will probably lose his market and is unlikely to have the resources or the inclination to pursue things to a full trial a year or two later. This power to restrain conduct without a full opportunity for the issues to be investigated is probably necessary but it is a serious infringement on liberty and it is occasionally modified, as in libel, where it is virtually impossible to get an interlocutory injunction if the plaintiff says he will justify what he has published. If the law were otherwise, it would be easy to stifle scandal with a "gagging writ."[35]

Other subsidiary forms of injunctive relief are mandatory injunctions (requiring the defendant to undo a wrong already done) and *quia timet* injunctions (restraining a wrong which is merely threatened) but the principal form of injunction available

---

[34] There are still unresolved problems here in relation to the supposed rule that the plaintiff's impecuniosity cannot increase damages (*ante*, p. 68): see *Dodd Properties* v. *Canterbury City Council* [1980] 1 W.L.R. 433.

[35] But compare the "Spycatcher" saga where interlocutory injunctions were fairly readily granted for breach of confidence even though the defendants contended they were exposing wrongdoing.

after trial is the prohibitory injunction, ordering the defendant to stop committing a legal wrong. Because of the equitable origin of the remedy it is "discretionary" but this is apt to be rather misleading. If the plaintiff's rights are being infringed he is prima facie entitled to an injunction unless the injury to him is trivial, it would be oppressive to grant the injunction and the injury, such as it is, is capable of being adequately compensated by a payment of damages. If the injury is substantial the defendant cannot claim to buy the plaintiff out without the latter's concurrence.[36] Each case turns very much upon its own facts but by way of illustration there have been cases in which the courts have refused injunctions against harmless trespassers on the plaintiff's land for the purpose of reaching the beach or sea. As the judge said in one of them[37]:

> "no doubt it is the law that upon the foreshore of this country and upon the rough cliff paths which exist in many places along the coast the public have not a right of way recognized by the law, and no doubt it is true that rights of property are as a general proposition entitled to protection by, if necessary an injunction of this Court. But it does not follow that if the owner of the foreshore—say at some well-known seaside resort—came to this Court for an injunction to restrain the nurserymaids from wheeling their perambulators on the sands or the children from playing on the rocks, this Court is bound to make, or in the absence of good reason should make, such an order."

On the other hand, the owner of a yard in residential or business premises would be entitled to an injunction to restrain others parking there without having to show that his own use of the yard was interfered with[38]: there is a great practical difference between transient passage in pursuit of immemorial recreational purposes and using someone else's property to store your goods.

In those cases where the court exercises its discretion not to award an injunction it has statutory power to award damages instead. Since this extends to a case where a *quia timet* injunction is sought against threatened harm it constitutes a form of compulsory purchase of the plaintiff's rights, but the practical impact of this is reduced by the fact that an injunction would be refused only in the most exceptional circumstances if the injury were substantial.

[36] See further in relation to nuisance, p. 124, *ante*.
[37] *Behrens* v. *Richards* [1905] 2 Ch. 614.
[38] See *Patel* v. *Smith* [1987] 1 W.L.R. 853.

B. LIMITATION OF ACTIONS

Most legal systems feel the practical need for a claim to become extinguished by the passage of time,[39] a matter known to the common law as limitation of actions.[40] The investigation of disputed issues of fact becomes more difficult as the recollections of witnesses are clouded and documents are mislaid and it is unfair on the defendant to have a claim hanging over him for a long period of time, with the consequent uncertainty about his financial future. The force of the last point is somewhat diminished where the defendant is a large corporation or is insured, but it may be thought that even these defendants are entitled eventually to "close the books" on a dispute. The subject goes far wider than the law of torts but even when confined to that sector it is of great practical importance and has become increasingly complicated as successive attempts have been made to strike a balance between the legitimate claims of defendants to protection from stale claims and the "hard cases" where the damage to the plaintiff appears only after a long period of time. The increasing incidence of tort claims for industrial diseases and for defective buildings have combined to produce a continuing crisis in limitation law. For Parliament to have legislated four times on a rather technical area of "lawyer's law" since 1962 is a sure sign that there are problems.

When we refer to the "limitation period" we meant that a writ must be issued (not served) within it: the actual trial may be delayed for long after that, though a defendant can get the proceedings dismissed for "want of prosecution" if the plaintiff drags his feet. The basic periods are three years for personal injury and death cases and six years for others (except defamation which now, though not formerly, is subject to the three year period). But the question arises, three years from when? Until 1963 the answer was simple,[41] from the time when the cause of action arose, *i.e.* from the first moment when the plaintiff could sue, which in the case of torts actionable *per se* (such as trespass) meant when the wrongful act was done but in the majority of cases (and especially negligence) meant when the damage was suffered, since until then there was no complete tort. However, if damage had been suffered it was irrelevant that the plaintiff was

---

[39] Though comparable societies seem able to tolerate very substantial differences in the time required. In England tort actions are barred after three to six years; in France the general period is 30 years, though reduced for many cases.

[40] Not to be confused with the concept of limitation of liability, *e.g.* by contract or under the Companies Act or the Merchant Shipping Act.

[41] Special rules have always applied to persons under legal disability (*e.g.* infancy) or to causes of action concealed by fraud etc.

unaware of it. Hence a claim for an insidious industrial disease like asbestosis might be barred before any symptoms arose to give the plaintiff reason to believe he was ill. It is still the law that time runs from the accrual of a cause of action but Parliament has now added an alternative basis for the running of time. At this point we must distinguish between personal injuries and other cases. In a personal injuries case (see the Limitation Act 1980, which on this point replaces earlier, unsuccessful legislation of 1963) time will start to run from the "date of knowledge" of the person injured. The precise definition of this is somewhat complicated but for our purposes it will do to say that it means when the plaintiff could reasonably have known that he had a significant injury and that it was attributable to the act of an identified defendant. Obviously, such a date may be difficult to determine, but no more so than, say, the time when the plaintiff first began to suffer from a particular disease. This may be thought to be a great deal fairer to the plaintiff, though it may expose the defendant to liability many years after the event. Many American courts of their own motion adopted such a "discovery date" approach to their limitation legislation but the problems which have arisen have led legislatures to enact "statutes of repose," that is longstop absolute limits which apply irrespective of the plaintiff's knowledge. As is explained below, such is the law in England for other types of harm, but far from introducing a statute of repose for personal injury cases generally[42] Parliament has moved further in favour of the plaintiff by giving the court power to "disapply" the limitation period altogether "if it appears to the court that it would be equitable to allow the action to proceed" having regard to the relative prejudice to the plaintiff and the defendant. This has not been interpreted (though it may have been intended) as a provision applicable only to rare, exceptional cases and, while it does have its limits, it casts doubt upon the necessity for the highly detailed provisions on discoverability. It must also be borne in mind that a not uncommon cause of the plaintiff's case being out of time is the failure of his legal advisers to proceed expeditiously with his claim and he may have an action for professional negligence against them. The provisions governing fatal accidents differ in detail but are similar enough to the above scheme to need no further mention here.

Other types of claim arising from negligence (but not other torts) are governed by the Latent Damage Act 1986. The catalyst of the 1986 Act was the building cases. Curiously, though the

---

[42] But see the 10-year long stop provision for product liability cases under the Consumer Protection Act 1987: *ante*, p. 110.

courts in personal injury cases had denied a power to apply a "date of discovery" rule until Parliament intervened, the case law on defective premises was developing just such a doctrine in the 1970s, until it was cut short by the decision of the House of Lords in *Pirelli* v. *Oscar Faber*.[43] This difficult and in parts obscure decision held that where premises were defectively constructed time ran from the moment when damage was done. This was, however, neither necessarily the time when the building was completed nor when the damage was discoverable. On the facts, cracks at the top of an industrial chimney constituted damage and hence triggered the running of the six-year period even though they were not discovered until seven years later. On to this rule the 1986 Act has now engrafted an alternative "date of discoverability" starting point modelled on that for personal injuries in the 1980 Act but the period under this head is three years not six. It is, therefore, quite possible for this alternative period to expire before the primary six-year period running from the damage. There are two very major differences from the personal injuries legislation. First, there is no discretionary power to disapply the limitation period even though it would cause no prejudice to the defendant. Secondly, an overriding provision extinguishes any claim 15 years from the last act of negligence by the defendant, even though the damage has not become discoverable or indeed has not yet even occurred.

[43] [1983] 2 A.C. 1.

CHAPTER FIFTEEN

Tort and Personal Injury Compensation

It is hard to imagine the legal system being structured with nothing in the shape of a law of torts, but it is not at all hard to contemplate one in which it plays a very much more limited and peripheral role than it does today. Certainly, there are many areas in which the growth of alternative legal mechanisms has already relatively diminished tort's significance. Actions for trespass to the person have never been particularly numerous in modern times in England but such actions, while they remain of some importance in the control of police powers, are insignificant in comparison with the number of claims handled under the Criminal Injuries Compensation Scheme.[1] Similarly, any lawyer with his client's interests at heart is likely to pursue complaints to environmental agencies or the local authority to their uttermost before embarking on a costly suit for the tort of nuisance. Tort claims of this nature are perhaps now playing an almost symbolic role as a remedy of last resort, but even the most ardent collectivist, convinced of the effectiveness of public regulatory and disciplinary agencies, would probably hesitate before altogether extinguishing the private tort right. Sometimes a private right of action will be created by legislation which leaves the tort remedy formally untouched but offers procedural or substantive advantages which will lead to the practical atrophy of the older remedy.[2] A good example is the Australian Trade

---

[1] See p. 143, *ante*.

[2] A process which has, of course, continually occurred *within* the common law of torts; see, *e.g.* the victory of conversion over detinue; *ante*, p. 148.

Practices Act 1974, which deals with "misleading or deceptive conduct" and which, because it contains an element of strict liability, is a more attractive proposition to the plaintiff than deceit or injurious falsehood.[3] Some form of "right of reply" *might* have a similar effect on the law of defamation, though that is more problematical.[4] But the story is by no means all one of retreat for as some areas of torts have declined, so others have grown in importance. Our system lacks the seemingly inexhaustible fertility of American law but nonetheless there are instances of expansion or of revival. We shall not now, it seems, see the immense expansion of negligence liability which most at first discerned in *Junior Books* v. *Veitchi*[5] but there certainly exists a wider liability for non-physical loss, particularly in the context of statements, than existed thirty years ago. Again, liability for interference with contract has enjoyed something of a renaissance in England since the restriction of trade union immunities by legislation in the 1980's. These ebbs and flows are, however, matters of comparatively minor significance in the picture as a whole, which is dominated by the controversy on personal injury compensation, a matter which has been foreshadowed at various points in this book and at which we must now look in more detail.

The two most widely accepted aims of the law of torts have been compensation and deterrence. Now there can be no doubt that in some areas of tort deterrence has the primary role and plays it to some effect—defamation and interference with contract are good examples[6]—but this function is much more problematical in the context of negligence and accidents. It is unlikely that empirical enquiries will be decisive one way or the other on the deterrent effect of negligence law, but the following somewhat impressionistic views are widely held among those who have discussed the matter. Tort law probably does have a limited effect in increasing safety in professional and industrial environments where there exists both the machinery for disseminating information about risks and claims and the capacity to modify processes and routines to meet particular dangers. Of course, the same function can be performed— perhaps better—by the investigations and reports of regulatory agencies, but at present tort's role cannot be dismissed altogether. With regard to road accidents, however (and these are

---

[3] See Trindade & Cane, *The Law of Torts in Australia*, p. 734.
[4] *Ante*, p. 182.
[5] *Ante*, p. 53.
[6] Of course deterrence is sometimes ineffective, but that does not invalidate the argument. Deterrence is unquestionably a major role of criminal law but it fails to deter a great deal of criminal behaviour.

the largest single source of tort claims) it seems most unlikely that tort plays any significant role in moulding behaviour when compared with simple self-preservation and the prospect of criminal prosecution. In any event, the very vagueness of the negligence formula makes it a dubious guide to the conduct required by law. Furthermore, the deterrent effect of the threat of liability must be considerably blunted in road and non-road cases alike by the prevalence—indeed the near universality—of liability insurance. The odd anecdotal indication can be found which even suggests that insurance may positively militate against taking care. In the case which first clearly stated the objective standard of the prudent or reasonable man the defendant, a farmer, had been warned that his rick was a fire hazard but he replied that he was insured and would "chance it"[7] and in an early American motoring case the defendant, moments before the crash and in reply to his passenger's protests about his driving said "don't worry, I carry insurance."[8] English legislation carries motor liability insurance in respect of personal injury to remarkable lengths, coming close to removing the contractual basis of the institution: it is compulsory[8a]; it is unlimited in amount; the plaintiff is given a direct right of enforcement of the policy notwithstanding the failure by the defendant insured to comply with its conditions; and in the last resort the bill for the liability of uninsured or untraceable defendants is picked up by motor insurers as a whole acting via the Motor Insurers' Bureau. No fault-based system can go further to ensure compensation. It may be an exaggeration to claim, as some have done, that insurance renders the defendant's liability nominal, for while this may be true as far as the particular suit is concerned (assuming the cover to be adequate) an adverse claims record may affect the defendant's premiums.[9] There are, however, wide variations in the burden of liability insurance. The crisis in some areas of American liability insurance is well known and malpractice premiums for certain medical specialisms can now run into scores of thousands of dollars a year. In England, by contrast, medical liability insurance is handled by a small number of agencies, operating exclusively in this area, which are in effect (though not in law) mutual insurance societies.[10] There is a no risk-rating by specialism or claims record and until a year or two

---

[7] *Vaughan* v. *Menlove* (1837) 3 Bing.N.C. 467.

[8] *Herschensohn* v. *Weisman* 119 A. 705 (1923).

[8a] As a result of E.E.C. requirements it will soon become compulsory for property damage, too.

[9] It must, however, be said that the evidence is that this operates on a rather crude and random basis.

[10] Where a health authority is involved there is an arrangement for sharing the liability between the authority (vicariously liable) and the doctor's insurer.

ago premiums were far less than those required to insure a family car. They have recently risen very sharply in response to a marked increase in medical negligence litigation, but they are still modest when compared with those paid by some other professional groups and they bear no resemblance to those of their American equivalents. The fundamentals of medical negligence law are much the same in England and the United States and the differing costs of the systems, as reflected in premiums, are to be explained by factors other than the formal rules of law: the level of damages awards; the mechanism for applying the formal rules, particularly the prevalence of jury trial in the United States; and the "hard-charging" nature of American litigation, perhaps contributed to by the fact that the plaintiff's lawyer will be paid a share of the proceeds, the so-called contingency fee system.

Outside the fields of operation of state agencies and a few major corporations (which may carry their own risks rather than insure) liability insurance is what makes the tort system go round, since few could bear from their own resources the financial consequences of a major award. With the possible exception of the shift to strict product liability, insurance has had comparatively little *overt* effect on the rules of negligence law but some have claimed that its prevalence has been responsible for constantly driving up the standards required of defendants (thereby weakening the moral force of a tort judgment) so that what is fault-based in name is strict in fact, what Professor Ehrenzweig called "negligence without fault." This view has been particularly prevalent among those who have seen loss-spreading as the primary aim of tort law in the accident field, but others have been more cautious, contending that the apparently greater strictness of liability is merely the product of the fact that experience reveals ever more risks, which thereafter become predictable. Professor Prosser concluded that rather than liability insurance having produced the expanded liability "it would be quite as reasonable to say that the spread of the...insurance itself is a consequence of the expanded liability, which is rather the result of a multitude of other factors."[11] Certainly, even English judges, who are normally reticent about such matters, can be found appealing to the existence of insurance as a reason for imposing liability, but there are just as many, if not more, reminders that the law currently rests upon

---

[11] *Torts*, 5th ed., p. 589.

the defendant's fault having caused damage, not upon his ability to pay.[12]

So far we have been looking at deterrence as if it were a matter of controlling the conduct of an individual defendant in particular circumstances ("if you won't slow down you are liable to cause an accident and be sued") but some American lawyer-economists have developed a theory of "general" or "market" deterrence which sees tort rules as a mechanism for reducing accident losses to the lowest level compatible with "efficiency." So long as the costs of an activity are borne by the person carrying it on rather than being left to fall on others, then he will have the incentive to maximise safety precautions until the point is reached where the cost of those precautions exceeds the cost of the accidents likely to be generated. Alternatively, if the activity cannot be made safer, the higher price attached to it by making it bear the costs of the accidents it generates may lead to a reduction in accidents by users turning to alternatives. This approach may seem to point towards a general regime of strict liability (provided, of course, that we can identify which costs can properly be attributed to which activity[13]) but another view is that the negligence formula is economically efficient in so far as it involves a balancing of risks against the cost of precautions. A huge literature has grown up around this topic but its influence upon the behaviour of the courts, even in the land of its birth, has hardly been noticeable.[14] Certainly, the arguments have been conducted at a theoretical level without reference to the practical difficulties inherent in determining who is the cheapest cost-avoider (and hence the best person to carry liability) in any particular situation.

If we turn to compensation, it cannot be denied for a moment that tort law compensates only some victims of personal injury and then does so at the expense of considerable administrative cost. By its own lights, and bearing in mind that it is a system created by judges out of the material of individual litigation, not an administrative scheme planned by a bureaucracy with power to tax and access to the legislative machine, that is not a criticism at all: to complain that tort law fails to function as an efficient and universal system of social insurance is rather like saying that Concorde is badly designed because it does not carry as many people as a Boeing 747. Nevertheless, while acknowledging Concorde for its technical sophistication it is a widespread point

---

[12] For an example of the first, see the judgment of Lord Denning M.R. in *Nettleship* v. *Weston* (see p. 77, *ante*). The decision of the House of Lords in *Wilsher* v. *Essex A.H.A.* (p. 23, *ante*) is an example of the second.

[13] See p. 103, *ante*.

[14] Of course, the school which says that negligence law *is* efficient would not regard this as a criticism!

of view that the money spent on its development might have been better spent on cheaper forms of air transport and in the same way many would contend that however well tort is operated its inherent limitations mean that it is not the sort of compensation system that society needs or can afford.

The practising lawyer is concerned with operating the system as it is for the resolution of individual cases and the law student, too, needs to understand the law as it is, but neither can ignore the fact that tort is also a *social* institution which involves the transfer of large amounts of money from liability insurers to accident victims and there is now a good deal of information available on its overall performance. The Royal Commission on Civil Liability and Compensation for Personal Injury[15] estimated that about £200 million a year was paid in this country in tort compensation for personal injuries at January 1977 prices and in the money of 1987 this would amount to £500 million. There is no reason to believe that the incidence of successful claims has fallen and it may well be that, given various developments in the law of damages and the undoubted increase in the number of claims in some areas (for example, medical negligence) the actual pay-out may be even greater than the figure produced by scaling up for inflation. This is by no means, however, the total cost of the *system*, for *Pearson* estimated that a further £170 million (or 85 per cent. of the total amount of compensation paid) was consumed in "operating costs," that is to say, the costs and general overheads of insurance companies, commissions to agents and legal fees and expenses. If we compare tort with social security, the other principal source of compensation for injury, where the overall cost of administration is perhaps 10 per cent. of the sums paid out, then tort is unquestionably comparatively inefficient. The point becomes even more significant if it is borne in mind that in England social security payments attributable to injury were estimated by *Pearson* to be two to two-and-a-half times as great as tort compensation. Moreover, this figure excludes benefits in kind, such as National Health Service treatment of victims. If these are brought into account, social security may push five times as much money in the direction of accident victims, making tort very much the junior partner in accident compensation. This is an important point which is often ignored in public discussion of these matters, where it seems often to be assumed that the only

---

[15] Hereafter *Pearson*. The Commission's report (1978, Cmnd. 7054) is still an indispensable source of data even though hardly any of its recommendations have been implemented. Harris *et al.*, *Compensation and Support for Illness & Injury*, considers the wider context of illness. Atiyah, *Accidents, Compensation and the Law*, 4th ed. is the best overview of the law and its operation.

true compensation is that which comes from the defendant or his insurer, whereas at the lower end of the income scale social security payments may wholly replace the financial losses attributable to an injury.

No doubt something could be done to make the tort system more efficient. For example, a more widespread incidence of strict liability might remove some disputes over the existence of fault, but, as explained in Chapter 6, the impact of such a change would be much smaller than might be expected because there would still be contentious issues of causation, damages and contributory negligence by the plaintiff. For this reason, the introduction of strict liability for defective products by the Consumer Protection Act 1987[16] may not be the royal road to speedy and widely distributed compensation it has been made out to be in some quarters. Nor is there likely to be more than a marginal gain in modifying court procedures for hearing personal injury claims, for the simple reason that hardly any cases come to court. Of 250,000 tort claims made in 1973, *Pearson* found that 86 per cent. were disposed of[17] without issue of legal proceedings and over 13 per cent. were subsequently disposed of before a court hearing, so that less than 1 per cent. were actually the subject of a judicial decision. It is a truism, indeed, that the legal system would be unable to cope if a larger number of cases were to be tried. The paucity of cases sued to judgment means of course that the rules of law stated by the courts and outlined in this book may not be a wholly reliable indicator of the basis upon which tort compensation really is obtained. The point that out of court settlements are influenced by factors other than formal rules of law and weight of evidence is certainly true of all litigation but the personal injuries area has the special characteristic that nearly always the plaintiff will be an individual with little or no knowledge of the law or the legal system and the defendant (in fact, if not in legal theory) an insurance company with large resources and enormous experience in handling such claims. This inequality is of course to some extent evened up by the plaintiff's access to legal advice[18] but at the end of the day an individual claim, large or small, is a comparatively minor feature of the insurer's landscape and, except in those rare cases where some significant point of law is at stake or a decision will affect many other claims (for example, a test case to establish causation of the side-effects of a drug), its outcome is only important to him

---

[16] See Chap. 6.
[17] That is to say, settled or abandoned.
[18] It cannot, however, be assumed that all lawyers will have the same expertise in handling personal injury claims.

in so far as it forms a single component in the year's profit and loss account; to the plaintiff his claim is unique and his whole financial future may depend upon it. It is not surprising, therefore, that there is considerable pressure upon the plaintiff to settle out of court for a sum which is lower than a judge might award and that insurers exploit their inherently superior position in this game of guess and bluff. A not untypical settlement might be the result of three or four offers, each slightly larger than the last, both sides keeping their cards as close to their respective chests as the law allows[19] with mounting pressure on the plaintiff as he faces increasing delay and the possibility that the offer may be withdrawn. This is in no way improper given the rules of the game as they are, for insurers are not charitable organisations with bottomless pockets, nor is any claim without an element of risk that it may founder at trial, but the substantial "discount" produced by the negotiating process involves a serious qualification upon the proposition that the aim of the tort system is the full compensation of the plaintiff's loss. Where the plaintiff has commenced proceedings one aspect of the system may be regarded as stacking the cards particularly heavily against him. The defendant can "pay money into court" and if the plaintiff refuses to accept this but proceeds to trial then, in the event of the judge (who does not know about the payment) failing to award a higher sum by way of damages, the plaintiff has to bear all costs of both parties from the date of the payment in. On one view this provides a rational and necessary incentive to the plaintiff not to persist unreasonably with litigation; but it must be said that it can be very difficult to make a precise estimate of damages likely to be awarded and a small misjudgment by the plaintiff's legal advisers can lead to a costs bill which entirely eats up the damages award. Apart from uncertainty, delay is a serious problem with the tort system, being singled out by *Pearson* as "the most important reason for dissatisfaction with the legal system," larger claims often taking years rather than months to disposal.

It is inherent in any tort liability system that there will be winners and losers but just what are the proportions in these categories? All the evidence indicates that there are more losers than winners. *Pearson* estimated that about six-and-a-half per cent. of all injury victims obtained something through the tort system, though with huge variations according to the source of the injury, with 10.5 per cent. for work accidents and no less

---

[19] But since 1970 the plaintiff has been able in personal injury cases to obtain disclosure of documents in the other party's possession even before an action is commenced.

than 25 per cent. for road accidents. An Oxford survey[20] produced slightly more favourable results (19 per cent. for work accidents and 29 per cent. for road accidents) but this does not really change the overall position. In one sense this is a misleading picture, for most "losers" in fact never start the race: the majority of victims of all types of accidents never even consider claiming damages and most of those that do fail to take the matter beyond consideration. Those that do get as far as taking legal advice, however, have a fairly high chance of recovering something, between 74 per cent. and 87 per cent. depending on the type of accident, according to the Oxford survey. There are many diverse reasons why the majority of victims do not pursue legal redress—ignorance, fears about cost or the consequences of legal action (for example, where the defendant is an employer) and the simple fact that in most non-road and non-work accidents there may be no one to whom the plaintiff can attribute responsibility[21]—but the major one may be that most injuries are comparatively minor. It is true that for the reasons outlined above in relation to the tactics of the settlement process it is not entirely safe to conclude that the sums recovered by claimants fully reflect their injuries, but overall there is likely to be some correlation between settlements and injuries and *Pearson* found that the average amount of tort compensation was about £1,000 (in 1987 money), with the average financial loss being about £720, though the net figure for the latter, when social security payments, sick pay and insurance are brought into account was only about £400. Given the expenses of the system it is in fact remarkable how many small claims there are.

Enough has been said to show that as a reasonably cost-effective method of compensating accident victims tort is a poor performer and is likely to remain so whatever substantive and procedural changes were to be introduced. Its deterrent role, too, seems limited. Are there any other justifications for continuing to give it a major role in compensating personal injuries? A cluster of reasons are sometimes advanced under the general rubric of responsibility or corrective justice.[22] The fundamental argument is that the idea of individual responsibility permeates our culture, that it is therefore morally right and "natural" that those at fault should be liable for the consequences of their actions and that we risk serious social harm if we remove that principle, however

---

[20] Harris et al., n. 15 *supra*.

[21] Injuries in the victims' own houses, for example, are more numerous than road accidents.

[22] For a vigorous exposition of these see Linden, *Canadian Tort Law*, 3rd ed., Chap. 1, pp. 11–26.

administratively inefficient and cumbersome the legal mechanism which reflects it. Further it is argued from this premise, the fundamental core of the tort system, the plaintiff's "day in court," permits the exposure of wrongdoing, enables public pressure to be brought on those guilty of it (what has been called the "ombudsman" function of tort) and acts as a safety valve in assuaging the resentment of victims. At this point we are in effect positing a retributive or vindicatory function for the law. This is the "romantic" view of tort, to stand in opposition to the rather lifeless compensation mechanisms of the economists and the proponents of social security, and it is not without its validity, for symbols and rituals are important to the functioning of society. A good deal of this can be accepted in relation to, say, defamation or assault and perhaps even in relation to "disaster" litigation, where the anecdotal evidence of what people say suggests a powerful retributive element in bringing a civil claim, but it is of very questionable validity in relation to the run of the mill road or work accident claim. The "day in court" idea certainly accords ill with the fact that under 1 per cent. of the cases ever get there, and the defendant is in a position to buy off unwanted publicity by prompt settlement. Furthermore, it is doubtful how far tort in practice accurately reflects the moral idea of responsibility. First, responsibility should presumably involve the defendant being subjected to some sanction, but the existence of liability insurance blunts that sanction as severely here as it does in the context of deterrence. Secondly, it is by no means easy wholly to subscribe to the view that tort involves wrongdoing as that term would commonly be understood. Not only is liability in some areas strict, but even where it is based on fault that fault is a single standard which draws no distinction between, for example, the reckless drunk and the motorist who has a momentary lapse of concentration. Nor, once the threshold of fault has been passed, is there any necessary correlation between the seriousness of the defendant's conduct and the extent of his liability for, as we have seen, provided the injury suffered is of the broad type he should have foreseen, he takes his victim as he finds him. It is arguable that the criminal law, with its flexibility as to punishment, is a much better mechanism for achieving the goal of allocating responsibility.[23] There does not seem to be any doubt that the belief that fault should entail civil responsibility is widely held, but its influence upon the initiation and conduct of claims arising out of ordinary, day-to-day accidents is difficult to gauge[24]: even

---

[23] Though it must be admitted that this operates haphazardly: there is no general offence of negligently causing injury.

[24] See Chap. 4 of the Oxford Survey, n. 20, *supra*.

someone who links responsibility with fault as an abstract principle is likely to modify his response in the light of competing factors. A minor injury caused by a friend or relative, for example, is likely to be looked on in a very different light from a serious injury caused by a stranger and it may be that even the abstract principle is a reflection of the system as it is rather than a deeper-seated moral imperative.

It is now time to turn to alternatives to the tort system for personal injuries. If one is primarily concerned with removing inequalities among different classes of victims of misfortune one could simply abolish it and put nothing in its place, leaving all losses to the existing social security system and whatever private loss insurance potential victims chose to effect. This is a non-starter. There are few votes in equality in the abstract and the marginal reduction in the direct cost of some activities could hardly be presented as matching the increase in disability-related poverty. It is most unlikely that potential accident victims would turn to private sickness and accident insurance on any large scale and the proposal would be an anathema to those economists who believe that making an activity bear the full costs of the losses it generates is an effective way of reducing accidents. Something has to be put in the place of tort and changes in the law in other jurisdictions suggest two possible avenues: the first based on *ad hoc* "no fault" schemes, the second a more radical social security based approach.

No Fault Systems

No definition could be framed which would accurately encompass all "no-fault" schemes. The Workmen's Compensation Scheme, abolished in England in 1948 and replaced by the National Insurance (Industrial Injuries) Scheme, but still in existence in the majority of common law jurisdictions, was a form of no fault compensation, for it required an employer to make payments to an employee suffering injury arising "out of and in the course of employment." Unlike tort, there was no requirement of fault or breach of statutory duty[25] but the requisite causal link between the employment and the injury had to be shown. In this sense it was closer to tort that to a social welfare system geared only to *need* and the similarity to tort was emphasised by the fact that most cases involved adversarial litigation. When discussion of the problem of accident

---

[25] Contributory negligence was not as such a defence but, except in cases of death or permanent disablement, no compensation was payable if the accident was due to the claimant's "serious and wilful default."

compensation became widespread in the 1950s and 1960s it was largely conducted in the context of road accidents and the consequence has been a proliferation of no-fault schemes for this area. Such schemes operate in about half of American states, in most provinces of Canada and in several Australian states. They vary enormously in detail, but most of them provide limited compensation without proof of fault for motor vehicle injuries, the compensation being paid either by a public agency created for the purpose or by requiring motorists to effect insurance policies which pay benefits directly to victims of accidents involving the vehicle. There are huge variations in the amount of compensation provided and in the extent to which the claimant is still allowed to bring a tort claim.[26] In some cases the tort claim is left untouched, save only that tort damages are reduced by any sums received under the no-fault cover. In others, the tort action is taken away until a "threshold" is reached, which may be measured by severity of injury or monetary loss, or both. Outside the common law world, Sweden provides an example of no-fault compensation for medical misadventure in the 1975 Patient Insurance Scheme. Proof of negligence is not required but the scheme is by no means a universal insurance against medical accidents. For example, there is no compensation if the injury was a natural or foreseeable result of acts which were medically justified and skilfully performed and over 40 per cent. of the claims presented are rejected. Tort rights are unaffected but such claims are, apparently, rarely pursued. It might be close to the mark to say that the Swedish scheme is less a full no-fault system than a transfer of the substance of negligence law into an informal and speedy adjudication process.

Social Security

No-fault schemes necessarily require a causal link between a particular activity (motoring, medical treatment etc.) and the claimant's injury. Further, they are in the nature of things limited to areas where it is economically feasible to create the necessary administrative or insurance structure, in practice those where tort and liability insurance now play a major role. More radical critics of the present compensation structure would sever the connection between the cause of the injury and compensation entitlement and steer instead by the needs of the victim. This is

---

[26] *Pearson* proposed a no-fault road scheme which would have coexisted with tort. The cost was to be kept down by the elimination of small tort claims and full offset of social security benefits against tort damages. The proposal has not been implemented.

the social security approach,[27] which finds its fullest expression
in the system which has operated in New Zealand since 1974.
The tort action for personal injury arising from accident has
been entirely abolished in New Zealand and compensation
is payable under a scheme administered by the Accident
Compensation Commission. There are three funds, covering
injured earners, motor vehicle accidents and other accidents
not falling into the other two categories and these are financed
by levies on employers and the self-employed, on motorists
and, in the case of the third fund, by general taxation. The
levy on employers is risk-related according to the nature of
the employment, but that on motor vehicles is fixed (though
in each category there is power to vary the levy according
to the accident record of the person subject to it). Administrative
costs compare very favourably with English social security
administrative costs and compensation payments are heavily
orientated towards replacing loss of earnings in the lower
and middle sectors of the income scale, 80 per cent. of proved
loss being recoverable (by way of periodical payments) up
to a statutory maximum revised from time to time in line with
inflation. Payments are made on a lump-sum basis for non-
pecuniary loss but these are much lower than those that would
be recoverable under the tort system in a comparable society.
For the average earner who suffers financial loss but no long-
term disablement or loss of amenity the scheme offers a high
level of pecuniary compensation (substantially above general
social security rates) and is an attractive proposition when
compared with the delay, expense and uncertainty of tort.
For the non-earner who suffers injury with long term effects
the outlook under the scheme is comparatively bleak. Another
"loser" is the victim who had substantially higher than average
earnings, but proponents of the scheme would argue that
neither of these cases amounts to a serious criticism given
the limited resources available. As to the first, non-pecuniary
loss is seen by them to occupy a lower level of social importance
than income replacement and should therefore be relegated
to a subsidiary level until income replacement needs can be
met. As to the second, high earners have the opportunity
to cover the "extra" by private insurance and there is no reason

[27] The line between no-fault and social security is sometimes arbitrary when
compensation is paid by a public agency. The Criminal Injuries Compensation
Scheme, for example (see p. 143 *ante*), would not normally be regarded as part
of the social security structure even though the money comes straight from
general taxation. On the other hand, the National Insurance (Industrial
Injuries) scheme is a central feature of social security, albeit that it pays
enhanced benefits by reference to the cause of the injury, *viz.* work accidents.

why they should be subsidised by the generality of people on lower incomes.[28]

No comparable society has yet followed New Zealand, though Australia came within an ace of doing so in the 1970's. But even the New Zealand scheme does not satisfy some critics because in the last resort, like tort and the *ad hoc* no-fault schemes it suffers from the "vice" of selectivity and preference according to the cause of the disability (accident),[29] whereas the needs of the disabled are the same whatever the cause. At the moment in England successful tort claimants are singled out as a particularly favoured class; elsewhere, this favour is extended to non-fault victims of road accidents; but even in New Zealand the victims of accidental injury are favoured over the much more numerous victims of disease and congenital disability. *Pearson* estimated that the contribution of injury to incapacity (however that was defined, whether permanent handicap or any restriction on activity during a short period) was about 10 per cent. and there is no reason to believe that this figure would be substantially different in New Zealand. Even if we add in the victims of occupational disease that leaves the overwhelmingly greater part of disability as attributable to illness, whether man-made (smoking, industrial pollution) or natural.

It is not clear why discussion of compensation has focussed so strongly upon the "minority risk" of accident. Perhaps there is something which leads us to believe that the accident risk is somehow more abnormal than that of disease and that the accident victim is therefore more "deserving," but it is equally likely that it is a by-product of concentration upon the inefficiencies of tort compensation. Since tort is for practical reasons, particularly reasons of proof of causation, largely confined to accident and occupational disease the reformers' activity in exposing the deficiences of tort has led them to behave as if accident and occupational disease were the *whole* problem.[30] The point was clearly perceived by the Australian Committee which prepared the abortive Accident Compensation Bill of 1974:

> "The needs of the sick are even more neglected. Except where entitlement can be established to a social security pension, the disparities that plague the injury field are avoided by the simple but drastic process of leaving every

---

[28] Under the tort system liability insurance premiums must of course take into account the fact that A on low earnings with a cheap car may crash into B on high earnings with an expensive car.

[29] Certain occupational diseases are included.

[30] See Stapleton, *Disease and the Compensation Debate*, especially Ch., 7, Part I.

loss to lie where it falls.[31] It is an incongruous situation. The needs of men and women are not mitigated by the chance visitation of sickness rather than injury. A man hit by a disease is not more able to resolve his problems than his neighbour hit by a car. In terms of equity, therefore, and as a matter of logic, there should be equal treatment for equal losses. There is an obvious need for the compensation scheme to include all persons who are physically handicapped."

However, acceptance of this premise has serious implications for any prospect of change. The fault-based tort system has a defensible *logical* basis upon which to discriminate between successful and unsuccessful claimants and attacks on it have largely focussed on its inefficiency as a means of transferring resources. Certainly, if tort transfers £500 million a year at an additional cost of £425 million and road accidents account for over half of that sum transferred then a good case can be made that to move over to a no-fault scheme for such accidents with low administrative costs would result in a worthwhile extension of adequate compensation to a substantial number of victims, albeit at the price of some reduction in compensation where the claimant has a high income and/or very severe injuries (and can, at the moment make out a tort claim). Since, however, the number of tort claims in respect of other types of accident is lower and the relative contribution of present social security therefore higher, the savings stemming from tort abolition would be spread a good deal more thinly if a scheme were to be devised for all accidental injury, unless new revenue were raised, or unless the scheme were structured so as to concentrate on long term disability. A scheme which was based on modest all-round increases would amount to an abandonment of the element of income-relation which has been at the root of virtually all reforms or proposed reforms of accident compensation and might be very difficult to "sell" unless we move into an overall climate of egalitarianism and redistribution. Virtually all *popular* discussion of compensation (which tends to be generated by disasters, such as Thalidomide or Opren) is conducted with a distressing absence of attention to the *amount* of costs and benefits but it seems that the amount of a full liability tort judgment is just the starting point of popular expectation and that there is a widespread (albeit perhaps misguided) attachment to substantial

---

[31] In England, some form of social security payment, even if only income support (formerly supplementary benefit) is likely to be payable if the disability arises from illness, but the system distinguishes between injury and illness, generally to the disadvantage of the latter.

lump sums for non-pecuniary loss. If, like the Australian Committee, we bring illness within the proposed new system then the costs start to become so great that we may as well abandon the idea of the savings stemming from the abolition of tort making any major contribution to the exercise. For practical reasons (principally money)[32] the radical view that illness should be equated with injury will probably not prevail in the foreseeable future and if there is to be change it is likely to come by way of limited, *ad hoc* schemes which can be presented as offering better coverage than tort without the threat of increased taxation. In some quarters this may be seen as a means of proceeding gradually to a more comprehensive system, though there is some risk that the creation of yet more enclaves of preferential treatment will make comprehensive reform even more difficult. The "radicals" have, however, performed the useful service of drawing attention to the fact that compensation for injury is part of the wider question of poverty and inequality, of how far the victims of misfortune have a claim for redress upon society. That question goes far wider even than illness and one's answer is more likely to be governed by political preferences than by assessment of the relative efficiency of tort.

---

[32] But there are other awkward questions inherent in any scheme extending to disease, most obviously that of "self induced" illness caused by tobacco or alcohol.

INDEX

241